THE EXPERIENCE OF ANXIETY
A Casebook

THE EXPERIENCE

OF ANXIETY

A Casebook

MICHAEL J. GOLDSTEIN, Ph.D.
DEPARTMENT OF PSYCHOLOGY
JAMES O. PALMER, Ph.D.
DEPARTMENT OF PSYCHIATRY
THE UNIVERSITY OF CALIFORNIA
LOS ANGELES

NEW YORK
OXFORD UNIVERSITY PRESS

To
VIDA AND MINERVA
*Whose encouragement and patient editing
made this book possible.*

Acknowledgments

Our primary indebtedness lies with our patients, who, in turn, have fascinated us, frustrated us, and taught us most of what we know about personality. A wider range of case materials was made possible through the invaluable contributions of our colleagues, Drs. Michael Rosow, Carl Younger, Herbert Eveloff, and Mr. Robert Jones. Our students struggled with us in the initial classroom use of these case materials and supported us with their enthusiasm. Last, but not least, we should like to express our appreciation to the secretaries of the Psychology Department, Alice Vollman, Helen Wiczenski, Valerie Durham, and Deborah Schilling, and to the secretarial staff of the Neuropsychiatric Institute, all at U.C.L.A., who patiently typed the many drafts until this book took final form.

December 1962   M.J.G.
                                                             J.O.P.

FOREWORD

Collections of case studies for the instruction of students of human behavior frequently have been published. Therefore, each new effort in this area must justify its existence by the relative uniqueness of its contribution. Some clinicians argue that each study has a unique individuality setting it apart from all other studies. Although individual differences are the basis of psychological studies, generalizability must be the promise and responsibility of a science; and acquired skills, experiences, and understanding the goals of instruction in the field of abnormal psychology.

Drs. Goldstein and Palmer have drawn a series of studies from their combined clinical and teaching experiences of more than a quarter of a century during the significant postwar years of enormous expansion of abnormal and clinical psychological teaching and training programs. The range of behavior sampled includes apparent successes and disappointments in the evaluation and treatment of a variety of psychological adjustments and maladjustments, illustrations of the trials and other situations which sorely trouble patients and even their therapists, and the vast complexities of behavioral adjustments as these are made with varying degrees of success in a multitude of situations and contexts.

The special contributions of this text are at least two. First, the student of human behavior does not have to wade through pages of inference, interpretation, and analysis by authors which, even though perhaps reliable and valid (often not a valid assumption), are a long jump ahead of the student's comprehension simply because he has not yet accumulated the background of experience of the text authors. Therefore the condensation of experience represented in interpretations of behavior may have little objective communication value.

The second significant contribution by Drs. Goldstein and Palmer rests in the carefully selected and designed questions at the close of each case study. The student may thus be taught to examine and consider various behaviors and adjustments; their import, antecedents, and consequences; and the possible roles of various efforts at intervention by both trained and untrained persons, family members, and other community persons. With directed discussions, students may systematically investigate the behaviors portrayed in these case studies, review their inferences about the behaviors, and test the hypotheses raised by these evaluations against the objective course of events and outcomes.

27 September 1962

IVAN N. MENSH, Ph.D.
Professor and Head
Division of Medical Psychology
Department of Psychiatry
UCLA School of Medicine

CONTENTS

III EMOTIONAL DISTURBANCES
OF CHILDHOOD

IV PSYCHOTIC REACTIONS

THE EXPERIENCE OF ANXIETY
A Casebook

INTRODUCTION

This book has developed from our experience in teaching the undergraduate course in abnormal psychology. We have attempted to achieve three objectives in this course: first, to introduce the student to the important theories of psychopathology; second, to review relevant research on abnormal behavior; and third, to provide the student with a variety of case materials illustrating concretely the theoretical abstractions, statistical averages, and experimental analogues read about and discussed.

We were unable to find much published case material that challenged the student's problem-solving ability. Most published case books seem to follow the traditional pattern of clinical teaching; a wealth of clinical detail and invariably, a point-by-point interpretation and analysis of the case by an expert. Such cases serve the purpose of introducing the student to analytic interpretation and to illustrate how case and theory may be integrated.

Our choice of unanalyzed case materials reflects a philosophy worth making explicit. It is our contention that students need direct experience in the process of hypothesis-raising and hypothesis-testing which is so essential to conceptualizing the organization of personality. Cases analyzed by others lead the student to believe that there is *one* correct method for integrating case material. Since we have always supported the view that there are a number of interpretations of a case, some more probable than others, exclusive exposure to interpreted case material seemed to defeat our teaching goals. Therefore, our purpose is to challenge the student with essentially unanalyzed, raw clinical data. By unanalyzed, we mean case descriptions that present a detailed history of a person and his own statements about himself, with little or no inference about the etiology of his condition. For example, it is a fact that a certain person is afraid of trains; it is an inference to assume repressed aggression or castration anxiety as a source of this fear.

This type of teaching requires that the student be provided with an opportunity to use raw material as the basis for defensible inference. In this book a series of essentially "programmed" questions are presented which are designed to encourage the student to develop a consistent and empirically defensible system of hypotheses. In devising these questions, the aim was the achievement of a delicate balance between giving a student guidance and yet permitting him the freedom of his hunches. In most instances, the questions are arranged along a continuum of generality, with the most general questions appearing earliest in the sequence. As the student progresses with the questions, he must deal with specific bits of information essential to the understanding of the case. In addition, we have used questions designed to move the student through a continuous process of hypothesis-raising and hypothesis-testing. If one question in the sequence leads to a consideration of one hypothesis or inference, the next requires him to weigh this against other data and to choose between possible interpretations. As this sequence of raising hypotheses and testing them against subsequent case material continues, the student is gradually forced to account for a larger body of case material. Thus, while two or three hypotheses are equally plausible early in the sequence of questions, some become less and less likely as more material is considered. Ultimately, the student should come up with one series of hypotheses that best accounts for the relevant case material.

It is, in our estimation, a valuable feature of these questions that there need not be only *one* good set of hypotheses which these questions can elicit. We have been amazed at the ingenuity of students in making original integrations of case materials, all of which are adequate but all of which differ markedly in approach. As long as we assume basic agreement that most psychopathology is learned, the questions provided can be answered quite adequately by students varying widely in their theoretical backgrounds.

Despite this flexible quality, it will be readily apparent to the reader that the questions do not arise from a theoretically neutral orientation. They reflect, through unconscious rather than conscious intention, a theoretical position lying halfway between social learning theory and psychoanalysis. Our questions consistently focus upon early family relationships and conflicts and require that the student project forward from these early relationships to later clinical behavior. Our debt to psychoanalysis is further evident in the emphasis in the questioning sequence upon modes of defense mechanisms and the conditions under which they were learned. Social learning theory is reflected on a number of levels. First, our questions frequently force the student to analyze the patterns of social learning reinforced within the family group. Second, our questions imply that the number of learning patterns possible is greater than those originally conceptualized by classical psychoanalysis. Third, and on a more subtle level, we have emphasized the role of learning, rather than innate forces, in shaping motivations and drives.

Those who desire to understand the logic of the questioning procedure should notice that a number of questioning programs exist in the book. The *retrospective pattern* forces the student to consider first in the sequence the pattern of current symptoms and the circumstances under which they originally appeared. From this point, the questions direct the student to project backwards, until he is confronted with questions emphasizing early family relationships. The *prospective pattern* of questioning places initial emphasis upon the early family relationships and then directs attention to the progressive development of the emotional conflict within the individual over the years. The *intermediate pattern*, only rarely used, requires the student to begin the analysis at some earlier period, typically post-puberty, and then requires both forward and backward analysis of data.

In these questions, understanding the dynamics of an emotional disorder is possibly more heavily weighted than symptomatic classification. While we cannot agree with a currently popular view that classification of abnormal behavior is futile and meaningless, we recognize that the fringe of vagueness surrounding most traditional diagnostic categories does not warrant excessive emphasis upon the niceties of differential diagnosis. Where an important diagnostic issue is presented by a case, however, the questions reflect the problem at some point. When the diagnosis is unambiguous, the emphasis in questioning is upon understanding rather than classification of behavior.

Despite the energy and time which have gone into the development of the questions, it is obvious that usage of the cases does not require usage of the accompanying questions. Most instructors will no doubt think of other questions which should be asked and other case data which should be emphasized. The case histories can be used in any fashion that the instructor desires.

The selection of cases for this book was a difficult problem. Puzzling or bizarre cases, however fascinating, are not always the most instructive ones. The cases in this book are intended to represent a wide variety of symptom syndromes and dynamic personality patterns. We have avoided the "classic" cases so common in the psychiatric textbook; these are rarely encountered either in everyday life or in the clinic. It is our hope that the student reading the cases in this book will gain an appreciation of the complexity of people and their lives and of the multiple interrelationships between the various facets of behavior and experience. Each case presents several important problems of psychodynamics and diagnosis and can be used to demonstrate any one of the problems illustrated by a case, while ignoring the others. In addition to presenting a wide variety of symptom and dynamic patterns, we have attempted to select cases that also illustrate special sociological and cultural problems. Thus, different racial and religious groups are represented as well as all phases of the life span. It is our hope that the cases selected are truly representative—representative of all social and ethnic groups as well as the types of cases genuinely encountered in the hospital or clinic.

It may be helpful for the reader to know how we have used these cases as supplemental teaching aids. When enrollments are large, the total class is broken up into discussion groups which meet at various points on campus. The selection of group members is ordinarily done at midterm because it gives the instructor the necessary period of time for introducing whatever general personality theory and theory of psychopathology he is trying to present. The group meetings are leaderless in character and are held once a week. Students are assigned to discuss one case each week, using the programmed questions as a guide. A written report is required following each group session, and typically a different student in the group is picked each week to write the report. This procedure gives everyone a chance to participate in the group discussions and to write at least one case report during the semester. While we have used individual reports by each student on a weekly basis in some instances, the reading time required seriously limits the efficiency of this procedure. It is our impression that these group sessions are extremely lively; discussion is vigorous, and students evidently do a great deal of preparation for them. The discussion is most productive when all students come to the meeting familiar with the case and the questions and use the group to test out their private theories. We have been impressed with the sophistication of these discussions and with the students' desire to check their hypotheses against current research and theory.

When enrollments have been small we have used the materials in this book in a workbook fashion. Students are assigned the task of answering one set of questions each week, and class time is set aside for discussing the various answers.

Material of this sort is always tentative and in need of change. The cases contained herein and the accompanying questions have been pretested in our own classes. However, it is inevitable that other instructors will think of questions that we did not mention which have proved effective with their classes. We welcome comments from both instructors and students who use this casebook so that we can refine and adapt our questioning procedures as indicated.

THE CASE OF POLLY J.

The Curse

Mrs. Polly J., a thirty-nine-year-old secretary, was referred from the medical clinic, where she had sought treatment for intermittent severe headaches. The clinic reported that a thorough medical and neurological examination had revealed no pathology. The patient had worn glasses for many years, and now complained of "lights swimming" before her eyes. An ophthalmological examination showed no complications other than the mild astigmatism which was already corrected. However, each medical examiner noted that Mrs. J. seemed physically tense. Her physician therefore suggested to her that the headaches were very likely an outcome of this general tension; in his opinion, the underlying cause of her complaints was emotional stress rather than organic pathology. He then referred her to the psychiatric clinic.

In appearance Mrs. J. was a slightly heavy-set, red-haired woman of average height, dressed conservatively but fashionably. She spoke softly and slowly in a conversational tone. Her occasional smile did little to offset a serious, although not severe, demeanor. She sat stiffly upright in the chair, her feet crossed underneath, and all during the interview repeatedly pulled at the hem of her skirt. She said that she had accepted the referral to the psychiatric clinic because she admittedly was "nervous" at times, and besides, "There seemed nothing left to do for my headaches." In her opinion, her nervousness stemmed directly from her headaches. She went on to explain that the headaches were occurring frequently; worse still, the attacks, which came without warning, had built up to such an intensity that she was immobilized during these intervals. She described the insistent throbbing, generally originating in the temple area, which would quickly spread throughout her head. Often, she would feel nauseous; other times there might be accompanying pains in the other parts of her body. She had tried aspirin and various kinds of self-medication to no avail. There were times when she could attribute the onset of the headaches to fatigue, or possibly incidental emotional strain, but just as often the episodes could appear when she thought she was feeling very fit. More recently, the duration of the headaches was beginning to extend to periods of several days. This frequently meant that she could not sleep easily, and therefore, she had resorted to taking sleeping pills.

She had suffered from headaches of "various kinds" most of her life. Her mother had had similar headaches, and Mrs. J. was of the opinion that possibly her headaches were inherited. Approximately a year earlier her headaches had begun to be much more frequent and severe. Up until then they had occurred about once or twice a month, and as a rule, had subsided after heavy doses of aspirin. Never before had it been necessary to stay home from work.

Mrs. J. freely discussed her physical complaints, but was reluctant to discuss other matters. Asked how her headaches affected her activities, she responded with a sardonic smile and a slight shrug. She had taken a leave of absence for the preceding three months from her position as secretary to one of the deans at a university, a job which she had held for over ten years. Prior to her leave of absence she had been forced to stay off the job almost one-third of the time because of her headaches; thus she had used up most of her sick leave. Also, up to a year before she had been active in church work and in the League of Women Voters, but now, with the persistent headaches, she had dropped these activities. Asked specifically how her headaches affected her home life, she hesitated; then she admitted that she felt guilty that she had not been able to keep her house as clean and neat as she was wont to do and that she had neglected her husband because she had often felt unable to cook meals or carry out other homemaking activities. She added quickly that her husband had been most understanding and, indeed, had waited on her, curtailing some of his business and social activities in order to be home with her when she was ill.

It was difficult for Mrs. J. to imagine any stresses or conflicts which might be related to her tension. True, she accepted her physician's diagnosis of "tension headaches"; after discussing the situation with him, she had come to realize that she often did feel tense and nervous, but as to the reasons, she had no idea. She said firmly that she saw no reason why she should be "unhappy." She enjoyed her job tremendously; it entailed considerable responsibility and she had built up the work and organized the procedure to such a point that she was known as the "unofficial dean." There had been several changes of deans during the past ten years, all of whom had depended on her to run the office smoothly. She volunteered the information that she was very fond of her present boss, who was about her own age and considered young for a dean. Aside from business, she also performed personal duties for him, such as taking care of his checkbook and writing personal letters. She felt particularly sorry for the dean because he had been divorced the year before. She added quickly that if this were *her* state she could understand having headaches, but she felt that her own marriage was more stable now than ever before.

She and her husband "never" quarreled. Political activities often kept him out until late at night or, at times, there would be out-of-town business trips. Mrs. J. felt that the remaining times they spent together seemed more intimate, and her husband more loving, even than prior to their marriage. She felt particularly disturbed about her headaches since she had been hoping for the past several years to find time to join her husband in his political activities. She explained that until three years ago she had felt she should be at home, mainly because of their teen-age son, who, after completing high school, had decided to go into military service. She wondered, in passing, if her tension might be associated with worry for him; however, she had to admit that it was a ridiculous idea since he was not in a dangerous area.

At the beginning of treatment about the only definite source of tension Mrs. J. could think of was her relationship with her mother and sisters, all three of whom lived nearby and with whom she had continued frequent contact. Her mother, now along in years, was often ill "as usual" and called her almost daily, complaining of *her* headaches and making small demands on Mrs. J. to run errands for her. Mrs. J. felt annoyed with her mother's frequent complaints and demands, particularly when she herself felt ill and wished that she had someone to sympathize with her. Her mother also relayed worries to Mrs. J. about Mrs. J.'s sisters. Mrs. J.'s next younger sister, two years her junior, was going through the throes of her third divorce. The other sister, four years younger, was having marital problems with an alcoholic husband. Mrs. J. worried about her sisters and wished she could do something for them, but she felt helpless and frustrated. And yet, her sisters, with all their troubles, seemed less tense and ill than she—and Mrs. J. wondered why. All in all, though, she could not see how her sisters' problems could have any bearing upon her current headaches. It seemed that all her life she had worried over them, and she was certain that some of their previous conflicts had been much more serious.

It was only with considerable more discussion that she was able to relate her life history. It was constructed very slowly and not in any definite chronological order, but only as it came to mind in respect to various associations.

Past History. Mrs. J. was born and reared in a village on the edge of Chicago which has since become part of the city. Her father's family had once been large landowners and social and political leaders of the community. By the time of Polly's childhood, however, the family fortunes had dwindled considerably. Her grandparents continued to live in the big Victorian mansion on top of the hill, and everyone referred to her grandfather as "The Judge." Polly's father was the village postmaster, a sinecure which her grandfather had obtained for him soon after her father was graduated from college. This political appointment afforded the family more social distinction than income; always there was the struggle in Mrs. J.'s parental home to make ends meet. But the financial problems never troubled her father very much. When his wife protested their limited budget, he would remark airily that he had no use for money. He was open-handed; often he lent money to friends while his own family was doing without. He could never deny the girls when they asked for money, much to the despair of his wife. Nor did he stint on himself; he wore only the finest clothing and drove the best and latest model automobiles. Consequently the family was usually deep in debt. He spent as little time in his office as possible; mostly he would be at his lodge, either playing cards or discussing with his lodge brothers "women, horses, the weather, and politics—in that order." Polly said that as a little girl she idolized her father. He was demonstratively affectionate with her and her sisters, although actually he spent very little time with the family.

Polly's mother came from a much poorer and socially lower background. Polly's maternal grandfather had been the town drunk, a fact which Polly's father never failed to bring up when his wife started to nag him. Her maternal grandfather died when her mother was in her early teens, leaving Polly's mother, the oldest of a large brood of children, to help support her mother and the younger ones. Not only did Polly's mother take over the main support of her brothers and sisters, but she also managed to complete high school and some nurse's training. Polly came to the conclusion that her mother, in her younger days, must have been very hardworking, driving, and ambitious. Also, it was quite possible that one of the chief attractions of Polly's father was his prominent, wealthy family. "I don't believe my mother was even in love with father," Polly said at one point, sadly and angrily.

Polly's most vivid memory of her parents was their constant battles, during which her mother would upbraid her father, while he, in turn, would become cynical and trade accusation for accusation. After the "fireworks" her father would stomp angrily from the house, sometimes staying away for several days. During these periods, Polly recalled that her mother was often ill with her "migraine" headaches. As the oldest, Polly had to try to comfort the other two girls; anxious and frightened, they would retreat to the other end of the house. Occasionally, Polly fled to the home of friends or to her grandmother's. She was too humiliated to discuss why she had to be away from her home and often wondered if people guessed the real reason.

Polly remembered very little else of her early childhood. She knew nothing of the conditions of her birth or early development. She had overheard her mother mention at one time that she had had a very difficult pregnancy and labor with one of her sisters; Polly wondered afterward if this had been true in her case. Indeed, all during her teen-age years Polly wondered why her mother had ever bothered to have children since her mother always made it clear that she regarded raising children as "a cross a woman has to bear"—a phrase which her mother applied to a great many situations. During her preschool years, Polly spent a great deal of time at the home of her paternal grandparents—possibly because of her mother's illness and pregnancies. Polly believes that in addition to the live births of her two younger sisters, her mother had one or possibly two miscarriages.

In any event, it was very common for Polly's father to take her along with him to his mother's and leave her there for the day until he was through work. She was very fond of her grandparents, who fawned over her and "spoiled" her. She remembered one of her parents' quarrels in which these visits to her grandparents was a central topic; her mother accused her father of giving Polly to the grandmother to raise—an act which she interpreted to mean that her husband did not regard her as capable of raising her children. Polly's father wearily replied that her "imagination" and, he conjectured, her inner guilt as usual were running away with her common sense. Although Polly continued to visit her grandparents she felt guilty, as if she were the cause of her parents' unhappiness. Polly's grandmother noticed that Polly seemed unhappy and depressed; when she inquired as to the reason, Polly was reputed to have replied that she had a headache. She does not remember whether she actually did have headaches at that time, but her father considered this a great joke and used it as further ammunition against his wife, saying, "See what you're teaching the girls."

After Polly began school her visits to her grandparents were much less frequent. When Polly was about seven or eight, both grandparents died. Polly remembered being very sad and demanding of her father some reassurance that they were not permanently gone. But her father, who prided himself on being an agnostic—another source of argument between him and his wife—took this opportunity to attempt an explanation of the reality and permanence of death. Polly believed that this incident may have been related to her later preoccupations with the possibility of her own death. She did remember asking anxiously other times later in her childhood if certain people were going to die, a question which annoyed and embarrassed her mother but seemed to amuse her father.

Polly's memories of her later childhood were somewhat inconsistent. Initially, she recalled being a relatively happy child who played very actively and had many playmates and few if any worries. She was quite a tomboy, who preferred playing with the boys in active games, wore jeans and boy shirts, and seldom cared about her appearance—much to her mother's despair. She loved nothing better than to ride her bicycle around town, play sand-lot baseball, or join the boys in an exploring trip down the river. She seldom returned home after school until almost dark. It was when she returned home, she remembered, that there was unhappiness.

Shortly after Polly's younger sister was born, her mother returned to nursing in order to supplement the family income. Polly's father protested that it was not necessary for his wife to go to work, as they could get by on his salary; furthermore, he felt that Polly's mother was merely avoiding her duties as a housewife and mother. Polly's mother argued that it was necessary for someone to bring in some extra income to pay off the ever increasing debts. She claimed that she had arranged her schedule so as not to neglect her family. She did not go to work until early evening, returning from the hospital at dawn. However tired she might have been at that time, Polly's mother thought it her duty to prepare breakfast and lunches for her husband and the children and to see the children off to school before she got any rest. Polly and her sisters soon learned that if they wanted to avoid their mother's irritable nagging, they should dress and eat and get out of the house as quietly and quickly as possible.

As soon as she was old enough, Polly gradually took over these early morning duties, cooking the breakfast and seeing that her younger sisters were dressed. More and more often, her mother would retreat to the bedroom with a headache. Polly's father constantly praised her, called her his "little housekeeper," and proclaimed loudly, so that his wife could hear, that breakfast was far more peaceful and delicious since Polly had taken over. Her mother said nothing. Polly accepted her father's praises with mixed feelings; although she enjoyed her father's praise, she again felt discomfited and guilty at being the object of her parents' dissension.

Polly remembered her thirteenth year as the point of her greatest unhappiness. "My body played me a dirty trick at this time." Overnight she seemed to change from a slim tomboy child to a young woman. What seemed to her large breasts and hips appeared quickly and embarrassed her considerably. Her first menstrual period was painful and the flow heavy. Although her father had tried to discuss sexual matters in an adult fashion in front of the children, he had always been shushed by his wife. Other than being curious as to what was so hush-hush, Polly could not remember being interested in anything relating to sex or receiving any information about it prior to the onset of her menstruation. Even at this time she could not recall that her mother told her more than how to keep herself clean; she gave her little sympathy for her discomfort.

Despite the amount of time spent playing with boys, Polly claimed that she had engaged in no sex play. Finally, she did remember one incident in which a little boy companion had exposed himself to her and requested her to do likewise. She had become silently angry, "though I cannot remember why," and although he was larger and physically stronger than she, she knocked him to the ground and beat on him "till he was bloody."

Polly's menstrual periods continued to be painful and accompanied by nausea throughout her adolescence and on into her adult years. She almost always suffered from premenstrual headaches. "When women refer to their menstrual period as the curse, I really know what they mean!" Polly said with feeling. Although she gave up her boyish clothes, she never dressed in the blouses and tight skirts the other girls wore to show off their developing figures. Instead, she tried to hide her burgeoning sexual development by wearing heavy clothing and, whenever possible, a coat. She recalled being questioned by her mother and teachers as to why she insisted on wearing a coat even on warm days, and, if permitted, in the classroom.

Using her headaches as an excuse, which her mother upheld, she avoided all participation in physical education as she was embarrassed to wear gym clothes or to undress for a shower in front of the other girls. Her father kept teasing her about her mode of dress and tried to get her to buy more feminine—what she equated as revealing—dresses. One summer he embarrassed her when he bought her a scanty bathing suit and practically demanded that she model it for him. When she burst into tears, her father apologized, but she felt even more guilty that she had in some way disappointed him.

It is very probable that as an adolescent her bright red hair, her pale complexion, and her fully developed figure made her very attractive to boys despite all her efforts to hide her physical attractions. She had many offers of dates, especially from her childhood companions, but as a rule she rejected them. When she went to a party or a dance she commonly suffered from a headache early in the evening and found it necessary to return home. She began to masturbate with increasing frequency and, though she felt very guilty about it, was unable to stop. Her family was not religious, but she voluntarily joined the church and became quite active in the youth group. Frequently, alone at night, she prayed for forgiveness for her many feelings of guilt, particularly regarding her sexual impulses.

At one time when she was about sixteen she tried to discuss some of her feelings with her mother, but instead her mother poured out to Polly her own feelings of disgust regarding sex, revealing to Polly the revulsion that she had always felt during her husband's sexual advances. It was then her mother admitted that one of the reasons she had taken up night nursing was to avoid her husband's bed. Polly was confused and shocked by her mother's revelations. Although this further confirmed Polly's feelings that sexuality was disgusting and unacceptable, she also felt sorry for her father; again her sympathetic feelings toward her father were accompanied by guilt.

Polly's sisters also developed sexually rapidly and even at a somewhat earlier age than Polly did. In contrast to Polly, her sisters were quite proud of their development, which they regarded as entree to adult status. They discussed their bodies and sexual feelings openly in front of Polly, often parading around the house nude and posturing in front of mirrors. This only served to embarrass Polly, and when she tried to bawl them out, they teased her for being a prude. Despite their mother's protests the younger sisters began to date in their early teens, and often they would boast of their sexual adventures with their boy friends. Polly's mother raged at her younger daughters' behavior and held up Polly's behavior as a model. Again Polly had ambivalent feelings about such praise, for she was not certain she wanted to identify with her mother's feelings about sex; also, she did not feel happy about being at odds with her sisters, with whom she had previously been very close. "Praise can be a double-edged sword," Polly remarked unhappily as these memories returned to her during her therapy.

It was also when Polly was thirteen that her parents separated permanently. At first the separation seemed somewhat of a relief, as Polly and her sisters were no longer subjected to their parents' bitter quarrels. Polly continued to see her father almost daily, dropping by his office on her way home from school. He would come by on weekends to pick up the girls and take them out to dinner. However, even before her parent's divorce was final, Polly's father began living with another woman, whom he subsequently married. Polly remembered feeling pangs of jealousy and anger; at first she stead-fastly refused her father's invitation to meet his second wife. After repeated invitations, she finally consented to spend a weekend with them. She found her stepmother a young and beautiful woman, warm-hearted and gay—"just what my father needed." Her jealousy of her stepmother seemed to vanish, and, instead, she developed al-most a girlhood crush on her. Polly would have dearly loved to dress in the casually stylish yet sensual fashion of her stepmother, but she did not dare. Her father quit his job as postmaster and went into business at the other end of town. It was at this time that the estate of his parents was finally settled after protracted litigation with his brothers and sisters. Polly's mother added to her store of bitterness the fact that her husband's new wife received the inheritance which she felt was rightfully hers. She continued to recite in front of Polly and her sisters her accusations of his injustices toward her and the children. Polly's father contributed nothing toward their support in-sofar as Polly was aware, but from time to time he privately sent her money, urging her to buy clothes or other items for herself. Polly did not know what to do with the money; she usually wound up giving it to her mother who, in her usual manner, accepted it with further words of abuse against Polly's father.

As Polly was of above average intelligence, schoolwork came easily for her. In high school she devoted all her energies to her studies and was one of the top students in her class. She seemed to express herself easily in words, took a special course in journalism, and was editor of the school paper. She dreamed of going on to col-lege and becoming a newspaper woman. She received a scholarship to a highly respected girls' school in the East, but at the last minute had to turn it down because there was no money for clothes or board and room. Later she realized she could have asked her father for help, as he then seemed to be prospering, but at the time, it had never occurred to her.

Instead, she considered it necessary to go to work immediately. Her next younger sister, having become pregnant illegitimately, had mar-ried and divorced all within one year. Polly felt it necessary to help support her younger sisters and the baby, all of whom were living at home. Although she had had no working experience, she found a job at which she worked very hard for a low salary. She had the com-bined duties of switchboard operator, typist, and bookkeeper in a small manufacturing firm. She was thrilled by what seemed to her to be the whirl of the business world and did not mind the multiple responsibilities thrust upon her; indeed, she frequently worked overtime without compensation, because "I've always felt that if you were going to do a job you had to do it right." Her boss and most of the office employees, salesmen, and customers were men. They kidded her, asked special favors, flirted with her, and offered her dates and open propositions. Although she turned them all down, for the first time in her life she found herself enjoying male attention. Her job was a relief from her home, which remained full of tension. She found herself increasingly at odds with her mother and less sympathetic with her mother's illnesses and bitterness.

During the next five years, between the ages of seventeen when she was graduated from high school and twenty-two when she married, she continued working at the same job. Within two years both of her sisters married and left home. Both of their marriages were precipitate, to men they had known only briefly. Polly's mother was very disapproving of their choices. Polly tried to warn her youngest sister that her boy friend, who was much older, was an alcoholic. Again she found herself siding with her mother, although she did not join her mother later in the "I told you so's." Her next younger sister's marriage was also unsatisfactory. Both women came to their elder sister with their complaints, seeking consolation. Polly was concerned for her sisters, helped them out with small loans which were never repaid, and tried to temper her mother's denunciation of them. At times she wondered if she herself could ever make a successful marriage. Left alone at home with her mother, she threw herself even more into her work and into various social activities, continuing with her church association and later, at the instigation of her stepmother, joining the League of Women Voters. She remembered her father's interest in politics and enjoyed being associated and identified with him again.

During World War II she was active in the USO. In this work she met her present husband, who was a soldier at a nearby army camp. Although he was approximately the same age as she, he seemed socially much less sophisticated and mature and at first she regarded him more as a younger brother. In contrast to most of the men she met at work or at the USO, he made no passes at her but acted much more like a high school boy, obsessed with sports and eager to discuss in idealistic fashion the affairs of the world. He was an excellent dancer and for the first time in her life she enjoyed dancing. She brought him home and cooked for him and found herself enjoying waiting on him. Her mother also seemed to like him and actually seemed bright and cheerful when he was around. Both of them were depressed when he was transferred overseas. Polly continued to write him regularly and daydreamed of the time that he would return and ask her to marry him, although he had never even mentioned that he was in love with her, much less made any proposal. His letters became less and less frequent and finally stopped. Two years passed and she worried that she would never see him again. She dated occasionally, but "it was always the same old thing. There is only one thing a man wants." Much to her surprise and joy this man returned discharged from the service a few weeks after V-J day, and they were married very shortly thereafter.

Polly had looked forward to her wedding night with a mixture of hope and apprehension. Intellectually, at least, she had tried to resolve some of her adolescent fears and disgust toward sex, rejecting the picture her mother had painted of it. Although she had had no previous sexual experience, she hoped that it might be something that she would enjoy. On the other hand, she was half aware that her sisters were not as sexy as they had made out to be and that they, like her mother, were probably not very satisfying sexual partners to their husbands. She worried a great deal lest she also might not please her husband. Her anxiety mounted and she was very tense. She found herself sexually aroused by his caresses but unable to relax and enjoy sexual intercourse. Indeed, intercourse was painful and unsatisfying. However, her husband was quickly and easily satisfied, and, even though she did not reach a sexual climax herself, she was at least gratified to find him content. She therefore kept her frustration to herself. Nor did she tell her husband of her premenstrual headaches and nausea. He seemed unaware of her suffering and she was just as glad, as she did not want anything to occur which might in any way disrupt her marriage.

This honeymoon state of affairs lasted almost two years. She had quit her job and enjoyed staying home and caring for their apartment and cooking. She dropped most of her activities at church and with the League of Women Voters and instead accompanied her husband to sports events. Despite her tomboy behavior as a little girl she knew little about sports and seemed unable to understand, even with all her husband's attempts to explain them to her. Occasionally they went to a movie together or out to dinner, but she realized that he did not really enjoy these things and went only to please her, so she did not press them on him. He had no friends in town and she had dropped most of her former acquaintances. He had quickly gotten a job selling insurance in association with an army buddy of his; he made a fair living although he did not seem to work very hard at it. Gradually Polly grew somewhat weary of his boyish manners and was less inclined to join him at ball games or all-day fishing trips, particularly when she had a headache. She was somewhat chagrined to find that her staying at home made very little difference to him.

After three years of marriage she became pregnant, an event which she had looked forward to. She was quite ill with nausea and vomiting throughout most of the pregnancy, and had a prolonged and difficult labor. Nevertheless she gave birth to a healthy boy. Both she and her husband were delighted. She devoted every minute to caring for the new baby, but almost from the moment of the boy's birth her husband kept admonishing her not to be an overprotective mother, which he feared would make a sissy of his son. During the day, she was able to enjoy the baby, feeding, bathing, and playing with him, but as soon as her husband came home at night he took over his son's care "in order to make a man of him." As the boy developed, her husband encouraged him in every physical activity, often before Polly felt the boy was ready to take the step, exposing him to what Polly felt were unnecessary dangers. However, her little boy seemed to thrive on his father's attention and encouragement, and Polly's protests were of no avail. By the time her son was eight, he and his father were constant companions, going everywhere together, often leaving Polly at home. With the boy at school Polly felt bored and discontent. She secured her present job as secretary to the dean, at first on a part-time basis, soon afterwards full-time. The money she made came in handy, as they always seemed to be making major purchases: a new home, furniture, a new car, and so forth.

Polly and her husband had hoped to have more children, but her second pregnancy, three years after the birth of the son, ended in a miscarriage. Her physician advised her that her uterus appeared to have been damaged at the time of her son's birth and that it would be inadvisable for her to have more children. For this reason and also because of her continued menstrual problems she accepted her physician's advice and had a hysterectomy. Although her physician had advised her and her husband that the surgery would not interfere with her sexual desires, she found herself less aroused by her husband's advances and less inclined to attempt to satisfy his desires. Again she was somewhat angry that her failure to go along with his wishes did not seem to bother him. She began to wonder if he might be finding sexual satisfaction elsewhere. She was unable to dismiss the idea from her mind, even though she had no evidence that he ever showed any interest in other women. She found herself puzzling why he had never answered her letters while he was overseas in service. Subsequently, Polly built up a private fantasy about a girl in Italy whom she imagined her husband might have lived with while he was in the service there and who had a baby by him. She would elaborate on this fantasy, imagining the situation of this mythical girl, thinking of the hardships of a woman raising a child in poverty, without a husband, putting herself in the girl's position in sympathetic fashion.

Course in Treatment. Polly continued in semi-weekly therapeutic sessions with the psychologist for approximately thirty months. Gradually she began to have time in which she was free from her headaches, at first briefly and then for more prolonged periods. During the last six months of treatment she was entirely symptom-free. After an initial reticence, she was able to talk quite easily about herself and her immediate problems and her past. However, after she had gone over her story once, she seemed to find it more difficult to think of anything to talk about. She became worried that the therapist would consider her unco-operative and then was piqued that he did not ask her questions nor offer her advice. She sighed and said, "I know I am supposed to solve my own problems, but you could do something besides just sit there." Later she admitted that she had developed another fantasy in which she was the psychologist helping others and was more successful at it than her therapist. She was upset at having this fantasy and felt guilty in telling her therapist about it. As she thought more of this, she realized that she had often felt that she was really more adequate in her work than many men are on their jobs. She expressed some feeling of sympathy for her mother who had worked so hard to support two sets of families because both her maternal grandfather and her father were inadequate. She began to express more overtly her feelings of anger toward her husband and to make more demands upon him for companionship without feelings of guilt. Although at first he was irritated by her anger, he gradually responded with more attention to her needs. She became more sexually aggressive in their marital relationship and found much to her amazement that both she and her husband had a renewed pleasure in it.

Questions for Polly J.

1. Polly mentioned that her headaches became particularly severe about one year before being referred to the psychologist. Search through the case history and locate all other events in Polly's life that were occurring around the time these headaches began.

2. What emotions or drives were these events likely to stimulate?

3. How did Polly handle the expression of these emotions or drives?

4. What relationship can you formulate between these emotions and drives and the form of Polly's symptoms (headaches)?

5. From your reading in the text, or elsewhere, can you understand what sort of *psycho-physiological* relationship can exist between these emotions or drives and the mechanisms believed to underly the type of headache which Polly describes (throbbing in forehead and temples which spreads to other parts of body)?

6. One of the important learning experiences for a young girl involves identifying with the adult female role, usually as represented by her mother. How did Polly learn to identify with a feminine role in her early childhood? Take into account the following in your answer:

    a. The relationship between her parents

    b. Polly's relationship with each parent individually

    c. Polly's role among her siblings

    d. Polly's preparation for her adult sexual role

7. How did this identification become manifest in her later life? List the aspects of Polly's behavior from early adolescence onward that support your answer.

8. What in her prospective husband seemed to attract Polly? Can you relate this to Polly's role conflicts?

9. In middle age, what aspects of her husband's behavior, which were originally attractive to her, became irritating to Polly?

10. How can you explain the fact that a particular pattern of behavior can be gratifying at one point in life and frustrating at another?

11. How did Polly's treatment by her husband apparently leave her feeling most of the time?

12. Can you see some relation between the chronic arousal of these feelings and Polly's symptoms?

13. What feelings or emotions did Polly express in her therapy? Why, in view of your above answers, should this expression lead to reduction in the severity and intensity of Polly's headaches?

References

WOLFF, H. G. *Headache and other head pain.* New York: Oxford Univer. Press, 2nd ed., 1963.

THE CASE OF SHIRLEY K.

Death in the Attic

Shirley K., a twenty-three-year-old housewife, came to the clinic with a complaint of frequent attacks of headaches and dizziness. During the preceding three months, she had been disturbed by recurring thoughts that she might harm her two-year-old son, Saul, either by stabbing or choking him. She constantly had to check to reassure herself that Saul was still alive; otherwise she became unbearably anxious. If she read a report in the daily paper of the murder of a child, she would become agitated, since this reinforced her fear that she too might act on her impulse. At one point, while relating her fears, Shirley turned to the interviewer and asked, with desperation, whether this meant that she was going crazy.

After describing these symptoms, Shirley added that she had other problems, mainly with her marriage. She had always considered herself sexually responsive to her husband, but lately, she had noticed a considerable decrease in her sexual drive; frequently she had not been able to achieve orgasm. Worse still, Shirley was beginning to find her husband's advances repugnant. Instead of finding satisfaction in their relations, Shirley was resorting to masturbation; during these times she achieved orgasm while fantasying violent sexual attack by men. Usually these were men of a physical type she had not before found attractive.

Shirley, a petite and attractive brunette, was dressed simply and in excellent taste. Her young and naturally pretty features were noticeably marred by her evident facial tension. She seemed visibly disturbed when she related her fears concerning her son. Yet her manner changed completely as she went on to her other problems. For instance, she appeared quite detached when she related the early events in her life; her tone was monotonous, and at times the interviewer had difficulty ascertaining if Shirley was discussing her own problems or those of a stranger, even when she recalled some particularly traumatic events.

As she became more comfortable in the interview situation, Shirley acted in numerous ways that indicated she was trying very hard to please the interviewer. She followed each statement with the phrase, "Is that right?"; when discussing future appointments she made it clear that she would come at any time convenient for the interviewer.

Current Life Situation. Shirley and her husband, Bill, had been married for almost two years. This was Shirley's second marriage and Bill's first. They had recently undergone some serious crises. Bill had just started his third job in four years, as a lawyer in a large manufacturing concern. He had lost his last job three months before because he was "overly ambitious." Shirley had been very upset when Bill was fired; she had started to wonder if he would ever straighten out and provide for the family. Shirley claimed that for once she would like to have a man who would take care of her. Although she had never been aware of wanting much in the way of material possessions, recently she had begun to have ambitions for a higher standard of living. For example, she wanted to move into a better neighborhood, where Saul could have "nicer friends." She found herself restricting Saul's playmates for various reasons, but this proved particularly upsetting since it repeated a pattern of her own childhood. Shirley found it virtually impossible to ask Bill for anything, and when she did bring herself to ask for anything, either for herself, Saul, or the house, she became so guilty that occasionally she ended up returning the item to the store. Shirley related that there were times, difficult to correlate with any external events, when her recurring thoughts concerning Saul subsided. During these periods, she enjoyed Saul immensely and derived much pleasure in taking care of him. These were the kind of "normal maternal feelings" which she felt she should be experiencing at all times.

Past History. Shirley grew up in a lower-class neighborhood of a medium-size city. She was an only child, and her parents were economically better off than their neighbors. Her father worked as

a railroad engineer and made an adequate lower-middle-class income. Shirley's parents impressed upon her that they regarded themselves socially above the rest of the neighborhood, and they controlled her playmates very rigidly. Thus, Shirley spent many days
in an enforced isolation while the other children played on the
streets. She described her father as a "good guy" who spent a good
deal of time with her. However, he was also quite strict and demanded a high standard of behavior from her. Shirley received an
occasional spanking from her father, but on the whole he was passive, and he left the actual disciplining to his wife. Her mother
attempted to control her by constantly screaming at her, which
Shirley found intolerable. She recognized that her parents were
concerned with her welfare although they found it difficult to be
openly affectionate. Shirley's mother was preoccupied with illness;
she would become "ill" whenever the pressures of family life became
too great. These illnesses, largely hypochondriacal, brought support
and sympathy from both Shirley and her father, and they were her
mother's most effective means of controlling the family. During the
periods of her mother's "illnesses" it became Shirley's duty to take
over the responsibility of the home. Her mother supervised her very
closely; from the vantage point of her bed she unabashedly criticized
Shirley's performance. Although often very annoyed with her mother's
illnesses, Shirley kept her irritation to herself, believing that there
was no alternative to this state of affairs.

Shirley's early physical and social development was essentially
normal. When the restrictiveness of her parents seriously limited her
friendships, she made up fantasy playmates to while away the time.
At the age of six Shirley started in a grade school which was composed of students from lower-class homes. Shirley regarded the
other students as much rougher than herself, and she found much
of their behavior difficult to reconcile with the standards of conduct
set in her home. During her school days, Shirley's parents continued
their policy of keeping her apart from the "bad" children of her
neighborhood. Though frustrated and lonely, Shirley never felt that
it was a matter which she could discuss with her parents.

As she approached puberty, Shirley's father in particular tended
to restrict her contact with boys very vigorously. Initially, as she
entered her teens, she was not permitted to associate with boys or
to be away from home after dark. There were numerous indirect

warnings about the dangers of sex, but she received little or no sex instruction. Shirley entered high school at fourteen and found herself at a loss in an essentially upper-middle-class school. Her clothes were inferior to those of the other children, and their poise and snobbish ways made her feel extremely uncomfortable. At this time, against her parents' wishes, she transferred to a vocational school, where she felt much more at ease. However, the expressed antisocial behavior of many of the children shocked her. Some of the boys already had police records and the girls were not ashamed of recounting their sexual adventures. It was at this time that Shirley began to date. Her father bitterly opposed this; it was only after a violent fight that permission was granted to be out until ten at night. During this period, Shirley met Don, who was her age. One evening, after a few dates, Don induced her into having sexual relations, using, as Shirley described it, "considerable force" to get his way. However, Shirley described the experience in rather bland terms, suggesting that she found the experience neither pleasurable nor unpleasurable. She also did not remember experiencing any guilt over this incident, but she did have a fear of social disapproval should the other kids find out. Shirley and Don continued to have sexual relations for the following two months, during which she submitted without pleasure to Don's demands. Then Don became interested in another girl and their relationship gradually dissolved. She remembers feeling relieved at the end of this affair. After the break-up with Don, Shirley continued to date boys, but she avoided intercourse. She was interested in kissing and petting, but was at a loss on how to communicate this to the boys in a respectable fashion. She finally hit on the solution of pretending to be asleep when alone with a boy. During these periods she would permit the boy to make advances, waking up when the advances went beyond what she desired.

Conflict and discord within the home remained intense during this period, and Shirley often had to fight with her father in order to obtain permission to go out on a date. Frequently she had to endure physical punishment from her father before he would relent and finally let her go. It was during this period that Shirley met Al, a man in his late twenties. Shirley was sixteen at the time and found Al quite attractive. After a brief courtship which involved some abortive sexual experiences, Al asked Shirley to marry him. Although aware that she was not completely in love with Al, Shirley found his proposal desirable as it would get her out of her oppressive home environment. They were married three months later with her parents' approval. Shirley described Al as a "nice guy'" who took care of her and was kind of fatherly toward her. At the beginning, she found sexual relations gratifying, but gradually she lost interest and became frigid. In many ways, Shirley's description of Al was very vague, and further questioning produced little additional information.

After a few months of marriage, Shirley found herself growing more distant from Al, and she began to look around for other interests. She signed up for a course in music appreciation given by a local musician of some repute. She found herself very much attracted to the teacher, James, and within a short time, they were involved in an affair. When she was eighteen Shirley divorced her husband and went to live with James. To help supplement the meager income James derived from his music appreciation courses, Shirley successfully operated a small record and sheet music store. She found James was a very bohemian type who cared little for material things and gradually left the financial support of the relationship up to Shirley. Shirley's relationship with James was a very tempestuous one. In addition to working infrequently, James conducted a number of affairs with other women, often flaunting them in front of Shirley. Shirley reported that she was jealous to a mild degree, but also, she felt more desirous of James and more interested in him because other women were. At times, Shirley threatened to leave James and he usually replied with an unconcerned "OK goodby." When this happened, Shirley became terribly upset and she would beg James to take her back. Throughout the affair, Shirley felt an intense sexual attraction for James and not once did she experience the loss of desire or the frigidity characteristic of the situation with her first husband. James constantly emphasized his inability to support her and his lack of desire to conform to society whenever Shirley raised the issue of marriage.

It was during the affair with James that Shirley's father became seriously ill. She received a telegram from a relative asking her to return to her home town; however, she did not want to go because she was having considerable difficulties with James at that time. Her father died shortly afterwards, and Shirley felt intense guilt because she failed to see her father before his death. Shortly after her father died, Shirley's mother became emotionally ill. She was going through the menopause and developed acute involutional symptoms. Shirley went back to her home town and found it necessary to have her mother committed to a state hospital for treatment. Again Shirley experienced intense guilt feelings about taking this action, particularly since she left her mother in the hospital shortly after commitment in order to return to James. Shirley's mother remained in the state hospital for one year at which time she was discharged as improved.

During the latter phase of her affair with James, Shirley tried several times to leave him, but eventually realized that it was impossible. She was amazed to see how intensely she was bound to James. At times, she felt that he could do anything to her, regardless of how cruel or humiliating, and she would endure it without complaint. At one point, James expressed a desire to have a child and shortly thereafter Shirley became pregnant. During this pregnancy, Shirley was often ill, suffering frequent bouts of nausea and headaches. James worked very little and Shirley continued to work part-time in the afternoons. She often longed to stay home in the mornings to rest, but James insisted that she should get away from the house. During the pregnancy Shirley found it possible to make some demands on James. One morning, Shirley and James had a particularly violent argument in which Shirley was annoyed that James wouldn't help her clean the house. She was particularly determined that James should clean the attic. Shortly after their argument, when Shirley got into the car to leave for work, James kissed her goodby and said, "Don't be angry at me." When Shirley returned home she found James dead, hanging from a rafter in an immaculately clean attic. Shirley was shocked, but recovered in a few hours without any visible disruption in her behavior. She called the police, and made arrangements for the funeral. Shirley was very surprised at her reaction to the whole affair. Although she had lived with James for three years, she believes that she must have been secretly relieved that the relationship came to an end. She found herself strangely unable to cry or to experience any emotion after James's death; however, at the funeral, she found it necessary to feign a grief reaction so that her friends would not think her peculiar. Shirley's behavior after James's death was so well controlled that her friends continuously praised her "for carrying on without going to pieces." Shortly after the funeral, Shirley left the city to return to her home town, where she moved in with her mother.

Six months later, Saul was born following a normal and easy delivery. Two months after Saul was born, Shirley went to work as a secretary at the large factory where she met her present husband. Their courtship was a stormy one but they decided to get married after six months of an on-again, off-again, engagement. Bill seemed to take to Saul very early in their relationship and was pleased with the idea of having a ready-made family. At the time treatment began the couple were trying to have a child of their own, but had not succeeded.

Course in Treatment. Shortly after an initial interview, Shirley L. entered intensive psychotherapy. Initially, she behaved in a deferent fashion to the therapist, obviously trying to please him at every turn. The ambiguity of therapy threatened her and she constantly asked the therapist to structure the situation for her. She claimed that she would talk about whatever the therapist indicated was of importance, but that she could not initiate lines of investigation. Gradually Shirley began to cautiously look into her relationship with James and into the meaning of his suicide to her. Shortly after this period, Shirley's disturbing thoughts and headaches disappeared. Her whole relationship with the therapist changed at this period. At this time, Shirley started reporting sexual fantasies about the therapist (a man), and spent hours expressing her frustration in not being able to have a more personal relationship with him. The therapist continually interpreted these feelings as representative of feelings from an earlier life period. Gradually and with much difficulty, Shirley became capable of exploring her feelings about her mother and father in detail. This phase of therapy lasted over two years at which time Shirley's level of discomfort was markedly reduced. Since her relationship with Bill and Saul had greatly improved, Shirley's therapy was terminated at this point.

Questions for Shirley K.

1. What events were going on at the time Shirley's obsessive symptoms first appeared?

2. What emotions or drives were most probably stimulated by these events?

3. What relationships may be seen between these emotions or drives and the type of symptoms Shirley developed?

4. What methods of coping with anxiety do Shirley's symptoms suggest?

5. Shirley's relationship with James was obviously very important to her. How would you characterize this relationship?

6. In particular, what emotions and what psychological mechanisms do we see operating in Shirley at the time of James's suicide?

7. How might Shirley's disturbing thoughts have been related to James's suicide?

8. Why did Saul become the object of Shirley's disturbing thoughts?

9. How would you characterize Shirley's relationships with men?

10. Do we see some evidence in Shirley's relationship with either of her parents which helps us to understand why she related to men as she did?

11. How would you characterize a relationship in which the partner suffers continual abuse from another, yet feels unable to break off the relationship?

12. What drives or motives appear to underly such behavior?

References

BERGLER, E. On pseudo-dependence. *Psychiatric Quarterly Supplement,* 1955, **29**: 239–247.

CHAPMAN, A. H. Obsessions of infanticide. *Archives of General Psychiatry,* 1959, **1**: 12–16.

LESSER, G. S. The relationship between overt and fantasy aggression as a function of maternal response to aggression. *Journal of Abnormal and Social Psychology,* 1957, **55**: 218–221.

REIK, T. *Masochism in Modern Man.* New York: Farrar and Rinehart, 1941.

WAHLER, H. J. Hostility and aversion for expression of hostility in neurotics and controls. *Journal of Abnormal and Social Psychology,* 1959, **59**: 193–198.

THE CASE OF VERONICA F.

The Invisible Net

For several months prior to her application for treatment Mrs. F. had been unable to leave her home without generalized feelings of panic, which she could not explain. "It is as if something dreadful would happen to me if I did not immediately go home." Even after she would return to the house, she would feel shaken inside and unable to speak to anyone or do anything for an hour or so. However, as long as she remained in her own home or garden, she was able to carry on her routine life without much problem. Otherwise she suffered no emotional or physical disturbance. Because of this agoraphobia, she had been unable to return to her position as a mathematics teacher in the local high school after the summer vacation.

In appearance, Mrs. F. was a tall, slim woman, neatly and conservatively dressed in a gray tweed suit. She wore little make-up, no nail polish, and her dark hair was bound neatly in a bun at the nape of her neck. Her expression suggested considerable depression; her face was taut with tension, her lips pursed, and her forehead had a perpetual frown. She spoke in a low voice which at times was almost inaudible, and she seemed to be constantly clearing her throat.

Mrs. F. stated that she had always been a somewhat shy person who generally preferred keeping to herself, but that up until approximately a year ago she had always been able to go to her job, shop, or go to church without any particular feelings of dread or uneasiness. It was difficult for her to recall the first time that she experienced this panic when in public, but it seemed to her that the first major experience was approximately a year before when she and her mother had been Christmas shopping. They were standing in the middle of a crowded department store when she suddenly felt the impulse to flee. She left her mother without explanation and drove home as fast as she could. Her mother was extremely angry, and she was unable to explain to her what had happened. She admitted that shopping with her mother was a trial, as her mother was a loud-voiced person who would badger store clerks and often "create a scene" if she did not get the immediate and complete service she demanded. Veronica said that she "just knew" that sooner or later her mother would embarrass her on this shopping tour. However, Veronica felt that this incident in itself did not explain her phobia, since it continued to occur whether or not her mother was present. She could not remember when it first might have occurred, but believed that this was not really the first time. Over the next several weeks, during the Christmas vacation, she had several similar attacks; at a church party, at a friend's house, on the way to the dentist, and even just going to the grocery store. After the Christmas vacation she seemed to recover for a while and was at least able to return to her classroom duties without any ill effect. During the ensuing several months she had several similar experiences, usually when she was off duty; but by late spring these fears were just as likely to occur in the classroom. Sometimes she would excuse herself and lie down in the teachers' room, but by the end of the spring semester, her panic states occurred almost once a week and made it necessary to return home. In thinking further about the occurrence of her phobia, it seemed to Veronica that there was actually no particular stress which might account for her fear. Often it seemed to come over her when she was momentarily relaxed, although always she was in public. For example, it might come over her while she was standing in the classroom watching her pupils during an examination, or, as in the initial experience, when she was standing in the middle of the ladies' dresses section of the store waiting for her mother to return from the restroom. She had no memory initially as to what she was thinking or feeling at the time the fear came over her.

At the end of the spring semester Veronica had hoped that her fears might disappear during the summer. She had stayed at home, rarely leaving the house during the entire summer vacation, and her symptoms seldom appeared. However, as soon as it was necessary for her to return to work, her phobia returned even more intensely; she realized that she must get help. She was rather ashamed to admit it to anyone and did not know where to turn. She had read about a woman with a similar condition in a newspaper article written by a man purporting to be a psychologist. She telephoned him and was given an appointment. At the end of the initial interview he told her confidently that he knew exactly what was wrong and would have her back to her normal state within a few weeks. She was encouraged by his confidence and requested a brief leave of absence from her school at the beginning of the semester for "health reasons." Her principal was reluctant to accede to her request, particularly because she would not state the nature of her illness, but because she was a highly respected and efficient teacher he agreed to this arrangement. She returned to see the newspaper columnist psychologist, who advised a regime in which she should leave the house for brief periods, going a short distance and telling herself that she had nothing to fear. He telephoned her each day, asking how she was progressing, and advising her to go a longer distance for a slightly longer period each day. She tried to follow his directions and, at first, suffered no ill effects. However, she still felt unable to return to her job at the end of several weeks, and when she tried to go to church, she re-experienced her phobia so intensely that she was unable to continue on the prescribed regime of the "psychologist" for the next several days. She went to see him and he scolded her for disobeying his orders. He then suggested that perhaps the whole problem was much deeper than he had originally estimated and suggested that she take a series of psychological tests, which would cost her $200. She had received a bill the day before from him for several hundred dollars, which he had explained covered not only the cost of her initial visit to see him but also his half a dozen phone calls. When she arrived the next day to take the tests, she discovered that the "psychologist" was out and the tests would be administered by his secretary. She became somewhat perturbed and rather angry, feeling that her case was being taken too casually. Nevertheless, with the encouragement of the secretary, she filled out a sheet with questions asking about her personal life and answered a series of true-false questions. A week later the "psychologist" telephoned to apologize for having been out of town and to ask that she come in to see him again. She was becoming more and more uneasy about seeing this man and asked what he had found out from the tests. He explained that he now realized that she had a serious sexual problem and that he felt that by exploring this he might help her. At this point she declined to see him further.

Later a fellow teacher called on her to see how she was, since she was missed at school. Although Veronica had not previously discussed her problem with anyone, she did confide in this friend, who advised her to check up on the alleged "psychologist" by calling the psychology department at the nearby university. She was advised that the man in question was not a member of any recognized professional group in either psychology or psychiatry and that his newspaper claims and his behavior, as Veronica and others had reported it, made it questionable that he was a qualified person. Veronica's friend visited the "psychologist's" office, pretending to seek help, and asked him about his qualifications. He pointed to his diploma on the wall, from a college of which neither Veronica nor her friend later could find any record. At that time there was no law in the state as to who could or could not hold himself to be a practicing psychologist. Veronica was considerably depressed by this experience and wondered where to turn next. She again telephoned the university and was given the names of three reputable psychologists in the community.

At this time Veronica was twenty-seven years old. She was living with her widowed mother at the same house in which she had spent most of her childhood years. Usually her schoolwork kept her fairly busy. Aside from her job she spent most of her time caring for her home and garden. She attended the local Protestant church fairly regularly, occasionally participating in some of the social events when requested to do so by a friend or the minister, although she was not a member of any of the church groups. She also enjoyed playing bridge with her friends each week, but had dropped even this social activity at the end of the summer.

Past History. Veronica's parents were in their early twenties when she was born. They had been married only a little over a year. Veronica knew well the story of her parents' wedding, for her mother had told it to her many times during Veronica's childhood. Furthermore, in her mother's bedroom, in a prominent place on the wall, was an enormous enlargement of her parents' wedding picture, which she had often studied in detail. Her mother was a very beautiful young woman, tall, blonde, and shapely. She had often wished that she had inherited her mother's looks. Even today, Veronica said, her mother is an attractive woman, who at fifty still had the complexion and figure of a much younger woman and who only recently stopped "touching up" her graying hair, to dye it a fashionable silver. Studying her father's features, and comparing herself in the mirror, Veronica long ago decided that she much more resembled her father. As far as she could ascertain, he was about the same height as her mother, slim, dark-complexioned, and boyish-looking. He had just finished his law degree and had started practice with a prominent firm, and was looking forward to a promising career. Both parents came from well-to-do families from whom they received many expensive presents at their elaborate wedding; their new home had been a gift from her father's family.

When Veronica was scarcely two years old, her father was called into the military service during World War I. Two years later, only a week before the end of the war in Europe, he was killed in action. One of Veronica's earliest memories was of the funeral (his body having been returned to the United States). She remembered being very puzzled by the collection of relatives who arrived solemnly at their home. She believed she did not know exactly what was going on but remembered crying in echo of her mother's tears. Her mother, who had previously been a fairly vivacious and sociable person, retreated into a prolonged mourning. She seldom went anywhere, continued to dress in black, and would break into tears at the sight of her husband's picture or mention of his name. At this time Veronica's maternal grandmother, who was also widowed, came to live with them.

Aside from her father's death and her mother's reaction to it, Veronica could not remember anything particularly unhappy or disturbing in her childhood. She remembered very little of her childhood prior to her father's death. As far as she knew, she and her mother had been very happy together, awaiting her father's return from service. Her mother had had many friends and was quite active in their church. They entertained frequently and their home was often full of friends. After her father's death, her mother invited no one in and seldom left the house. Veronica believed she had few or no playmates prior to attending school but rather spent all her playtime with her mother, who was fond of making up little games and entertaining her.

After Veronica's father died her mother seemed less inclined to spend so much time playing with her or amusing her. When she was not in school Veronica was at home with her mother and grandmother, but Veronica could remember little exchange among the three of them. Grandmother busied herself with the housework, mother seemed preoccupied with her own thoughts, and Veronica retired to her room with her collection of dolls. Although Veronica had schoolmates who lived in the neighborhood, she does not remember playing with them very much. By and large she was encouraged to stay at home and play. If other children came over either her mother would discourage them from staying, telling Veronica that the other children would bother grandmother, or grandmother would scurry them out on the excuse that Veronica's mother wasn't feeling well. In some way it became an accepted fact among the three of them that anyone else entering the house was an intruder who would upset things. Veronica herself would become annoyed if some child would enter her room and disturb her playthings. She had had many gifts over the years of dolls and stuffed animals, all of which she kept displayed in a set fashion across the shelves, dresser, and bed. Each of these dolls had a name and almost an identity. Her favorite fantasy was that she was the princess of the court in which she commanded these dolls, each of whom had some way of disobeying her which she had to correct. Her mother and grandmother commented on how strict a disciplinarian she was with her dolls. She spent many hours dressing and redressing them. Even as an adult, some of these dolls remained in her room.

In many ways Veronica's mother and grandmother appear to have had an overprotective attitude toward her. For many years, one or the other of them always walked with her to school and was there waiting to meet her to see that she got home safely. She was warned again and again about staying on her own side of the street and having some adult to guide her across the street when it was necessary for her to go anywhere. She was the only child in school who always had a raincoat whenever a cloud appeared in the sky. Moreover, it was a very special raincoat with large multicolored polka dots, which her mother thought was very pretty but which Veronica came to hate. Veronica loved animals but was not allowed to have pets because mother and grandmother said they would carry germs. However, at one time she was allowed to keep a kitten, which was killed soon afterwards by a truck. To console Veronica, her grandmother helped her conduct an elaborate play funeral with a cement block headstone for the grave in the garden. Later in treatment Veronica remembered having a repetitive dream in which the kitten seemed to be a monster of some kind which was attacking the polka dot raincoat and ripping it up. Veronica would awake disturbed and check in the closet to make sure the raincoat was all right. Although Veronica was concerned about discipline with her dolls, she could not remember ever having been disciplined by her mother or grandmother. "I always did what I was told without question; I have always been a good girl, I guess I still am," Veronica said, a little sadly.

Aside from the fancy raincoat, Veronica was usually dressed in very plain clothes. At the girls' school she attended she wore the middy blouse and skirt uniform of the day. For church she was dressed in dark clothes like her mother and grandmother, and even her play clothes were, in Veronica's memory, drab. Until her late adolescence, her hair was cut in a Dutch bob. She gained in height very rapidly, was always taller than most of the children in her class, and reached her present height of five feet, six inches by the time she was thirteen, when she was head and shoulders above all the girls and taller than many of the boys. From approximately age seven her mild astigmatism was corrected by glasses in steel frames much like her grandmother's spectacles. At about age nine she began the long orthodontic correction of her dental malocclusion with a series of braces which she wore for the next three or four years.

Her feeling that she was not like the other children in looks and behavior was further added to socially by the fact that, although she was a Protestant, she was sent to a Catholic girls' school. It was her mother's idea that this school would offer a more intensive education and "better discipline" than the public school. Her grandmother frequently "spoke her mind" on this topic, declaring that this was a mistake because of the difference in the religious background. At the grandmother's insistence, it was specified that Veronica need not attend the hours of religious training at the Catholic school. Each day while the other children were in the chapel, she sat alone in the classroom; she was thus in yet another way marked as apart from the other children. Her grandmother frequently queried her about what they taught at school, maintaining that it was necessary to "clear the child's mind of any funny ideas." When grandmother remarked that she did not understand how unmarried women like the nuns could possibly understand children, Veronica's mother became irritated and told her to be quiet. Veronica heard that the Sisters were considered "brides of the church"; she asked one of her teachers about this but did not remember the answer except that it seemed confusing to her. One of her teachers gave her a colored and detailed calendar picture of the crucifixion, which she kept in her room. She remembered regarding this figure of Christ in agony on the cross with a mixed feeling of attraction and horror. Although she attended Sunday school regularly, she remembers little of her training and does not believe that she ever felt very religious. In some way, however, this portrayal of the crucifixion stuck in her mind; she often wondered about it but felt prohibited from asking either her grandmother or the Sisters about it. Later, in adolescence, she was somewhat fascinated with the idea of death and violence, secretly reading mystery and murder stories and being particularly concerned with the manner of the death of the victim.

When Veronica was graduated from the eighth grade, the Catholic high school proved to be too distant, and her mother agreed with her grandmother's protest against continuing her in school where the religious training was not compatible with that at home. She was allowed to go to public high school, but there was considerable concern in her home about this move. Veronica had been allowed to go to school by herself for a number of years, but the idea that she might not be able to take care of herself out on the streets was renewed when she had to go almost a mile to high school. In this instance Veronica did protest her mother's overprotectiveness and was met with repeating warnings about "knowing how to take care of yourself." Exactly what her mother meant by this Veronica was not sure. Both her mother and grandmother repeated these warnings in various ways to indicate that they disapproved of children who attended public school, as if the children were of a different social class. Though Veronica was allowed to get some new clothes to start high school, she soon discovered that her mother's taste was much different from that of the girls at public school. She felt different from the other children, was socially shy, and felt very much the ugly duckling. Although she had been an above-average student in the Catholic girls' school, at public high school she was so embarrassed that she found it difficult even to recite in class, much less to take part in any extracurricular activities. Her grades fell off slightly although her achievement remained above average. She did absolutely no dating throughout high school and had very few girl friends.

In her senior year she did form one very close friendship with another girl, Eloise, who also was a social isolate, heavy-set, and aggressive, and in manner quite opposite from Veronica. Her friend was much more likely to tell others off, to say what she thought, and to use vulgar language to which Veronica had not been exposed. Veronica's mother and grandmother made it clear that they thoroughly disapproved of Veronica's friend, but Veronica secretly defied them by spending as much time with this girl at school or at the girl's home as she could without causing too much disruption with her elders.

Prior to meeting Eloise, Veronica does not remember having any knowledge whatever of sex or even any curiosity about it. She had had her first menstrual period at age thirteen, for which she was entirely unprepared. She remembered being puzzled and uneasy, but was somewhat reassured by the casual attitude of her mother and grandmother. Her mother actually said little about it, and her grandmother explained only that it was "the curse of all women" and gave her instructions in caring for herself hygienically. Eloise told Veronica the "facts of life" in vulgar terms, which both fascinated and upset Veronica. As her mother and grandmother never mentioned anything regarding sex, Veronica understood from their attitude that this was a prohibited topic and did not dare to ask them about it. Eloise further initiated Veronica into mutual masturbation which excited Veronica and which, for reasons she could not fathom, left her feeling guilty. Eloise moved away just before Veronica was graduated from high school. Veronica again felt lonely and depressed and left out of the rush of social affairs.

For the next two years Veronica attended the local two-year college. Her social habits changed little. Shortly before the end of this college training her grandmother died and her mother went into a second intense period of mourning. Veronica could not remember exactly how she felt about her grandmother's death. "I don't remember that I really felt sad, but my mother's mourning was depressing." Upon her grandmother's death Veronica was given a great deal more responsibility for their financial affairs. She discovered that both her paternal and maternal grandparents had been fairly well-to-do and that she and her mother were owners of a considerable amount of income property and other assets. Her mother loudly proclaimed that she knew nothing about business and felt very helpless. Veronica became involved in straightening out the financial affairs for herself and her mother and prided herself on being a good businesswoman. Her grandmother had specified in her will that part of the inheritance should be used for Veronica to continue her education. Veronica went on to the university where she completed her A.B. in mathematics and obtained a teaching credential in secondary education. Although it was unnecessary for her to work for a living, she wanted to go to work, if for no other reason than to get out of the house. She kept herself busy teaching school and tending to the many business affairs associated with the family property.

It was through one of the attorneys who helped her handle her business affairs that she met her husband. He was the son of another attorney, tall, slim, blond, and, like herself, shy and socially withdrawn. "The main thing we seemed to have in common was that we had no social interests," Veronica said sadly. She could not recall that there was really any courtship between them. She would see him in his office and would be invited to his home, or she would invite him to hers. Her mother encouraged their association and made it clear to Veronica that this was the type of man who would be a good son-in-law. Veronica was also aware that her future mother-in-law was very determined that she marry this man. The wedding was a social affair, planned by her husband's parents, which made the newlyweds quite uncomfortable, but since neither of them had ever made any protest against any plans of their parents they meekly submitted. She remembered that it was only the day before the wedding that she thought to ask her husband where they would live and found that he assumed that they would stay with his parents while she was assuming that they would live with her mother. It was she who made the suggestion they find an apartment of their own. The whole marriage seemed to Veronica to be artificial, as she looked back on it. She did not believe that either she or her husband were at all prepared to get married or were really interested in one another.

After their wedding she discovered that he was very difficult to communicate with, that he seldom volunteered any conversation, and that she herself did not know what to say to him or to do with him. Their sexual life was almost nil. He made no sexual advances toward her and the few times they had sexual relationships it was almost entirely on her initiative—which embarrassed and angered her. She tried pleasing him with cooking and housekeeping, but he seemed unaware of her efforts. Very often he would excuse himself in the evening and leave without explanation, to return late at night after she had gone to bed. At one time she angrily demanded an account of his behavior, but he shrugged it off and ignored her. She began to feel desperate. She did not want to confess her unhappiness to her mother, and she knew of no place to seek help. When she finally pressed the matter with her husband, he coldly told her that he felt it was useless to continue the pretense of their marriage. He informed her that furthermore he had made an homosexual adjustment before their marriage and he wished to maintain it. After she recovered from her initial shock, she was depressed and even ashamed, feeling that in some way she had been at fault for getting herself into such a situation. Her depression was partially relieved when her husband voluntarily left. She was thus able to file suit for divorce on grounds of desertion, so that no one knew the real reason for the break-up of their marriage.

Upon returning to live with her mother, Veronica tried to assume her previous life. Although she had stopped working during the year of her marriage, she was easily able to obtain another teaching position. Nevertheless, she began to feel extremely restless and dissatisfied at home. For the first time in her life she began to resist some of her mother's many petty demands to be waited on and cared for. "I felt as if my mother had an invisible net spread over me." She made plans for a trip abroad with a schoolteacher friend, but at the last minute cancelled them, as she felt that she could not leave her mother alone. "I don't really know why I felt that since my mother is still a young woman and is physically quite capable of caring for herself." Her mother had many friends in church and in the bridge club. When Veronica's phobia appeared and became worse, Veronica's mother was at first startled and then annoyed, but not at all sympathetic. She regarded Veronica's symptom as something which Veronica had "made up" and advised her to "snap out of it."

Course in Treatment. After her experience with the previous "psychologist," Veronica was apprehensive about further treatment. She admitted that she was not quite sure of what she did expect but felt that perhaps something more than "just talking" was the answer. She was able to leave the house and come to the therapist's office without difficulty, but sometimes experienced her panic attacks in the reception room. Veronica also felt shy and embarrassed when talking about herself, but soon found considerable relief in being able to express some of her feelings of frustration. In discussing her symptom further, she found that she did have the feeling that if she did not immediately return home, something awful would happen to her. It seemed connected with her feelings about death and her experiences of loss of various objects and peoples. Later she became conscious that her real fear was that something would happen to her mother. She began to discuss the restrictions which her mother had placed on her throughout her childhood and her mother's current demands on her. On a day following a treatment hour in which she had expressed considerable anger toward her mother, she was unable to come for her therapy session, and re-experienced her panic with a renewed intensity. Veronica also realized that she was very close to her mother and admitted that despite occasional hopes of living some kind of life of her own, she could not really bring herself to take any definite step to do so.

It was sometime before Veronica could begin to discuss any of her feelings of a need for independence, and even longer before she could mention her sexual conflicts and desires. She admitted that she often felt inadequate as a woman, and wondered whether she really ever could make a successful marriage. "I've lived with women so much I don't think I know how to associate with men." She expressed a fear that her marriage to a homosexual might mean that she herself was in some way homosexual. It was with this thought in mind that she remembered her childhood association with Eloise.

After two years of psychotherapy Veronica was no longer experiencing her phobic attacks. She became softer in manner and more feminine in her dress and appearance. She remained socially shy and despaired of trying to make friends beyond her narrow circle of school and church. She did accompany one of her teacher friends to a dancing class and seemed to enjoy some of the men she met there.

During the summer two years after she began therapy, she took her long-planned trip abroad. She did not return to treatment, but shortly before that Christmas she telephoned her therapist to announce that she was getting married to a man she had met at the dancing class.

Questions for Veronica F.

1. Examine the circumstances surrounding Veronica's *first* anxiety attack in detail. List the events occurring at that time and the people present.

2. What impulses or feelings, which might have been considered dangerous by Veronica, could have been stimulated in that situation? Toward whom might these impulses have been directed?

3. After this initial episode, Veronica's anxiety attacks were elicited by a wider and wider variety of situations. What does this fact suggest about Veronica's ability to keep these impulses or feelings out of her awareness?

4. The danger that Veronica feared was evidently an internal one (the arousal of dangerous feelings or impulses in herself). However, her exclusive fear became one of leaving the house. What transformation in the object of her fear took place following the development of the phobia?

5. What psychological mechanism or mechanisms appear implicit in your answer to question 4?

6. What might have been the hidden or symbolic meaning of staying at home versus going out that made the former a means of reducing anxiety for Veronica?

7. Do we see any continuity over the course of Veronica's life in coping with conflict? Can you present any examples from Veronica's earlier history that suggest the operation of similar ways of coping with anxiety?

8. Although it is not always easy to specify an answer to this question, can you suggest some hypotheses about why Veronica was unable to handle her conflicts without resorting to a phobic reaction during the particular Christmas vacation when her symptoms first began?

9. How would you characterize the pattern of relationships which existed among Veronica, her mother, and her grandmother during most of her early life?

10. In view of your answer to question 9, can you now understand why Veronica would have difficulty in openly expressing certain feelings and impulses? *Explain your answer.*

11. All you know about Veronica's psychotherapy is that it was successful. Extrapolating from your answers to the above questions, what changes do you feel should have taken place in Veronica (aside from remission of her phobia) for the therapy to be labeled as successful? In particular, consider what changes in attitudes, feelings, and behavior Veronica might have shown which might act to insulate Veronica against a future neurotic breakdown.

References

FREUD, S. Analysis of a phobia in a five-year-old boy, *Collected Papers of Sigmund Freud,* Vol. 13, New York: Basic Books, 1959. Pp. 149–289.

KATAN, A. The role of displacement in agoraphobia. *International Journal of Psychoanalysis,* 1951, **32:** 41–50.

MURRAY, E. J., & BERKUN, M. M. Displacement as a function of conflict. *Journal of Abnormal and Social Psychology,* 1955, **51:** 47–56.

THE CASE OF GEORGE P.

The Flower Garden

George P., a single, white male, age fifty years, had requested re-admission to a Veterans' Administration general and surgical hospital, "Because my stomach had been acting up again." On admission, George had given a detailed description of his complaint, using many medical terms with which he had become familiar in his previous hospitalizations. At this time his disability had become so severe that he had been unable to work for the previous three months. Almost constantly during his waking hours he was aware of pains in his stomach, a steady "heartburn," and a generalized feeling of weakness and malaise. He was unable to eat any solid food comfortably without fear of vomiting. For the past several weeks he had lived chiefly on skimmed milk. During this time he had lost the fifteen-pound weight gain which he had assiduously accumulated over the year since his last hospitalization.

In appearance Mr. P. was a slight-built man, five feet, four inches tall, hollow-cheeked but bronzed in complexion. He walked jauntily around the hospital, sat relaxed in a chair as he talked, and seemed in general good spirits; in fact, at first glance, with the exception of his notable thinness of face, he appeared to be in the best of health. Indeed, although he said he was somewhat depressed by having to return to the hospital, he seemed most cheerful. He was quite friendly toward the examiner, although he admitted that he didn't see any connection between his physical illness and any possible "nervousness" and was merely being co-operative because his physician had recommended it. He himself felt sure that "nervousness" would be ruled out as a cause of his illness and that he would be continued on a regime of medication, with the possibility of surgery, as had been the case in his previous contacts with the hospital.

Usually wearing a hospital robe, even though not confined to bed, he was always neatly attired. His thinning, dark hair was plastered down against his skull and the nurses reported that he spent a great deal of time in his personal care and grooming. When not wearing his hospital robe he dressed in his working khakis and sported a bright-colored necktie and highly polished shoes.

This was the sixth admission to this hospital for George. He had first been admitted in 1947 shortly after his discharge from the military service, with the same complaint. He was admitted the second time ten years later and he had been readmitted annually since 1957 with the exception of one year. A stomach ulcer had been discovered on his second admission in 1957, and in 1958 he had a resection of the stomach wall. Since that time he had been treated by various medications but there had been no signs of an active ulcer in the last several hospital admissions.

One of the reasons George was referred for a psychological consultation was that his physician suspected in his current complaint signs of possible external emotional stress from which George might be seeking relief. At the time of this hospitalization George was living alone in a tiny one-room apartment near the hospital, as he had been since his mother's death in 1956. He had been employed steadily for the past three years as a serviceman for an automatic food machine company, refilling the coffee and other food machines in various business establishments and institutions in the local region. George went into detail in explaining his job and some of the difficulties involved. He had obtained the job through a friend who owned the company when it opened. He was the company's most experienced worker, having outlasted all other men who had worked for them. In his opinion, other men quit because the work was fairly demanding, keeping a person on his feet all day long and on the move, going from building to building. Not only was he responsible for seeing that the machines were stocked but also that they were in good repair; in addition he had to collect the receipts and make sure the machine was full of change. He had to answer the complaints of the customers vis-à-vis and was on call whenever a machine broke down. He was also charged with trying to sell the machine service to new firms throughout his area. His work was salaried, but he made extra commissions whenever he sold the service to a new firm. He found the work challenging, was proud of his service, and had made many friends by his cheerful and co-operative manner. He claimed that his customers were all very fond of him, called him by his first name, and looked forward to his visits. He boasted that he had expanded the firm's business in his area some ten times in his period of employment by the company. According to George his job occupied approximately ten hours a day, but he didn't mind because he had very little else to do and the job afforded him a great deal of social contact, which he lacked elsewhere. However, shortly after he joined the company his friend was stricken with a heart attack and a young relative of the friend took over the company. He felt that this new employer was letting the business deteriorate through disinterest and that George's own efforts to build up the business in his particular area were unappreciated. At times George felt that his new young employer actually did not want to see the business expanded and interfered with some of George's efforts to see new business built up. During George's previous periods of illness his employer had been most understanding and had not docked his pay although there was no definite sick leave provision on his job. However, during the past year George's employer was much less sympathetic with his occasional illness. George felt he had to struggle even harder to be there every day as there was not always a replacement for him and his customers were becoming dissatisfied. Thus he often went to work when he was really feeling quite ill and struggled through the day. He found the lifting of heavy boxes of supplies and the pushing around of large food-vending machines becoming almost impossible. He finally asked for a two-week vacation, which he had coming to him but which ordinarily he would have taken in midsummer rather than at this time, just after Christmas. His employer refused him the vacation, whereupon George suddenly resigned in a fit of anger. For the following six weeks' period he stayed at home, living at first on his severance pay and then on unemployment insurance. The week before his unemployment insurance ran out George applied for admission to the hospital.

Past History. George was the fourth of five children born in a small, Midwestern town to a veterinarian and his schoolteacher wife. His older brother and two sisters were respectively fifteen, twelve, and ten years older than himself, and his younger brother was one year his junior. George spoke in glowing terms of his father. He initially described him as a very kindly man whom everyone loved and admired. His extensive veterinarian practice left him little time for his family. As a mark of his father's prowess, George told how his father had been one of the first to utilize artificial insemination with cattle and was in George's words "the father of 5000 cows in southern Ohio." George claimed that "kindness and service to others" was the principle of his own life, which he had learned from his father in watching his father's work with animals. He described his father as a silent person who, in his firm and yet kindly manner, was able to subdue and win over the most recalcitrant or vicious animal. He remarked that his father probably regarded animals as more intelligent and as having more feeling than people, and indicated indirectly that his father was fairly impatient with human stupidity.

Another "virtue" which George claimed to have learned in his childhood was "hard work." From school age on he was responsible for many of the chores around their small farm, particularly as both his parents were employed and his older brothers and sisters were already grown and had left the family. George denied that he resented having to spend most of his after-school hours at these chores, saying he often wished he were back on the farm. He spoke with considerable nostalgia of his childhood years, particularly of the rewards of outdoor life and of "good, fresh farm food." He emphasized that although his mother taught school, she was always at home to take care of the house and to provide generous meals for the family and to entertain many friends. He spoke longingly of homemade butter, pork chops for breakfast, and his mother's baked goods. He learned to cook from his mother and enjoyed helping her around the kitchen. He volunteered that despite all of this good, rich food he never gained any weight and was always a slight build, and wiry. His lean build concerned his mother a great deal and she was always anxious to fatten him up. However, he said, he was built much like his father and up until the time of his illness had always been able to eat everything and anything without fear of becoming overweight.

George was a slightly above-average student throughout his primary-school years, when he was constantly coached by his mother. He admitted readily that this coaching by his schoolteacher-mother was a point of irritation to him, although he quickly added that this was the only thing he could think of about which he had actually been at odds with her. Apparently he was able to convince his mother when he began high school that he should be free of her teachings, but he was much less successful as a student in high school, where he was much more interested in sports. Despite his size he had been an active athlete, was always on the baseball team, and even played basketball until he reached an age when he did not have the required height. He had many companions and despite his home duties and extra studies he had plenty of time to play and to get into mischief. He admitted with a laugh that he often embarrassed his parents by his mischievous and somewhat destructive acts —which he thought all young boys did. Occasionally, his mischief brought him to the attention of the town constable, who took a special delight in hunting him down because he was the schoolteacher's son. His parents attempted to discipline him, chiefly by adding to his chores and attempting to restrict him to the confines of the family property. Occasionally his father administered the traditional corporal punishment in the woodshed. He described himself as being "a young rebel" during his teen-age years, who "gave the teachers a bad time at school." Approximately three months prior to the time he would have been graduated from high school he was called to the principal's office for infraction of one of the school rules, at which time in a peak of anger he threw his locker key on the principal's desk and demanded his twenty-five cents' deposit as an indication that he was quitting school. When he announced this decision later that evening to his parents, his father's response was that if he were old enough to make such a decision he was old enough to earn his own living and from there on his father would require room and board money from him.

George decided angrily to leave home. After a tearful scene with his mother he packed his bags and took the next freight train out of town. This was the first year of the depression of the 1930's and George found it difficult to find permanent employment anywhere. He roamed back and forth across the United States, often living in hobo jungles, picking up work where he could or living temporarily off of various kinds of relief from government agencies. Despite the many deprivations which he endured then, George talked about this period of his life as if it were actually enjoyable. When unemployed, he would go sightseeing, talk to people from every walk of life, and live a life of general freedom even though he no longer enjoyed the relative luxury he had been used to in his childhood. Some three years later, when he was approximately twenty-one, he returned home for a brief visit to find his father on the verge of death. His father had long suffered from an undiagnosed stomach problem. Some months before George's return home the elder Mr. P. had been told he had stomach cancer, whereupon he suddenly dropped his entire practice and sat around home in what must have been a deep depression. George was shocked to find his father so depressed and urged him to seek medical care, but the father adamantly refused, saying that he did not trust doctors. Finally the family almost forced the elder Mr. P. into the hospital, where over his protests he underwent surgery. Shortly thereafter George's father died from pneumonia.

After the death of his father, George attempted to operate the family farm for a short period. His older siblings were married and had families of their own and could not, at that point, contribute to his mother's support. His younger brother had gone on to college and was beginning a career in the theater in New York. After approximately a year, George convinced his mother to sell the family property. They then moved to Southern California, where George had spent some time during his travels around the country. Until World War II, George earned his living at various odd jobs, chiefly as a short-order cook and baker. He was drafted into the navy in 1942 and served for four years as a cook and baker. He was aboard ship a great deal of the time but saw no combat other than the constant strain of possible submarine warfare or occasional threat of air attack. He claims to have been deafened at one time by gunnery practice and was given a 10 per cent disability for hearing loss. After his discharge from the service in 1946, he returned again to live with his mother. Using some of his veterans' benefits, he borrowed money and went into the restaurant business. He operated two different restaurants and bars over the next five years, both of which failed. He explained that he had misfortune in the first such venture when the partner ran off with the funds. In the second venture, he foresaw the approaching depression of the mid-1950's and sold out because he was afraid of losing funds which he had borrowed from his mother. Although George never mentioned his inheritance directly, it appeared that his father's estate had been left under the control of his mother, who bought a home and was able to live on the income from investments whether or not George himself brought in any income.

George described his twenty years of living with his mother as almost idyllic. "She was my buddy." He spent all his spare time making sure she was comfortable, that she got where she wanted to go, and that she had all the comforts of home. He described in detail the flower and vegetable garden that he worked on year after year for her satisfaction. He was an avid fisherman and outdoor sportsman and he always took his mother along. He had a special "camper" built for her comfort and always brought back his fishing catch for her approval.

Despite his portrayal of himself as a good boy devoted to his mother, George gave many hints that his adult social adjustment was at times marginal. He admitted that he was in frequent trouble with the law because of his driving habits. He had numerous tickets for speeding, for driving under the influence of alcohol, and later, when his license was taken away, for driving without a license. He bemoaned the rising costs of fines for his illegal driving practices. Although he said that he had lost his business because of the depression, VA records indicated that he also had been in trouble for selling liquor to a minor. He later admitted that his business partner was a professional gambler and that he himself had tried to make money through gambling at various times.

When asked about his use of alcohol, George became tight-lipped and somewhat irritated, saying that he had better admit that he drank at least a six-pack of beer a day because this was already in his record. He explained that he had been in an altercation with a night nurse just the previous evening because she had suggested that he might go to an Alcoholics Anonymous meeting; he felt that it was unfair that he had any reputation as an alcoholic. On the other hand, in discussing his mother he admitted that the one thing she would never do was open a can of beer for him. He strongly denied that he drank anything stronger than beer, but then added with a smile that this was because he couldn't afford it.

In discussing his family, George repeatedly mentioned the successes of his younger brother, David. He described how his brother had become a major theatrical producer, with frequent plays on Broadway and productions in Los Angeles, and more recently in Las Vegas. He remarked how extremely proud his mother was of David and how David would send her theater tickets and a plane ticket to go to the opening nights of his new productions. George admitted that he himself had seen only one or two of David's plays. He admitted with a wink that when his mother was away from home he was able to get in a little extra fishing and drinking which she might not otherwise have approved of. He also described David's success as particularly amazing because, "frankly, David was a sniveling little brat" as a child, whom no one presumed would ever amount to anything. As he looked back on it, George remembered that when they were children David spent most of his time with his books instead of sharing the farm chores with George.

Asked why he had never married, George laughed and said he had always asked himself that question. He decided that he had been left with the responsibility for his mother and that life had been so easy and wonderful with her that he had just never gotten around to hunting for a wife. He went on to reflect that he had been so interested in sports as a youngster in high school that he did very little dating. He had had one girl he was very fond of, but always had to struggle with several other rivals. He recalled an incident in which he had lost his temper and beaten up a rival for this girl, and subsequently the girl's father had forbidden him to come around the house because of this. The girl married another man and many years later George heard that her husband had died. On hearing this, he made a trip back to his home town to visit her. He described her with considerable disgust, saying that she had grown obese and sloppy and "was wearing nothing but a thin dress." Asked more directly about his sexual adjustment, George shrugged and said he guessed he was about normal for a bachelor, explaining that he visited houses of prostitution once or twice a year "to get it out of my system."

George's mother died in 1956. Although he was able to discuss the details of her death and his feelings about it in the same garrulous fashion he had discussed other facets of his life, there was a noticeable lowering and depression in his voice and his eyes seemed near to tears once or twice. He overtly denied being depressed, saying that it was almost fortunate that she had lingered on for a long period because he had that way been able to get used to the idea that she was going to die. He explained that she had been an extremely active and independent person until the time of the accident which led to her death, even though she was approaching eighty. She had been shopping by herself, had slipped, fallen, and broken her hip. She was hospitalized for many months and returned home, where he had to nurse her. Shortly thereafter she suffered an embolism which left her paralyzed and necessitated putting her in a nursing home. His mother continued to "fight off death" for another six months while she lay paralyzed and almost unconscious. George had quit his job as a cook at the time of her injury and had stayed at home caring for her, living off the income of some of her investments. For the following year he continued to be unemployed. After his second hospitalization in 1957 for his stomach complaint, he went back to work as a baker. After his 1958 operation he obtained his present job.

Course in Hospital. The chief psychological problem with which the hospital was faced concerning George was the fact that his attitude toward medical care was becoming more and more resistant and demanding. Most of the staff physicians, nurses, and others knew George well but all were beginning to be despairing and even disgusted with him. His current physical examination and laboratory reports showed that he continued to have hyperacidity in his digestive system but that in general he was not in any gross physical danger nor suffering from any disabling disfunctions. The referring physician remarked that it was often difficult for the staff to understand the fact that the patient might suffer considerable subjective pain even when their examinations did not reveal gross pathology. He said that the nurses and other staff at times expressed open resentment that George required so much physical care from the Veterans' Administration so frequently. George made himself at home in the VA hospital and tended to order nurses and other staff around as if such care were his deserved right. George himself recited how he had previously been in altercations with the nurses over his rights in the hospital and had maneuvered a physician to be on his side to override the nurses' rulings. George's physician was very much interested in George because he felt that the management of such patients was a particular type of problem that needed to be solved.

Both the physician and the psychologist agreed that it was unlikely that George would accept any formal psychological treatment, but that perhaps some regime could be worked out where support by the physician would be of benefit to the patient. It was decided to recommend discharge from the hospital with outpatient medical care to be carried on by the interested physician. This outpatient care was to consist of both medication and supportive counseling. At the same time George was referred to the vocational rehabilitation section of the hospital, where the possibilities of physically lighter jobs were reviewed with him. Through a contact made partly by the vocational rehabilitation counselor and partly independently by George he found a position in a nearby sports repair shop, restringing tennis rackets. George, in his usual good humor, made the wisecrack, "It's a job I've got the guts for."

Questions for George P.

Note: In some instances, it is valuable to start an analysis of a case in the middle and attempt to work both forward and backward in your analysis. George P. is one such case in which this approach will be used in the questions.

1. Looking at George's life during the twenty-year period that he lived with his mother, what patterns of interaction do we see occurring between mother and son?

2. Which of George's needs appeared to have been met by these patterns of interaction listed in your answer to question 1?

3. What appeared to be George's reaction to his mother's death, both at the time of her death and in the years following?

4. In what way can we see George expressing the same needs in the years following his mother's death that were formerly gratified in his relationship with his mother?

5. Looking at George's earlier years, state what you see in regard to the following:

    a. Training in autonomy and independence.

    b. Indulgence of dependency needs by mother and/or father.

    c. The degree of contact between the parents and George.

6. Looking at your answer to question 5, what sort of emotional conflicts appeared likely to develop under these conditions?

7. Can you see any relationship between this conflict or conflicts and

George's physical symptom of stomach ulcer? Attempt to link up the conflict and the symptom on both a psychological and physiological level.

8. At various points in the case history, it is noted that George was happy, unconcerned about his illness, even pleased with his life situation.

 a. What defense mechanism do these attitudes appear to reflect?

 b. What emotions or drives did these attitudes appear designed to inhibit or avoid?

9. Consider the following points:

 a. George worked most of the time with food or in a food related industry.

 b. George tended to drink rather heavily.

 c. George had little to do with women sexually during his adult life.

In what way might these facts be related theoretically?

10. In what ways was George's behavior in the hospital consistent with his earlier personality?

11. Search in your textbook or in any other book on abnormal psychology for a theoretical discussion of the causes of stomach ulcers. Outline some of these theories. Which of them best fits George?

12. What suggestions can you offer as to how hospitals might better deal with patients who act like George while hospitalized?

References

KAPP, F. T., ROSCHBAUM, M., & ROMANO, J. Psychological factors in men with peptic ulcers. *American Journal of Psychiatry*, 1947, **103**: 700.

MAHL, G. F. Anxiety, HCl secretion and peptic ulcer etiology. *Psychosomatic Medicine*, 1950, **12**: 158.

WEINER, H., THALER, M., REISER, M. F., & MIRSKY, I. A. Etiology of duodenal ulcer: I. Relation of specific psychological characteristics to rate of gastric secretion (serum pepsinogen). *Psychosomatic Medicine*, 1957, **19**: Issue I.

THE CASE OF PRUDENCE W.

The Mask of Respectability

Mrs. W., a thirty-seven-year-old Negro woman, sat in the clinic waiting room, stiffly upright in her chair, staring straight ahead, and rubbing a handkerchief between her hands. Although somewhat obese, her general appearance was attractive. Her complexion was clear, dark brown in color, and her features were a blend of the Negro and Caucasian races. She was dressed modestly but fashionably in a beige suit with matching accessories and a tiny hat perched on her carefully arranged hair. When she was addressed, she jumped, startled, and caught her breath before responding. In the interview room she settled herself carefully in her chair and tried to smile pleasantly, but she looked obviously ill at ease. When asked what her complaint was she began to cry. She wiped her face and apologized for crying.

Mrs. W. explained that over the past year she had been experiencing multiple symptoms of what she guessed was nerves. She said that many things made her jumpy, that tears came to her eyes readily, and that she often felt anxious without quite knowing why. She also suffered multiple physical symptoms. She perspired excessively. This symptom embarrassed her considerably because she was hypersensitive to the stereotype that Negroes had a strong body odor. She also suffered from insomnia: she could not fall asleep even though she went to bed early and tired. She would lie awake tossing, then get up, read and eat, but often would be unable to get to sleep until long after midnight. She had taken sleeping pills, both on her own initiative and on prescription from her physician. These had helped for a while, but were no longer effective. She had been advised by her physician that over-use of these tranquilizers would lead to an addiction. Her appetite also had been sporadic; at times she would not feel like eating at all and could not join her family in regular meals; yet at other times she would find herself voraciously hungry and would be at the ice box at odd hours. Her weight had varied considerably, changing as much as eight to ten pounds over a month's period. Sometimes she felt rather dizzy with spots before her eyes but, although she had felt faint, she had never lost consciousness. Since she seemed to suffer these symptom more frequently during her menstrual periods, she thought that she might be undergoing the menopause. Although her menses were regular, they had always been a painful source of tension. She had recently had a complete physical examination, including a consultation with a gynecologist. He had advised her that he had found no organic causes for her symptoms and had suggested that she seek psychiatric treatment.

Mrs. W. was made even more uneasy by this advice as she had always regarded psychiatry as dealing with severe mental illness. She wondered if there was something mentally wrong with her. This concern was exacerbated by the fact that her grandmother had been "put away" and had died in a mental hospital. She began to worry that she might have inherited "a weak mind." However, she tried to dismiss this as a "silly idea" because she knew that several of her friends who did not appear to be mentally ill were under psychiatric treatment. In addition, she had read various articles in women's magazines about psychological guidance. She asked anxiously if the clinic were largely concerned with "mental illness" or if she could receive some kind of "guidance" here.

She also explained that despite her reluctance to be classed as "mentally ill" her symptoms had become so disturbing and so interfering with her life that she felt it was necessary to do something about them. She was afraid to drive her car lest one of her panic-like attacks occur that would cause her to lose control of the automobile. She also felt that she would become embarrassed if she began to cry or "have the jitters" in public. She had dropped her bridge club and the "Great Books Discussion Group." She continued to attend church but avoided the social events there. She was employed full-time as a file clerk with a government agency and continued to work even though she was afraid that she was making many mistakes which sooner or later would be discovered. She had to make extra efforts to get to work every day and felt so fatigued that she had to push herself to do her work and was always glad when the day ended. Asked how her family regarded her symptoms, she began to cry again. She stated that she felt guilty that she might be neglecting her husband and son and that it was also a strain to keep up with her housekeeping and cooking. She added quickly that neither her husband nor her son had complained, but seemed very understanding. She was too often irritable with them, especially with her teen-age son, with whom she found herself growing increasingly impatient. "He's the nicest boy, most polite, and he has his own life to live." Regarding her husband, she was less explicit, saying that she did not believe that he was aware of her discomfort and that she did not want to bother him with it.

During the first few interviews, Mrs. W. denied that she had any idea what she might be nervous about. She volunteered that "many people worry about their families," but she wanted it made clear that she had nothing to worry about in this regard. She stated that her son was "just an average boy" who "loved his mother very much" and "did what his father told him to do." Sonny (Roger Jr.) was fifteen years old and was in his first year in high school. Her husband, Roger Sr., age forty-eight, was a porter at one of the local airline terminals. Their combined incomes gave them a modestly comfortable standard of living. They owned their own home in a Negro district of the city. Mr. W. had just finished completely painting the entire interior and exterior of the house. He also maintained both of their cars, his seven-year-old Cadillac and her five-year-old Plymouth. Sonny also was very interested in cars. "The two of them are always out in the garage and I scarcely see them even at mealtime," she said, with a laugh. Her husband loved to "go places and do things"; he was a good dancer and an active member of several lodges. And, "of course, Sonny is always on the go."

In Mrs. W.'s initial search for some reasons for her anxiety, she remarked that she "guessed" that she might feel some stress on her job. She could not exactly say what she meant, for she had been working in the same office for eight years and neither her duties nor the nature of the work had really changed. She sat at a desk in a large room with many other people and was responsible for one section of the claims files. She had originally had a file-clerk rating but after she had been on the job for a little over two years she was given a rating as clerical supervisor over two assistants. Her main stress on the job came from the fact that these assistant file clerks came and went; sometimes she had only one girl, sometimes no girls at all, to help her out. During the times that she had the entire responsibility her work basket often became filled and she became anxious lest she be criticized for not meeting her responsibilities. Over the past several years there had been one woman who had worked with her consistently toward whom she felt friendly and yet uneasy. She described her assistant as a slightly older woman who had emigrated from Germany when Hitler persecuted the Jews. She liked this woman, who sought in many ways to be friendly to her, yet she also felt uneasy whenever this assistant engaged her in conversation or was in any way intimate with her beyond the needs of the job. She felt that her assistant was not too competent and made many little mistakes in filing and posting which Mrs. W. had to go back over and correct. Mrs. W. did not want to embarrass her assistant by calling her attention to these errors, yet felt that if they were not corrected she herself might be criticized by her employer. She was most uncomfortable whenever her assistant was friendly or intimate with other people in the office, particularly with Mrs. W.'s superiors. "She just doesn't seem to know her place." Mrs. W. thought that perhaps part of her frustration on her job was due to the fact that her immediate supervisors and the directors of the local government office also had changed frequently. For the past six months the position of her supervisor had remained unfilled. This had occurred several times during her employment in this agency. On question, she denied that she had ever been interested in a promotion beyond her present rating and felt that she was not qualified for that position.

Mrs. W. was asked if she met with prejudice or discrimination in her job. She denied this vigorously, saying that everyone treated her very nicely. She voluntarily explained that she felt that here in this city Negroes need not meet with discrimination unless they themselves create the situation by being aggressive and "pushy." She gave as an example her Jewish assistant whom she felt evoked anti-Semitic remarks from others in the office by her social aggressiveness. "You know how some Jews are." She went on to add that this did not mean that she was an "Uncle Tom," that she went where she pleased, never thought where she sat down in a bus, and had just as many white friends as she had Negro friends. All this she announced in a vehement, argumentative tone which contrasted sharply with her almost obsequious manner of responding during previous interviews. When the interviewer indicated that it was natural that she have some feelings about discrimination, Mrs. W. grew even sharper. She remarked fiercely that a psychologist of all people should be aware that discrimination was the problem of the white person and that it had no bearing on her anxieties.

Although Mrs. W. continued to assert that her life at home was without stress, and continued for some time to recite repetitively her physical symptoms, she gradually began to reveal a network of feelings of frustration and tension within her immediate family situation. She began by expressing some worries about Sonny who "is growing up too fast." She revealed that he was not obedient to his father as she wished, and that he was frequently impudent to both parents. As she discussed this further, she admitted tearfully that the dissension between Roger Jr. and Roger Sr. not infrequently reached the point of blows, and that violent, angry scenes between them had been typical of their relationship over the last five years. Within the past several months, Sonny had left home after one of these outbursts and had stayed away for several days without his parents' knowledge of where he was. She described her husband as a hard-headed man, who felt the only way to handle his son was to put his foot down firmly and demand immediate obedience. She often tried to intervene but had been told by her husband that Sonny demanded far too much freedom. She recognized that he came and went without telling them where he was going. They were both afraid he would get into trouble. The W.'s lived in an area where there was a high rate of delinquency and although Mrs. W. tried desperately to restrict Sonny's associations, she was largely unsuccessful. She regarded most of his friends as either openly delinquent or prone to delinquency.

A great deal of the fighting between her husband and son centered on the use of the car. She admitted that she and her husband were extremely inconsistent in granting Sonny the use of either car. Sometimes she would allow Sonny to have the car when she felt sorry for him; at other times she would be at odds with her husband when he permitted Sonny to use the car, as she felt that Sonny should not be trusted with it. She was also afraid that Sonny might get into some sexual trouble with a girl. In her opinion, many of the girls in the neighborhood, who were Sonny's age, were already in sexual difficulties. She was particularly upset currently because her friends had told her that Sonny had been seen frequently with a Japanese girl, which "is something I just can't understand." Sonny was very proficient in sports and had won prizes in track. His parents were quite proud of him for this. His schoolwork, however, was less than acceptable, and his father had intervened with the school authorities to have him reduce his athletic activities and concentrate on his studies. Many of the quarrels began when Mr. and Mrs. W. insisted that Sonny remain at home to do homework. Mrs. W. volunteered that she had high hopes that Sonny would go on to college, adding that it was only through education that a Negro had any hope of achieving social equality. She also regretted that Sonny would no longer accompany her to church and had dropped out of the church group there.

It was at this point that Mrs. W. began to verbalize complaints about her husband. She felt it was her husband's fault that Sonny did not go to church since Mr. W. had long disdained any religion. He had, in fact, made fun of her for her church-going, saying it was just part of her "uppity ways." She felt that Sonny's problems all stemmed from his trying to imitate his father. She said that the two of them looked very much alike, that her husband, a tall, muscularly built man, had been a prize-fighter in his younger days and still had a violent temper. He had gotten into trouble because of his temper and fighting when he was a youngster, and she was afraid that Sonny would imitate him. She admitted that her husband also became angry at her about many things and, in the past, had physically beaten her. This had not happened in recent years as she had told him that if he ever did it again, she would leave him. However, she knew that when Sonny was young he had seen his father attack her and she had always feared that this had been a bad influence on him. She went on to remark that she had many differences with her husband. He liked to socialize with " a crowd I don't approve of." He drank, at least socially, whereas she did not, and he liked to lounge around the house, drink beer, and watch TV, such that she was ashamed when her friends dropped in. She enjoyed accompanying him to his lodge meetings, but was always embarrassed when he became tipsy and loud.

Discussing this further, she became tearful and admitted that she had long been aware that her husband was unfaithful to her. Despite the fact that she and Mr. W. had been married for more than nineteen years, he still had sexual relations with his previous wife. She was always embarrassed and upset when he flirted with other women in public, and she knew that other people in the community were quite aware of his extramarital affairs. Although no one had ever mentioned it directly to her, she felt that she and her husband were often the subject of gossip. However, again, she denied that these stresses had anything to do with her anxiety, since she felt that her husband had reformed in recent years, particularly since the death of his previous wife two years ago. In discussing her marital relationship further, she admitted, with some feeling of guilt, that she had become increasingly frigid. She said that earlier in her marriage she had enjoyed their sexual relations a great deal, and that her husband had often complimented her, saying that in contrast to his previous wife he found her more sexually willing and exciting. Secretly jealous of Mr. W.'s first wife, she felt somewhat flattered when he made this type of comparison. Over the past several years she found herself less and less interested in sexual contact with her husband, especially after they had had some quarrel which, she said with a laugh, they had formerly been able to settle in bed. Mrs. W. felt disgusted with her husband's social behavior, and his lack of attention to social amenities grew more and more irritating to her. In addition, their sexual relationship had been interrupted by his job, which began at ten at night and lasted until six in the morning. She herself arose soon after six to get to work and did not return home until almost six in the evening. They did not even have the same day off. Often Mr. W. would give Sonny the car and some money to get him out of the house so that he could demand sexual relations with Mrs. W. Although Mrs. W. submitted to her husband upon his demand, she admitted she was angry at him and thus could not relax and enjoy herself, or reach climax. These incidents served to increase their marital tension. At first she denied believing that Mr. W. was finding sexual satisfaction elsewhere, but finally admitted, in a burst of tears, that Sonny, in a fit of anger with his father, had revealed that he had followed his father to a house of prostitution. She felt again that Mr. W.'s behavior was an evil influence on Sonny and had urged him to avoid setting a bad example for his son, but Mr. W. said she was imagining things and reacted by not speaking to Sonny for almost a week. She had also urged him to discuss "the facts of life" with his son, but Mr. W. had retorted that it was far too late for that—that Sonny knew everything anyhow.

Past History. Prudence W. was born and reared in Memphis, Tennessee, the oldest of three daughters of a pullman porter and a housemaid. She described her father in glowing terms as a kindly man, devoted to his family, religiously devout, and a good provider. She had less kind words for her mother, whom she described as a nagging, complaining woman who always felt overworked. Her mother had been excessively suspicious of her father, especially when he was away from home for several days on trips across the continent working for the railroad. She felt her father bore many unjust accusations from her mother, that her mother was unduly suspicious of her father's relationships with other women and unreasonably harsh in her demands that he provide more money so that her mother would not have to work. She felt that her mother complained excessively about her employment, since in reality she was employed only irregularly and in many different places. When any demands were made upon her by her employers to do any kind of heavy labor, she quit. She felt that her mother expected to do only the barest housekeeping duties, "really, just to answer the door," and resented the way Negro servants were treated in Memphis, "just as if we were still slaves." Mrs. W. admitted that in the South "no Negro feels like a human being," and that she could never bring herself to leave the West Coast to live in the South again.

Prudence's mother often used illness as an excuse not to go to work or to avoid housework, which became Prudence's responsibility in the home "as soon as I was able to hold a broom or peer over the edge of the sink." However, Prudence never minded doing the housework for she received considerable praise from her father. She also quickly learned that if she was obedient she received less criticism from her mother. She was resentful when her sisters did not immediately join in to help her with the housework and she quarreled frequently with them over this. Whereas she tried her best to play the role of a good girl and be compliant to her mother's wishes, her sisters, Amelia, three years her junior, and Rose, six years younger, took no such pains and were in much more frequent conflict with her mother. However, her mother was no less critical of Prudence, and

Prudence felt her sisters "got away with murder." Her mother's illnesses were never so severe as to prevent her from attending church, lodge, or other social events, and she was one of the community leaders in women's groups. She had high ambitions for her children and pushed them to succeed in school. Prudence was a top student throughout grade school and high school. Her mother devoted considerable time to sewing for the girls and they were always dressed in the latest fashion.

Prudence described herself as shy and retiring throughout her childhood and adolescence. Even as a little girl she had little time for play as her studies and housework occupied most of her time after school. Her mother was critical of her neighbors and their children and would not allow her or her sisters to play with many of the other children in the neighborhood. Even when she reached adolescence Prudence had little social life. Her mother was always preaching about the wild life that young people led, drilling into the girls the proprieties of social behavior. Not only was Prudence uninterested in boys and dating but she did not show any signs of sexual maturity nor have her first menses until she was almost sixteen. "After that, I had a very good figure—until I began to gain weight a few years ago." Although in her last years of high school she had many opportunities for dates, she never went on a date by herself. Her only associations with boys were at dances at her father's lodge. Her sisters, however, began dating at a much earlier age, defying their mother's restrictions. Both married and left home in their early teens. Prudence finished high school at age seventeen and remained at home for the next two years while she attended a nearby college for Negro women, preparing to become a schoolteacher. At age nineteen she went to Chicago to live with an aunt and attend the University of Chicago. Although she had made superior grades in high school and was an above average student in her first two years of college, she barely made passing grades in her first semester at the university, and by the second semester she realized that she was failing. She blamed part of her failure on the fact that she was lonely away from home, although her aunt and uncle were very kind and encouraging to her.

It was during this last part of her year at the University of Chicago that she met her husband. She found him to be a handsome and debonair man who swept her off her feet. She loved to dance and found that she enjoyed the parties and nightclubs, which she had never known before. Her aunt and her mother also were very impressed with her husband. Only later did her mother become excessively critical when she discovered that Mr. W.'s family was from a lower socio-economic stratum. After a whirlwind courtship the W.'s were married in an elaborate church wedding to which the whole community was invited. Immediately after the wedding she discovered that Mr. W. had no intention of living in Memphis and that he was not really eager to stay in Chicago either, as he did not get along well with his own family. They moved to California where he joined his brother in running a small grocery store. However, Mr. W. did not seem content with this work either. He seemed excessively restless and irritable and they had many quarrels during their first year of marriage. Twice, after they had come to physical blows, Mrs. W. returned to her parents. Each time, however, they were reconciled and she returned to California. Sonny was born in the fourth year of their marriage, her first and only pregnancy. Mr. W. seemed overjoyed at the birth of a son and this seemed to help him settle down. He had had no children by his previous marriage and had often expressed a wish for children. He began work as a porter for the airlines and had worked fairly steadily ever since.

Mrs. W. suffered nausea during her pregnancy and her labor was prolonged. Sonny was a sickly child and during his first five years of life had many illnesses, so that care of the baby occupied a great deal of Mrs. W.'s time and energy. With her devotion to the child and Mr. W.'s irregular hours, "there was little that we had to do with one another." Sonny's poor health seemed to clear up about the time he started school. Soon afterwards Mrs. W. obtained her present job with the government. She explained that working in a civil service job provided considerable security as did her husband's job with the airlines. Despite their occasional violent quarrels, Mrs. W. described the first ten to twelve years of her marriage as relatively peaceful compared to the many more frequent dissensions over the past several years.

She admitted that throughout her marriage she made trips back to Memphis to visit her parents as frequently as possible. Her husband seldom accompanied her on these trips. The last of these trips occurred two years ago on the occasion of her father's death. Again she wept as she mentioned her father's death. She said she often thought of him, dreamed of him, and could see his face before her even when she was trying to get to sleep.

Course in Treatment. Many of Mrs. W.'s symptoms disappeared rather quickly after treatment began. She remained, however, at odds with her husband and unable to deal with her son. Gradually she began to express more directly to her husband some of her feelings of anger and to be less fearful of his retaliation. She was able to communicate to him more of her fears about Sonny and obtained his co-operation in being less punitive with the boy. Between them they were able to set limits for Sonny which he could accept. In exploring her own feelings, she became more aware of many of her own fears and fantasies regarding sexuality and realized she had imposed these on her husband and son. She went out of her way to meet Sonny's Japanese girl friend and even to become acquainted with the girl's parents. Much to her surprise and chagrin she discovered that they were as upset as she regarding the racial mixture. She admitted that she had been very angry when the therapist had brought up the problems of race prejudice and discrimination which she could not discuss because she felt that the white therapist would have no understanding. She admitted also that she felt very ashamed of discussing her husband's sexual and social behavior which she felt would only add to the white man's concept of Negroes as irresponsible and sexually loose.

At the end of almost two years of treatment she had been symptom-free for well over a year. She was not particularly upset when Sonny failed to complete high school and took instead a special course in drafting, which his father made plans for. She reported that her sexual relations with her husband were occurring more naturally and were more enjoyable to her and that her husband seemed less aggressive toward her, although she added with a smile, "He'll probably never be a gentleman."

Questions for Prudence W.

1.   *a.* List all of the symptoms, physical and mental, which Mrs. W. expressed when she came to the clinic.

    b. Which standard diagnostic category best fits this cluster of symptoms?

2. A number of general conditions are believed to precipitate manifestations of chronic anxiety. Some that have been suggested are:

    a. the threatened breakthrough of dangerous desires.

    b. threats of the loss of self-esteem.

    c. fear of punishment for the past expression of unacceptable impulses.

To what extent do each of these categories fit Mrs. W.'s situation? Specify and elaborate.

3. What ways did Prudence adopt in her early life to maintain her self-esteem and to minimize anxiety within her home environment?

4. During the year prior to coming to the clinic what stresses existed in Prudence's environment that threatened to shatter her life-long mode of maintaining self-esteem and reducing anxiety?

5. What impulses and feelings, which had been warded off for years, were likely to reach expression if the life-long coping mechanisms (cited in your answer to question 3) failed to function effectively?

6. Can you understand why these feelings should have been so difficult for Prudence to tolerate? In your answer, consider the following:

    a. Prudence's early relationships with her *father and mother.*

    b. Prudence's role as a Negro in a white society and her perception of the ideal role for her racial group?

7. Consider the following data from Prudence's history:

    a. the division of the sexes in her parental family and that in her marital family.

    b. her painful menses.

    c. her mother's fears of her father's infidelity.

    d. her husband's infidelity.

    e. her opinion of Sonny's girl friends in the neighborhood.

    f. her subservience to her husband and son.

What kind of a general emotional conflict do these data suggest? In what ways did Prudence seek to cover and counteract this source of anxiety?

8. Would Prudence be in less conflict with her husband if they were white? What role did her minority caste status play in her anxieties?

9. In what ways are Prudence's conflicts typical of any social group striving desperately for upward mobility and social respectability; in what ways atypical? Generally, to what extent can we say that

Prudence's neurosis is as much a sociological problem as a problem resulting from personal conflict?

10. Prudence admitted that she felt uneasy revealing her problems to a white interviewer. In view of her personal and social conflicts, what difficulties might she have experienced in talking about her problems had the interviewer been Negro? To what extent was the race of the interviewer irrelevant?

References

FREUD, S. *The problem of anxiety.* New York: The Psychoanalytic Quarterly Press and W. W. Norton, Co., 1936.

REDLICH, F. C., HOLLINGSHEAD, A. B., ROBERTS, B. H., ROBINSON, H. A., FREEDMAN, L. Z., & MYERS, J. K. Social structure and psychiatric disorders. *American Journal of Psychiatry,* 1953, **109:** 729.

SEWARD, G. *Psychotherapy and culture conflict.* New York: Ronald Press, 1956. Read Chap. 6, Negro portraits, and Chap. 7, Color and conflict.

THE CASE OF BARBARA Y.

Too Much To Remember

When Mrs. Y. was brought to the hospital by her husband, she was dazed, confused, and weeping. Apparently aware of her surroundings and able to answer brief questions in filling out the admitting form, she could not, at the time, discuss any of her problems with the admitting physician. Her husband reported that she had left their home two weeks previously while he was at work. All the efforts of her husband and the police to trace her had failed until approximately twenty-four hours prior to her admission to the hospital when Mr. Y. received a report that a woman of her description had been arrested in a nearby city. When he arrived and identified her, she did not at first recognize him, did not know her own name, and could not remember what had happened to her or anything about her past. The police informed Mr. Y. that she had been arrested for "resorting" after a motel owner had called the police to complain that several different men had visited the motel room she had rented three days before in the company of a sailor. Mrs. Y. seemed unable to remember any of these alleged events. Gradually she came to recognize her husband as he talked anxiously with her whereupon she began to weep and requested to be brought home. Their attorney was able to arrange a voluntary commitment to the hospital.

In appearance, Mrs. Y. was a short, buxom woman whose dress and demeanor gave the impression of a girl just out of high school rather than a woman of thirty-one. She wore her hair in a pony-tail and was dressed in a simple white blouse and dark skirt, bobby-sox, and low-heeled shoes. On admission to the hospital, her dress was disheveled and dirty, and she wore no make-up. Her face was flushed and her eyes were red from crying. Mr. Y. was a tall, heavy-set, gray-haired man who might be considered handsome. He was quite concerned about his wife's condition, and anxiously asked if the doctors thought she could be helped. He waved aside any questions about his possible concern over her arrest, saying that he cared only that she receive the best treatment possible.

Mrs. Y. was very fatigued, and for the next three days she slept a great deal of the time. When awake, she remained dazed, but responded if addressed by nurses or other patients. She ate very little at first, but then became quite hungry, requesting extra food between meals. Once she became severely nauseous and vomited several times but denied that she was at all ill and seemed very ashamed to have vomited. On the fourth day she became much more alert, joked with the other patients, watched TV, and joined in a card game. Her doctor attempted to interview her and she seemed eager to co-operate, but soon after entering the room she burst into tears and fled back to her bed. Her condition continued to improve, and two days later she was able to talk at length with her doctor about her marriage and her childhood, but remained amnesic about the events immediately preceding her hospitalization.

Only much later in treatment did the patient have any recollection at all of what had occurred during the previous two weeks and even then her memories were spotty. Pieced together with reports from her husband, it appeared that she had left the house with only enough money to purchase a bus ticket to the city where she had lived during most of her childhood. Much later the patient vaguely remembered spending much of one day walking the streets in the neighborhood where she had grown up, and standing several hours in front of the building where her father used to have his office. Further reports by the police indicated that she had taken a hotel room which was later paid for by an unidentified man. The patient believed that she had eaten very little during these two weeks and that she spent at least one night on a park bench along the beach. She had no memory of the man who allegedly paid her hotel bill, or of the other men later at the motel. She was very ashamed to hear of her behavior but did not express any disbelief or denial. She was very afraid at first that her husband would disown her because of these reports and was not relieved by his reassurance for many months.

Past History. Barbara's parents were in their mid-forties when she was born; as they had been childless, they were overjoyed at her arrival. From all of her accounts, they were very doting parents who lavished everything on her and made few demands. She knew nothing of the conditions of her birth, except that her mother was quite ill afterwards and remained in poor health during most of Barbara's childhood. Her mother would take to bed with malaise and headaches and remain there for several days, during which time Barbara was admonished to be quiet and was cared for chiefly by her father. However, she remembered these periods with fondness as her father was a very gentle and good-humored man who went out of his way to amuse her, take her places with him, and buy and cook special things for her. On the other hand, she remembered her mother as a rather fussy woman who always seemed to be afraid something might happen to Barbara, especially that she might become ill or have an accident. For example, her mother never permitted Barbara to play in front of the house because of the danger of being run over in the street. For the first several years after Barbara started school her mother would accompany her on the two-block walk to the grade school. As Barbara thought back, she could visualize her mother hovering over her with a sweater.

Barbara's health in general was fair throughout her childhood, except that she always vomited very easily. She would have brief periods of nausea frequently and vomit several times during an evening. Her mother took her to several different doctors who could find no physical cause for this. One pediatrician suggested that Barbara consciously induced the vomiting, and, although her mother overtly rejected the doctor's opinion, Barbara felt that perhaps she really did believe the doctor. When it was suggested during psychotherapy that perhaps this childhood vomiting might in some way have been associated with emotional disturbance, Barbara agreed that this might be true but could not immediately associate it with any particular disturbance. "If anything, I seemed to vomit more often after having a good time with my father." As far as she could remember the vomiting had gradually disappeared by the time she was twelve or thirteen.

She was a good student at school, made above average grades, and was a favorite of her teachers. The only trouble she remembers ever getting into was for whispering in class. "I was a great talker and Daddy used to tickle me, saying he was trying to find the button which would turn me off." She claimed she had many friends "and went to lots of parties" during her grade school and junior high school years. However, because of her mother's illnesses, she seldom could invite any playmates into the house, and because of her mother's fears she seldom was allowed to go to play in someone else's house. Her favorite game when playing by herself was "dressing up, usually in mother's old clothes." She loved to make up stories, "usually romantic stories," and act them out in front of the mirror. Later in junior high and high school she was quite active in amateur dramatics. She played the lead in the senior class play, "Mrs. Moonlight," a fantasy about a woman who never aged. She claimed that in her early years at high school she was very popular with the boys and was asked many times for dates. However, her father insisted on driving her and her date to and from the dance or movie, on the excuse that he did not trust teen-age driving. The boys seldom asked her a second time and gradually she had fewer and fewer dates. Asked if she resented her father's chaperoning, she laughed and agreed he was probably pretty old-fashioned but that she appreciated his protection and respected his advice. She said that she felt that her parents prevented her from becoming "real wild" like many of her high school peers, adding, "I probably would have gotten myself into some kind of a mess if it hadn't been for my father." She maintained that she had many good times despite the fact that she did not date much during her last year or so at high school, for she became quite active in the debutante auxiliary of her father's lodge. She was elected to several different offices including the presidency, and continued to be active in this debutante organization as "past matron" until her marriage a year ago.

Barbara claimed that the main reason for cutting down on dating activities was her "seizures." These "seizures" consisted of a feeling of vertigo and mild paralysis, but without loss of consciousness. "I would feel warm all over and then feel like I was about to faint and would crumple to the floor." The first of these seizures occurred just prior to her second menstrual period at age thirteen and seemed thereafter to be frequently, but not always, associated with her periods. She said that the relation between these seizures and her menstruation was difficult to ascertain because of the irregularity of her menses. Her menses were also accompanied by severe cramps and feelings of weakness. She remembered her initial seizure very clearly as it had occurred while her father was driving her to a very special teen-age party; he pulled to the curb and laid her out on the lawn where he administered artificial respiration. Throughout her adolescence and early twenties she was under the care of a local neurologist, who later was a consultant at the hospital where she was currently hospitalized. He reported that he had seen several of her seizures wherein she lay rather rigid on the floor, with her eyes rolled back, but that she had shown no clonic movements nor other indications of grand mal seizures. He was also puzzled by the fact that he found no abnormal neurological signs either in his examination or in the electroencephalographic record. Nevertheless for many years he considered her seizures and her childhood vomiting as "epileptic equivalents" and treated her with anti-convulsant medications. In later years he suspected that her seizures might have had some emotional etiology although he had no direct evidence for this hypothesis. However, on the basis of his guess, he told her that he had come across a new medicine which would completely eradicate her seizures if she took it faithfully every day for a month; he prescribed a placebo and she remained free of seizures from then on.

Barbara's mother died of lung cancer shortly after Barbara was graduated from high school. Barbara shrugged cynically as she mentioned her mother's death, saying, "Mother was a nervous chain-smoker and Daddy and I always told her that she would burn herself out." She took over the housekeeping duties at home after her mother died because "father would have just been lost without me." Soon afterwards she became her father's administrative assistant in his real estate business. Her father had always had a "weak heart" and after the death of his wife he suffered several coronary attacks. She assumed increasing responsibility in her father's business so that he could take afternoons off and rest. During this ten-year period "I was the man at the office and the mother at home."

Her father's death a little over two years ago was not entirely unexpected but was a very great shock to her. "I almost had a nervous breakdown then." She became very depressed, felt sick and weak, and thought she might die. She could not leave the house and for many days stayed home alone weeping. Her physician and friends advised her to take a long trip. She sold her father's interest in the business and used part of the money to take a tour of the Caribbean. Though she denied having any sexual experiences prior to this time, on the trip she had brief sexual affairs with three different men. The last of these affairs resulted in a pregnancy and abortion. In mentioning these episodes she said, "I guess I was just so upset by my father's death that I didn't care what I did or what happened to me." The abortion, which was done by a Cuban "doctor," left her with considerable pain and a serious infection which, when she returned home, required hospitalization for surgical repair and medical treatment.

This episode left Barbara depressed, but she was determined to break her depression and immediately sought employment in a real estate firm owned by her father's former partner. Soon afterwards she accepted an offer of marriage from this man, some seventeen years her senior. She had always admired her husband and had been secretly in love with him when she was a little girl and he a young man entering her father's business. At first she had many qualms about getting married, primarily because of her guilt feelings over the incidents on her Caribbean trip. Also she felt that she wanted eventually to have children and worried that the seizures which she had had previously might be an inherited epilepsy. However, her husband conducted an ardent courtship in a gracious manner, was quite affectionate, and aware of her every little need. As the wedding date approached she found herself more and more anxious and postponed it twice on flimsy excuses. On the night following her wedding she had her menstrual period one week prior to the time she expected it. She was very tearful and apologetic to her husband, but rejected his sexual advances. "He was so nice and understanding about it all." However, she discovered that she was completely unable to be sexually aroused by her husband; indeed, she felt disgusted by his sexual advances even though he was a much more gentle and undemanding lover than the men she had met on her Caribbean tour. She tried hard not to show her feelings about their sexual relations to her husband, and at first he made no complaint. It was obvious to her, however, that he was not really satisfied. One night he got her to drink rather heavily and became quite drunk himself. She permitted him to attempt intercourse but he was so inebriated and she so disgusted that it was a complete failure. He swore at her and compared her to a "rubber mat." She felt very guilty and tearful about this incident but did not remind him of it, and the next day he appeared not to remember it. The following week she disappeared.

Course in Treatment. During the ensuing two and half years Barbara was seen in outpatient psychotherapy interviews three times weekly. At first, she was quite loquacious, reciting much of the above history with many brief intellectual insights. She attributed much of her problem to the fact that she was "Daddy's little girl," saying that she had never really grown up. She began to dress in a more adult fashion, using more cosmetics and wearing revealing blouses or knit dresses that emphasized her shapely figure. Her walk and mannerisms became markedly seductive. She made many slips of speech, particularly referring to her father as her husband or vice versa. Once she slipped and said "daddy" instead of doctor in addressing her therapist. When these slips were called to her attention, and it was suggested that she confused her husband, father, and therapist, she would either smile sweetly and remain silent or attempt to make a joke of it, saying, "Oh you and your psychology!" After several months she reported that her sexual relations with her husband had improved markedly, "I'm so sexy every night that poor Bobby just can't keep up with me." She interpreted this change in her feelings to mean that her main problem had been resolved. She had about decided to stop treatment, but changed her mind saying, "I guess you've just become a habit with me." Shortly thereafter she became increasingly silent and obviously depressed. Whereas previously she had always been prompt for her appointments now she was frequently late and several times cancelled the appointment. It was suggested to her that her resistance might be the result of some feelings she might have regarding the therapist. She hotly denied this interpretation and became increasingly angry at the therapist, saying that she felt that he was pressuring her into something, to the extent that she felt as if she were being raped. Attempts to get her to explore these feelings further met with stormy silence. Finally, in tears, she admitted that she had recently had several dreams wherein she imagined the therapist making love to her. Following this revelation she had another brief amnesic period which lasted one day. She wandered the streets not remembering who she was, and finally found herself standing in front of the clinic. Thereafter, she was able to remember and relate several other sexual fantasies which had persisted from childhood. For example she had imagined that impregnation occurred orally and that the fetus developed in the abdomen. Her father had told her "the facts of life" soon after her first menstrual period, but did not say anything regarding the actual act of impregnation. Even after she learned about impregnation (in a physiology class), "it really never made sense to me."

Approximately two years later, she became pregnant, but failed to mention this fact to her therapist for several months, finally divulging it in a defiant, rebellious fashion. Her pregnancy proceeded without abnormal physiological difficulty, but she had several bouts of depression, even entertaining suicidal ideas, for which at first she could not account, though later associated with earlier guilt feelings regarding her love for the therapist and then for her father. She dropped out of treatment shortly before giving birth, returning for only three visits during the ensuing six months. She was wrapped up in the care of her baby boy, indeed, seemed a little too obsessed with the child and inclined to be overprotective. However, she declared she was happier than ever before in her life. She suffered no further symptoms. On the last contact with the hospital, she announced that she and her husband were planning a second child.

Questions for Barbara Y.

1. What is the technical term used for describing Barbara's condition during the two-week period after she left her husband?

2. What event or events were taking place in Barbara's life immediately prior to this two-week episode?

3. What events were occurring during Barbara's psychotherapy immediately prior to her brief amnesic episode at that time?

4. Taking into account your answer to 2 and 3 above, what feelings or impulses of a conflictual sort were most likely coming close to awareness immediately prior to both episodes?

5. If we view the amnesic state as a radical attempt to escape from an internal conflict, in what way did these episodes serve to help Barbara escape from awareness of her conflictual desires? Consider the following components of the amnesic episodes:

    a. the loss of the sense of identity.

    b. the amnesia for actions taken.

    c. the actions taken during the amnesic period.

6. Consider the following types of symptom patterns:

    a. a dissociated state.

    b. a blindness of psychogenic origin.

    c. a paralysis of psychogenic origin.

What common features can you discern in these three ways of handling intense psychological conflict?

7. Do you see other examples of reaction patterns illustrating this common feature or features, suggested in your answer to question 6, in Barbara's early life? List these other reaction patterns.

8. What conditions appeared to exist in Barbara's early home environment which reinforced her ways of reacting to conflict instead of some other ways (i.e. phobic reactions, obsessional symptoms, chronic anxiety states)?

9. What impulses and feelings appeared most conflictual for Barbara?

10. What conditions in Barbara's early home environment facilitated the development of these conflicts about her impulses? Consider, in your answer Barbara's relationship to both her mother and father and Barbara's early sex instruction.

11. Psychoanalysis, in particular, has focused upon the type of conflict which Barbara struggled with.

    a. What name does psychoanalysis give to this conflict?

    b. According to psychoanalytic theory, how does this conflict arise and grow?

    c. To what extent does Barbara's background fit the theory cited in your answer to *b*?

12. Is Barbara's selection of a mate consistent with your answer to question 11. In what way? Is it now clear why Barbara's conflicts were so intensified following this marriage?

13. Also, can you understand and explain, in light of your answer to question 11, Barbara's reaction

    a. prior to the delivery of her first child

    b. following the delivery of her first child?

References

ABSE, D. W. Hysteria. In ARIETI, S., *American Handbook of Psychiatry.* New York: Basic Books, 1959. Pp. 275–277, 283–288.

STENGEL, E. On the etiology of fugue states. *Journal of Mental Science,* 1941, **87:** 572–599.

STENGEL, E. Further studies on pathological wanderings. *Journal of Mental Science,* 1943, **89:** 224–241.

THE CASE OF LEONARD E.

The Prodigal Son

In the initial interview, as Leonard E. contemplated undergoing psychoanalysis, he began by stating it seemed almost unreasonable for him to take such a step. At thirty-seven he was a successful novelist and screenwriter. His royalties enabled him to live luxuriously. His marriage of seven years was, at least on the surface, peaceful and happy. He adored his two children, a boy age four and a girl age one and a half. He had a wide circle of friends in all walks of life, from every part of the globe. He was well liked; people sought him out for his advice and companionship. In appearance he was a tall, handsome man, of wiry build, who could have easily played the juvenile lead in some of his screenplays. He was dressed in a fashionable, expensive tailor-made suit and drove a foreign sportscar. He recounted these facts not with an air of boasting but rather one of incredulity. He argued with himself that anyone with such advantages should be happy and content rather than considering an extensive and intensive re-evaluation of his life. He added that he knew many neurotic artists and scientists who either were in psychoanalysis or should be, but he did not regard himself in the same class and had been told by his friends that he stood markedly apart from them. "Everybody in Hollywood thinks I'm so well adjusted that it is almost a joke."

Yet, for reasons he could not immediately fathom, Leonard E. had felt for some time a growing discontent with himself. This self-discontent had been most manifest in his inability to write. Leonard had not written a major work for the past seven years. His screenwriting, which at best had been sporadic, had consisted of rewriting some of his earlier short stories or someone else's work. Even this screenwriting had not been accomplished without the help of several assistant writers who did most of the work, while Leonard, who had the "name," received the credits and the major share of the royalties. He had tried various ways to get back to writing. He had taken off for nine months and rented a villa in the Balearic Islands, isolating himself from the world and his family, but produced nothing. He spent another vacation in his hometown in Arizona, hanging around poolhalls which he had frequented as an adolescent and from which he had drawn several characters for his previous novels. Again to no avail. "I'm just dried out," he remarked unhappily. He and his friends often discussed the position of the novelist and playwright in American culture; many of his friends felt they were reduced to the position of "hack-writers" who merely turned out something for television and sooner or later were unable to become creative in the way that would satisfy themselves. He did not feel this was exactly true of himself, although the year before he had had the experience of becoming fairly excited about writing a set of TV programs, the hero of which would be a serious and struggling adolescent. He submitted the outline of this series to the network management and it was rejected. He had planned to go ahead and write it anyhow, but could not bring himself to fill in the outline. He was currently employed as the chief writer of a TV crime series which was being considered for a national award but to which, he admitted, he had contributed little.

In the second interview, Leonard confessed that he was not only unhappy about his inability to write, but that he was increasingly discontent with his marriage. Again, there seemed no good reason to be unhappy with his wife and children. He felt that he made a mistake in his marriage in the first place, that his wife was not the kind of person for whom he had any high regard. "She's just another Hollywood doll." He described her as a beautiful woman who dressed in the latest fashion, attended the socially "in" functions, and called the "names" of Hollywood her friends. However, Leonard and his wife had never been sexually compatible and over the past several years, they had—without ever discussing it—dropped sexual relations. Leonard did not feel that his wife was unfaithful to him; "She's too frigid to be interested in sex and too narcissistic to be interested in anyone except herself." Although his wife gave nominal attention and care to the children, he felt that she really didn't want to be bothered with them any more than was socially necessary, and most of their physical care was left to the maid. Leonard himself took extra pains to be with the children and pay attention to their needs.

His wife performed the perfunctory role of the gracious hostess when the E.'s were called upon to entertain but otherwise offered him no companionship. He much preferred the company of his casual and less pretentious friends, his old army buddies, broke and neurotic writers, poolhall companions of an earlier age, or people he had met when he bummed his way around the world. His wife, characteristically, left the house in mid-morning for her beauty shop and stayed away from home with luncheons and bridge, and even dined away from home fairly frequently apart from her husband. They saw little of one another, discussed almost nothing, and thus had no open dissension. He felt his children missed having a mother and worried about the effect upon them. His own sexual life was considerably frustrated by this state of affiairs. He occasionally sought out old girl friends he had known casually prior to his marriage and had brief affairs with them, but without satisfaction. He had met no women since his marriage in whom he had any particular interest.

Prior History. Leonard, the second eldest of five boys, was born and reared in a medium-sized city in Arizona, where his father was owner of a successful, grocery-specialty firm. In the beginning of his analysis, Leonard dwelt on his father at length. In Leonard's mind his father was a model of intellectual, spiritual, and physical strength. The elder Mr. E. had emigrated from the ghettos of Warsaw as a youth and had settled in the Arizona territory when it was still developing. Lacking the friends and financial backing which he might have had had he settled in a community in which there were other Polish Jews, Mr. E. had built up a small business into a successful firm. He had helped to found the local synagogue and became one of the leaders in the Jewish community. He was also highly respected by Gentiles and was looked to by everyone for both financial advice and personal counsel. Although the elder Mr. E. had little formal education, he had become a Talmudic scholar. He had not married until he was almost forty and was thus sixty by the time the boys were grown. Leonard described his father as being a quiet, unassuming, kindly man, one who immediately sensed the feelings of others and was able to give them emotional support. He was an immense man, well over six feet tall and over 200 pounds in weight. He enjoyed physical labor and encouraged physical prowess in his sons, joining in competition with them in games he had never known as a child, even though he was in his fifties. Leonard remembered seeing him split a log over two feet in diameter with one blow of an axe.

At first Leonard spoke less of his mother. He described her as "always being busy with something." She was a constant joiner of every new club and every new movement. Though she was a well-educated woman who had a college degree from a private girl's school, she never used her education. The elder Mrs. E. was at least twenty years younger than her husband. Leonard knew nothing about how his parents met and often wondered how they had ever gotten together, for they seemed such opposites. "While my father never seemed to let anything worry him, mother was always in a stew about something." He described her as quick-tempered and easily excited; her moods seemed to shift constantly. He could remember her as being almost seductively affectionate one moment, and raging in anger the next. Her many social affairs kept her away from home much of the day, and he and his brothers were left in the care of a maid. Yet, at times, she would devote herself to a splurge of cooking and was always worried whether or not the boys got enough to eat. Leonard felt his father was most patient with his wife and he and his brothers often wondered how his father put up with "mother's antics." She was very ambitious for her children, insisted that they make the best grades at school, and scraped together every cent of the family fortunes to ensure that each of them would receive a professional education.

Leonard always felt distinctly set apart from his four brothers. For one thing, he was more separated in age; his older brother, Herschel, was almost five years his senior and his next younger brother, David, was four years younger. In contrast, David, Marvin, and Emil were just about a year apart. Thus Herschel always had his older group of friends and Leonard's younger brothers formed a coterie of their own. Leonard had considerable admiration for Herschel, "who was very much like my father," a serious and quiet person, a top student who completed high school at the age of sixteen and medical school when he was twenty-three, and was also a track star. Leonard's younger brothers were a noisy and mischievous gang, leaders in their group at school and in the neigborhood as children, and in social and community affairs as adolescents and young adults. All of them were bright in school and outstanding athletes.

In contrast, Leonard was the weakling and aesthete. His mother made much of this difference, often recalling that he was the son who "scarcely got born." Herschel's birth had left his mother weakened and the following year she had a miscarriage. She had considerable trouble during her pregnancy with Leonard and his birth necessitated a caesarean section. He was under-sized as a newborn, and was kept in an incubator for several weeks before he could be taken home. He remembered also that his mother described him as difficult to care for; he cried a great deal and was a fussy eater. He did not seem to thrive on either breast-feeding or special formulas. Leonard felt embarrassed as his mother recited to her many friends the story of the difficulties of his early years. He himself had no memory of his infancy; his earliest recollection was the birth of his next younger brother, David. Leonard believed that his mother had a miscarriage between his own birth and David's. In any case, it seemed to Leonard that his mother had been ill and irritable for a long time before David was born. He remembered that he knew some event was forthcoming; very likely he had been told that his mother was going to have a baby, but he had imagined that some dreadful event was going to happen wherein he would lose her. His apprehension was heightened when he and his older brother were sent away to his maternal grandmother for the summer when David was born. He remembered being so unhappy and surly that his grandmother complained to his parents that he was unmanageable. Although he was at home when his younger two brothers were born, he remembered having similar feelings of fear and depression on both occasions.

Like his brothers, Leonard was very bright and intellectually curious. However, his record of academic achievement was far more erratic. He had learned to read before he had started school and made even more rapid progress than had his older brother. His parents seemed amazed at his precocity and contrasted his rapid achievement with Herschel's more plodding progress. Soon after Leonard began school, however, he seemed inclined to disregard the lessons set out by the teacher and often failed to do his homework. At the same time he was the youngest member of the community ever to have obtained a library card, and he read everything he could lay his hands on. He also loved to join adult conversations and amused his elders with his acute perceptions and witty remarks. "Still compared with Herschel, he was the student and I was a flash in the pan." Very early in the boys' lives, the parents planned out their adult careers. It was predetermined by them that Herschel should become a physician. Leonard was to follow in his father's business. The younger boys were to be a lawyer, an architect, a scientist. Consequently Leonard was encouraged to spend a great deal of time with his father at his place of business. Even in grade school, he was sent over to "the store" and was expected to do some kind of work, carrying in supplies or sweeping up. In addition, both he and Herschel spent a great deal of time in religious training, studying Hebrew and preparing for their Bar Miztvahs. Their evenings were filled with homework, from the public school and from Hebrew school. Their father supervised their religious training and their mother, their public education. At one time Leonard's father secretly told him that he would be just as pleased if Leonard became a rabbi, which attracted Leonard a great deal more than going into business.

Leonard remained slim and even a little shorter than many other boys of his age, until late adolescence. "I certainly was the shrimp in my family." He had no ability nor interest in athletics. His health was fair but his mother was always concerned because he was underweight and tried stuffing him with various foods, constantly looking up new diets and carting him off to the pediatrician for advice. Everything that came on the market in the way of health foods she purchased for Leonard in an effort to fatten him up.

One incident from his middle childhood years which Leonard remembered particularly vividly and as having both physiological and psychological impact on him, was the accident in which his nose was broken. Even before this accident, Leonard had felt uncomfortable about his nose; all the family had noses which were large with a prominent hump. Leonard felt his nose was the largest and most distorted in shape. He remembered as a very young child looking in a mirror and worrying about his nose, and being told not to be concerned with it. He was approximately eight when driving with his parents, his father was forced to stop very suddenly and Leonard's head was smashed against the dashboard, breaking his nose. This accident was overshadowed by the fact that at that moment, for the first and only time in Leonard's memory his parents were openly quarreling. His father had said, very sharply, to his mother that if she had not been bothering him with all her "yaketty-yak" he could have avoided the accident. Leonard was very upset at hearing his parents quarrel and this, in some way, enhanced his feelings of conflict about his nose. Actually, in the ensuing surgery, the hump was removed and his nose was reset in a much more "perfect" alignment. Nevertheless, for years Leonard continued to worry about his nose and his looks.

Fairly early in childhood Leonard, in his relationship to others, first to his family and then to his friends, began to play the role of being the person to whom they could look for various kinds of help. If his mother needed something she knew that Leonard would get it for her. At the store, Leonard would volunteer to help out his father or the employees in many little ways. He was always offering to do something for his brothers, sharing his possessions with them, lending them money, giving up a prized piece of food, or taking on some onerous household chore they didn't want to do. He would give the extra food, which his mother loaded in his lunch, to his friends at school. He begged money from his father to get presents for his teachers, even though the other children didn't bother to bring them presents at Christmas or at the end of the year. It was Leonard who volunteered to be the school monitor. Sometimes he would go so far as to take the blame for things that his brothers or friends did, but he was not a very successful liar and the adult authorities seldom believed him. From childhood on, he seemed to accumulate a great many friends who, in one way or another, were underdogs. His closest companion at the store was the Negro janitor. At age eleven, he interceded with his father to stop the prosecution of an employee who had stolen a considerable amount of money from the firm, basing his argument on quotations from the Talmud regarding forgiveness. Even his pets were tramps which he rescued and brought home and cared for—defending them against his mother and brothers who couldn't understand why he took so much trouble with dogs and cats that seemed so beaten up and unlovable. One of his teachers at one time called his mother in for a long talk to complain about the type of boys that "Leonard plays with" since they were all "from the other side of the tracks." There were many itinerant farmworkers and hobos who floated through his town during the winter and Leonard loved to listen to their tales of travel and woe. His parents were somewhat concerned about his interest in these people, but his father praised him for his "interest in humanity." His mother, who also had many liberal political interests, was only afraid that in some way he might accidentally be harmed.

In high school Leonard was on a friendly basis with all his peers and occasionally attended social events with his companions, but "in reality I was a lone wolf." He much preferred to hang around the poolroom next door to his father's place of business in the company of adult acquaintances. His mother became more fearful that he might become delinquent and was less certain that she wanted him to take over his father's business. It became obvious to Leonard that his mother did not regard his father's grocery business as at all prestigeful and that she had some higher status in mind for him. Although the elder Mr. E.'s business had been the prominent, "fancy" grocery of town at one time, in later years it was enveloped by the slums and did not meet the competition of the newer supermarkets. By the time Leonard was eighteen and was finishing high school, his father sold the business and retired. It was then the middle of World War II at this time and many foodstuffs were difficult to obtain. The question of Leonard's further career was at least temporarily set to one side after his graduation from high school when he was drafted into the army.

Prior to entering the service, Leonard's sexual experiences had been limited to masturbation and talking about sex with his adult companions around the poolroom and the hobo jungles. Sex was a topic which was implicitly tabooed in his home, never mentioned by his parents nor even by his brothers. Leonard believed that there had been some mutual sex play among his younger brothers from which he was excluded. As an adolescent he felt very guilty about masturbating, tried many times to stop, and worried that there might be something wrong with him that he felt compelled to continue. He heard many tales of sexual adventure related in ribald terms by his poolhall friends, especially about their associations with prostitutes or women they met in their travels. He often daydreamed of the supposedly sexually uninhibited lives that these men led. He was approached once or twice by one of them inviting him to a homosexual relationship, but in both instances another older man intervened and drove off the would-be seducer. It was at one of these times that he learned that these men talked a great deal about sexual license and sexual adventure while their lives in reality were sexually empty. He was somewhat disillusioned but continued in his masturbatory daydreams. Although he occasionally went to a party or a dance with his high school companions, he never had a date alone with a girl in high school and, as he looked back on it, he seemed strangely uninterested in dating. All the girls in high school seemed far too nice and proper in contrast to the women he heard of from his adult friends at the poolhall. He believed that if he so much as put an arm around a girl to dance with her, he would sully her because of his own "dirty mind." He would purposely torture himself by watching the movement of girls' bodies as they walked, trying to see which girls had the largest breasts; then at night he would lay awake, remembering these observations and trying to keep himself from masturbating.

While in the military service Leonard had many heterosexual experiences both with prostitutes and other women he met. It was as if there were some ban on sexuality lifted when he left home. These experiences were relatively uneventful and he enjoyed himself without feelings of guilt. He entered the service late in the war and was shipped initially to the Pacific theater of operations, where he was stationed in Australia, the Philippines, and Japan. While stationed in Japan he lived with one Japanese girl for several months. "I almost fell in love with her." This relationship caused him more feelings of conflict. He felt obligated to this Japanese girl, for their relationship did not seem to be quite as casual as his previous experiences had been. After approximately eighteen months in the Orient he was transferred to the European theater, where he spent another year before being discharged. Here again, he was relatively free from military duty and spent a great deal of time traveling around the countryside meeting people and having a good time. He was also deeply affected by the poverty and misery which the war had left, both in the Orient and in Europe. "It was as if there was some mass injustice of which I had been a part all my life."

After Leonard returned home, he attended the state college for a year. Although he had made at least above-average grades he had been quite bored. So he quit and bummed his way across the country, looking up old army buddies and friends he had known among the itinerants in his childhood. He joined a friend who had been a reporter on an army newspaper and was founding a small newspaper in the Midwest. Leonard had been on the staff of his high school paper and had written several short stories, one of which had won a prize in a contest. He worked briefly on his friend's paper until it folded. He and his friend then obtained jobs as reporters on a large city newspaper where they continued to eke out a living. The following year, at his mother's insistence, he resumed his college education, but enrolled at the University of Chicago instead of returning to Arizona. He made top grades in those courses which interested him— classes in writing techniques and in English and French literature —but otherwise "I had to drag myself to class." After three semesters it became evident that he was not really working toward any degree and he dropped out of school.

Even before he went to the University of Chicago, Leonard had begun writing fiction. He turned out several short stories and circulated them among various magazines but they were rejected for publication. Editors commented on his creative imagination but called his writing "sloppy" and advised extensive rewriting. Despite this advice, Leonard found it all but impossible to rework his creations independently, even in his later novels and screen plays. "I let it go to the point of passive resistance." About the time he left Chicago he resubmitted two of these stories which he had reworked slightly with the help of one of his professors and they were accepted by prominent literary journals. His professor encouraged him to work on a novel which Leonard had begun writing and offered him the use of a beach cottage in Southern California where he could be isolated and do nothing but write. By devoting every ounce of his energy day and night Leonard completed his novel in approximately four months. The theme of the novel concerned a man's relationship with his wayward son. The hero was the father who gave to the son in every way, expecting no return, only to be rejected by the son who wasted his father's gifts and his own talents, but was still accepted by the father. The novel ended much as it began with the father continuing to support the son and the son unrepentant and still demanding. Much to Leonard's surprise the novel was accepted by the first publisher to whom he submitted it. He received high commedations from literary reviewers, but several critics remarked on the "morality" of the theme, suggesting that although Leonard had picked out a social problem of our age, he had made it into an approved way of life. Although the book was not a popular best-seller, Leonard became immediately known as one of the up-and-coming writers of the day. One of his published short stories with the theme of the restlessness and purposelessness of adolescence was purchased by a new and experimental movie producer and made into a film. This experimental film was considered very daring and received acclaim as an art film, and in the ensuing year won an international film prize. Thus at twenty-eight Leonard found himself an accepted and famous writer.

His novel was published in the spring of his twenty-seventh year and thereafter he went home to Arizona. Ostensibly he wanted to rest, but he found himself engaged in writing a second novel. The second novel had the theme of a mother who was a failure, with—as he explained it—a "twist on Momism." Here the heroine was a well-meaning woman who did all the expected things for her children and husband but underneath did not really care for them, and they sensed it. He continued writing this novel while living at home with his parents. Since none of his brothers lived at home any longer and his parents were busy with their own lives, he had plenty of privacy. During the summer he also met a girl he had known in high school and had admired secretly from afar. He described her as a soft, feminine, and quiet person and he fell very much in love with her. She seemed also to accept him and by late fall they had made plans to get married. However, he found himself becoming increasingly anxious and finally, after postponing the wedding several times, he left for New York City two days before the wedding was to take place. He could not account for his action except that he felt that he was not worthy of this girl's affections; he was unable to explain his feelings to her. Considerably depressed he felt he had to "get away from it all." He therefore spent the next year idly traveling across Europe, looking up old friends, and then back to Japan for a few weeks before ending up in Hollywood. Here he found enough energy to write a new screenplay.

On Leonard's thirtieth birthday he received notice that his father was dying. He returned home just in time for the funeral. Here again he reacted to his depression by restlessness and a feeling of a need to escape. However, his screenwriting demanded his return to Hollywood. Several producers had sought his permission to film his first novel but he had demurred. Now he threw himself into rewriting the novel as a screenplay. It was at this time also that he met his present wife. As he described it, this was a marriage of "convenience." He felt that he should marry, that there was something lacking in his life. "It was as if my childhood were now behind me and I should find some substitute for it." His wife, Maria, was the daughter of one of the producers of Leonard's movies, a man whom he revered very highly although he never felt very close to him. In many ways Leonard's description of his father-in-law was quite similar to his description of his own father. Maria was approximately ten years younger than Leonard; she had just finished college at a private girl's school in the East and had returned home, idly considering a career as an actress but with no real professional or vocational aims. Leonard had the impression that his marriage was arranged by Maria's parents and his friends, yet he accepted these arrangements not only out of his own needs but also to please everyone concerned. He sometimes wondered why Maria had accepted the arrangements made for them, since he recognized almost from the beginning of their marriage that there was little romantic exchange between them. Nevertheless, he found that he was not really disappointed with this arranged marriage. His wife made few demands on him of any kind. She carried out all their social obligations independently, leaving him free to his work and his own way of life. She saw that a home was purchased and furnished. She made all the living arrangements and asked him no questions. Even their sexual life seemed automatic. He felt less bound to her sexually than he had to his Japanese girl friend. She accepted his sexual needs in a casual manner but seemed to get no particular enjoyment from them herself. He found himself making fewer demands upon her over the years until they reached their present stage of abstinence. She never seemed to complain about this. She expressed no feeling about having the children and seemed to accept both of her pregnancies in a natural fashion but without any expression of delight. Nor did the fact that they had children together create any further bond between them. From time to time he would give her presents or do little favors for her as he used to do for his friends and relatives. She accepted his gifts and his graciousness without question or comment. Finally, he began to wonder whether or not he wanted to be closer to her.

Course in Treatment. The psychoanalyst advised Mr. E. that he could be accepted for psychoanalysis only on the condition that he delay any decision on his marital problems for the period of treatment. The psychoanalyst explained that during such a period of thorough re-evaluation of his life-motivations it would not be realistic to make such a major decision. Since Leonard had no immediate plans for making any change in his marriage despite his dissatisfaction with it, he accepted this condition. During the first period of analysis he became considerably more depressed as he reviewed his life history. He often questioned the analyst about his progress, asking for reassurance that he was carrying out the requirements of self-evaluation. As his depression became more marked, he suddenly began to write again. About this time he discovered that his wife was also in psychoanalysis; indeed, she had started treatment before he had. He realized that this was a fact he had really known but had in some way ignored or forgotten. He was angry with her for not telling him or making it evident to him, but could not quite understand why he felt so angry about it. Increasingly he began to express some of his anger toward her directly. She in turn expressed to him her sense of frustration with him. She accused him of being narcissistic, of never caring for her needs, and of treating her as if she were just someone to have around the house, like a piece of furniture. He was amazed that she felt this way about him and was at first confused and then somewhat pleased that she had any feelings at all about him. Within the analysis he became more demanding of answers from the analyst and then angry with the analyst, as if the analyst had made some demands on him or had rejected him. Then he became very guilty and again depressed. At the end of two years he broke off analysis and left for New York City where he lived for approximately six months by himself before he returned to Hollywood and resumed his treatment. During the next year of treatment there were continued storms at home between him and his wife and during the treatment hours against his analyst. However, his feelings of anger seemed gradually to be drained to the point that he showed no depression and was much more at peace with himself. He complained less and less of his wife"s neglect of the children and began to feel that perhaps he had neglected his wife and children. In his last round of accusations against his analyst he found himself believing that the analyst had denied him the right to start another novel while he was in analysis. When he recognized this to be an irrational idea, it seemed to relieve him of his feelings that he was not quite his own master. Shortly after this third novel was accepted for publication, he and his analyst both agreed that he had reached the conclusion of his treatment. At this time he had no more complaints about his marriage and seemed to feel that his life with his wife and children was entirely acceptable to him.

Questions for Leonard E.

1. From your reading of Leonard's history, what, in your estimation are the basic conflicts pervading his life?

2. Defend your answer to question one by showing how the conflict which you have mentioned derives from the relationships listed below:

    a. Leonard's treatment by, and relationship with, his mother

    b. Leonard's relationship with his father

    c. Leonard's feelings about his brothers, particularly the younger three.

3. Consider the following:

    a. Leonard's interest in the underdog and the marginal members of society

    b. Leonard's need to give gifts to people

    c. the themes of Leonard's first two novels

Are these behaviors also compatible with your answer to question 1? In what way are they compatible?

(*Note:* At this point if your answer to question 1 fails to account for the behaviors listed in questions 2 and 3, then you are probably on the wrong track and should think of some other conflicts that would tie things together psychologically.)

4. What behaviors manifested by Leonard's mother reinforced or nurtured Leonard's basic conflicts?

5. How would you describe Leonard's relationship with women in

    a. his high school days

    b. his service days

    c. during his marriage

Does the quality of these relationships follow from your answer to question 1 or must we postulate another conflict area to account for Leonard's relationship with women?

6. Considering your answer to question 5 above, what hypotheses can you raise about Leonard's need to run away from the girl he loved two days before his marriage? What was the threat here?

7. In looking over Leonard's history, when do you notice that he stopped writing meaningfully? What else happened about that time?

8. What hypotheses are suggested from your previous answers which could explain why Leonard could no longer write? (*Hint:*

First, you might consider which of Leonard's needs were met by writing before considering why these needs were either no longer present or became too difficult to express at the time they did.)

9. Can you understand why Leonard became so upset when he faced up to the fact that his wife was in analysis?

10. How would you characterize Leonard's behavior toward his analyst?

11. Does this behavior appear related to Leonard's basic conflict as outlined by you in question 1? In what way is it a direct expression of this conflict?

12. During the latter stages of his analysis, "Leonard found himself believing that the analyst had denied him the right to start another novel while he was in analysis. When he recognized how this irrational idea had arisen, it seemed to relieve him of his feelings that he was not his own master." What, in the light of your above answers, might Leonard have discovered about the origin of this idea that might have led to a greater sense of being his own master?

13. Since we are dealing with a talented man who was also quite neurotic, it might be interesting to give some thought to the relation between neurosis and creativity. From what you have read or might be able to locate on this subject, attempt to answer the following questions:

    a. Is the known incidence of neurosis greater in creative artists than in other subgroups of the general population?

    b. What, if any, relationship might exist between creativity and neurosis? (That is, is neurosis necessary to be creative, or are creative people more likely to develop involved emotional conflicts?)

    c. What is likely to happen to a creative, but neurotic, artist who is cured of his neurosis through psychotherapy? (In the case of Leonard, will he still desire to write when his conflicts are resolved?)

References

FREUD, S. The relation of the poet to daydreaming. *Collected papers of Sigmund Freud,* New York: Basic Books, 1959.

MASLOW, A. Emotional blocks to creativity. *Journal of Individual Psychology,* 1958, **14:** 1–56.

PART II CHARACTER DISORDERS

THE CASE OF LEWIS C.*

The Recoil

When Mr. C. telephoned the psychologist for an appointment, he explained haltingly that he had been referred by his physician whom he had consulted regarding his sexual impotency. His appearance and behavior as he presented himself at the office was not particularly remarkable. His face was round and chubby, almost boyish, so that he might have been taken for less than his stated age of twenty-nine, except that his blond hair was beginning to thin. One of his eyes did not move, although it was not immediately noticeable; later it was determined that he had one glass eye. His build and height were average. He wore a well-pressed, dark, pin-stripe suit, and his shoes were highly polished. Initially, he sat tensely, bolt upright in the chair, gradually relaxing after he began talking. His voice was low-pitched, and he spoke so softly that occasionally he was almost inaudible and had to be asked to repeat.

Mr. C. began by stating that he first experienced sexual impotency on his wedding night approximately five years previously. He had become sexually aroused in love making with his bride but had been unable to maintain an erection and thus did not attain a sexual climax in intercourse. This condition persisted for the next three months of his marriage at which time his wife left him, chiefly because of her sexual frustration. Shortly thereafter she had the marriage annulled on the grounds that it was not consummated. Although depressed by this marital failure Mr. C did not immediately do anything about it. He wondered anxiously if there might be something wrong with him but reassured himself by the fact that he had had no

---

* In contrast to the other cases, in which the main body of the report consists of a chronologically arranged life history, this case of Lewis C. is reported interview by interview, in order to provide an illustration of the importance of the sequence of behavioral clues and associations.

difficulty in his premarital sexual experiences with prostitutes and casual girl friends. Some time later, with considerable trepidation, he tested himself by going to a prostitute and was again reassured when he found his potency returned.

His immediate concern was the fact that he was again engaged to be married. He was very apprehensive that his impotency would return although he could not exactly justify his fear. He and his fiancée frequently had engaged in heavy petting which excited him, and he believed that she would welcome premarital sexual relationships and was probably frustrated by his reluctance. Mr. C. was convinced that he would be a failure. This problem preyed so constantly on Mr. C.'s mind that he had to drag himself to work, "barely made it through the day" and was even more depressed in the evenings. His friends at work had remarked on his general apathy, and his girl friend was becoming concerned about him. Nevertheless he had not missed any work, and the quality of his work seemed unaffected. He rarely felt like going any place with his girl friend but did visit her almost nightly and spent his weekends with her. The wedding was scheduled to occur about a month from the time of Mr. C's first appointment, and his anxiety was mounting. At this time he was living at home with his parents who also noted his depression and expressed their concern but were preoccupied with their own activities and did not press him much on the matter. He denied that there was any conflict with his parents nor could he think of any other areas of stress in his life.

He had had a complete physical examination and no psychological defect or disease was uncovered. His physician had told him "it was all in his mind" and had summarily advised him to seek psychiatric help in a manner which implied to Mr. C. "that I was some kind of a nut or other." Although almost angered enough by the physician's brusque manner to reject his advice, it had occurred to him that he had heard of men who suffered from impotency because of "nerves." However, he couldn't see that he was nervous in any way. As he made this statement he sat in silence for a moment and loudly cracked his knuckles. "There!" he exclaimed, "I guess I really am nervous! I used to crack my knuckles a lot when I was a kid whenever I was upset over anything. It would drive my mother wild."

However, when asked how he had been nervous, he couldn't think of any way that he was currently nervous or of anything he had been

anxious about as a child. He continued to mull over the possibility
that he was the victim of some unknown disease but could not entertain this long because he had always been in the best of health. "I
can't remember when I was ever sick." Then he corrected himself to
say that he did have a vivid memory of having his tonsils out when
he was about three years old. Indeed, he had been in an argument
recently about whether people could remember things when they
were very young, which had brought to mind this early memory. He
recalled being quite ill and feverish and being taken to the doctor's
office. He had an eidetic visual image of the doctor and his father
peering in his face while the ether mask was applied. This had been
a very frightening experience to him and one which recurred off and
on throughout the rest of his life in his dreams in various forms. In
these dreams the doctor and his father seemed to be the same person
or to be some kind of a threatening animal-like figure which was trying to choke him. Sometimes he awoke from these dreams screaming.
He believed that the operation was not really adequate and he was
quite ill following the surgery. He was not taken to the hospital but
returned home afterwards. Several times later the family doctor advised a second operation as there were some roots to the tonsils remaining, but Lewis had always expressed such terror of a second
operation that the parents had demurred. He laughed anxiously as
he recalled this incident, remarking again how funny it was to think
of these things.

This memory revived the memory of a second incident when he
lost his right eye. He explained that his father was an outdoor man
who loved fishing and hunting and had enjoyed taking him and his
brother Jim, a few years his senior, on trips into the woods. His father had bought them rifles and had given them some instruction in
shooting. Lewis was very anxious to use his father's shotgun although his father had forbidden it. Early in the morning he left camp
with a shotgun but when he fired it he was unable to hold on to it.
In the recoil the gun butt hit him in the face, injuring his eye which
later had to be removed. He felt very guilty about disobeying his
father's orders. His father, although very concerned about Lewis's
injury, took advantage of the situation to repeat sternly his warnings
about safety in the use of firearms and repeated his lesson on how to
hold a rifle correctly and particularly how to squeeze the trigger.
After recalling this memory Lewis went on to say how much he ad-

mired his father and what an excellent and persistent teacher he had been. He continued to hold the highest respect for everything that his father had said, and remarked "There isn't a kinder man in the world."

While Mr. C. was on the subject of his medical history, he was asked if he could remember having any other illness or injury. He hesitated, seemed thoughtful, but could not immediately think of anything. His physician in making the referral to the psychologist had noted that the patient had said that he had had an appendectomy but the physician could see no scar; when asked about it, Mr. C. seemed a little confused and mumbled something about the possibility that "maybe" he was wrong. The physician noticed that in a previous examination several years before Mr. C. had also mentioned an appendectomy without giving the date of the operation. When he was reminded of this, Mr. C. admitted that he had always thought he had an appendectomy until recently when his physician had noticed that he did not have a scar. He was even more puzzled because he could not really remember ever having an operation or even suffering from appendicitis. As he thought more about it, he exclaimed "Gee, there must be something crazy about me!" He now recalled that when he was about twelve his brother had had an emergency appendectomy and had almost died. However, Lewis could not explain why he had told two different psyicians that he himself had had such an operation; yet indeed, it seemed to him that he had believed this to be the truth when he gave this information in previous medical histories.

In the second interview, Lewis returned to considering the possible causes of his symptom. After the first interview he had gone back over his sexual history in his own mind as it had occurred to him that in some way he had "gotten off on the wrong track without knowing it." He mentioned his marriage first. He had become acquainted with his wife approximately six months prior to their marriage. Lewis had just finished barber school and was employed in his father's shop, which he subsequently took over. She was employed in the beauty shop next door as a trainee hairdresser. His friends had always kidded him about being a little bashful, and, when the new girl arrived in the shop, the owner of the beauty shop made it public that she was determined to match them up. He described his wife as petite, buxom, and attractive, so he didn't mind the match-making by the beauty shop owner. Even before he met his wife he had been thinking that he really should get married and had been wondering how to go about it. He had been living at home for approximately a year after he had returned from three years of military service. Most of his high school buddies were married and had children, and the other fellows in the shop, who were somewhat older, also had families. He was very attracted by this new girl friend and considered himself in love with her. He had wondered if she were a virgin and there had been considerable discussion among the barbers in his shop about his fiancée's virginity, which embarrassed him but also made him more curious. At that time he was firmly convinced that he would never marry a woman who was not a virgin, although he joined in the cynicism of his male friends regarding virginity in adult women. In thinking back over his engagement period with this girl he remembered that she seemed to take the lead in their love making and that he was uncomfortably aware that she probably would have been willing to have premarital sexual intercourse even though he had never taken up any of her hints. He had felt attracted by her seductiveness and looked forward to the wedding night. He wondered at times if in some way she had done something that repelled him, but he could not think of anything in particular. On the contrary, he felt at fault that he had frustrated her. Nevertheless he remained angry that she had broken up the marriage entirely on the basis of his sexual failure. He added that he felt too many people placed too much emphasis on sex, and he was firmly of the opinion that sex should not be the major factor in marital adjustment. "Too many people let their animal nature take them over!"

This remark led Lewis to explain that his father had always sought to teach the boys "self-control" in everything. He said that his father always wanted the boys to try everything but always preached moderation. He added that this was something very hard to teach children. He felt that he himself had learned his lesson quite early, but his brother Jim always seemed in conflict with his father over it. He said that he didn't want anyone to get the wrong impression, that Jim was "a very wonderful guy," but his brother had always felt cheated by life and always wanted something more than was allowed him. Even as a child Jim had always been the one to demand a second helping at the dinner table or to ask for something extra when there was an outing or a good time to be had. Lewis admitted that he himself would also have liked to have asked for things, but "I knew better." In contrasting himself further with his brother, Lewis remarked that "Jim was always shooting off his mouth about something while I was the quiet one." Jim was the one who always asserted his rights and rebelled against his parents while Lewis was much more compliant. Consequently there was increasing dissension between Jim and his father which during the boys' adolescence rose to a pitch of dissension. Once Lewis and his mother actually had to intervene between Jim and the father when their anger reached the boiling point of fisticuffs. Lewis could not remember ever seeing his father so angry. In addition, Jim was often in scrapes in school or in some other kind of trouble or mischief. Asked if he and Jim quarreled much, Lewis smiled and remarked that he couldn't remember ever being angry at his brother, but then Jim was always bigger and quicker so that there was no use picking a fight with him. "Oh I could get roused up all right, but I always had to back down, 'cause father wouldn't stand for us beating on one another."

At this point Mr. C. paused and apologized for getting off the topic, saying that he had meant to talk about his sexual history rather than about his father and brother. "I guess I better be frank and begin at the beginning," he said brightly. His earliest sexual experience occurred in play with a neighbor girl when Lewis was in kindergarten. As he recalled the details of this incident it had chiefly involved bodily exploration between his brother Jim and the little girl, while Lewis observed. He remembered this incident vividly because the children had been discovered by the little girl's father, who reported it to the boys' parents. Lewis's father had been very stern with the boys and had told them that they would both be spanked; however, Lewis's brother had protected him, telling their father that Lewis had not really been involved. Thus only Jim was spanked. Afterward Lewis felt a little guilty and thought maybe he should have been spanked too. At first he declared that this was about the only time he could remember his father physically punishing either one of them. Then he corrected himself when he remembered another incident in which Jim had gotten angry and had expressed himself in profane sexual language in front of his parents; Jim's behavior aroused their father not only to spank Jim but to lecture both of the boys about the use of any sexual terms or references in front of their mother. "The one thing my father insisted on most of all was respect for my mother." Asked how his mother reacted to either of the incidents and Lewis said he couldn't remember exactly what she did or said, if anything. As far as he could remember she usually let his father "handle the boys."

The patient was asked to describe his mother further. He paused and at first seemed unable to say much about her. He eulogized her rather than described her, "a very fine lady with high moral standards" and "she always gave us the best of care." He pulled out his wallet to show the psychologist a picture of his mother that he carried with him. Accompanying this picture was a card with the painting of the Virgin Mary. He explained that he had been reared a Catholic although currently he did not attend church as faithfully as he should. His mother was devoutly religious and had insisted that the boys go to Catholic school, learn their catechism, and attend mass regularly. His father had been converted to Catholicism at the time his parents were married, but it was his mother who had laid emphasis on their religious training.

Again Lewis felt it necessary to return to the topic of his sexual history. He said that his father had told the boys as they reached adolescence that "they should keep themselves clean and respect their bodies." In high school Lewis heard many of the boys boast of their sexual exploits with their girl friends, including his brother Jim. However, Lewis, himself, "never went that far with a girl." He was socially active, "went wherever the crowd did," and had several steady girl friends. He admitted it was sometimes difficult to follow his father's advice because "all the kids went in for petting." Asked specifically about masturbation, Lewis flushed and admitted that he masturbated quite frequently as an adolescent and asked anxiously if perhaps, that had something to do with his fear of impotence. However he could not associate the two in his own mind.

After Lewis was graduated from high school, he enlisted for the three years of peacetime service in the navy. While in the navy he accompanied his buddies to houses of prostitution several times. He did not feel that he had particularly violated his moral standards because "those women are no good anyway." Besides he knew of several boys of good moral standard who had been to prostitutes. He also learned "how to make a pick-up at a bar." He laughed as he reported these facts, saying that as far as he could remember that was all he had learned in the navy. His principal duty assignment was as the ship's barber—a job he had requested. On his return home he joined his father in the family barber shop; two years ago his father retired.

In the fifth and last interview, Lewis began by saying that he needed some advice as to whether or not to go ahead with the wedding. He was asked to tell a little more about his fiancée. He said that she was about the same age as he, that she had been married once before but that her husband had been killed in an automobile accident. He had met her several years previously and at that time had sensed that she was somewhat depressed, her husband's death having occurred only shortly before. However, as far as he could observe now she seemed to be over her grief. His main association with her was that she was "lots of fun" but also could be serious. They had many interests in common; they both enjoyed dancing and seemed to like the same shows. She enjoyed cooking and housekeeping and had already engaged him in apartment hunting and shopping for furniture. Asked what he liked best about her, he said that it was that she was "lively and full of spirit." He continued to press the psychologist for some opinion as to whether he should go through with the wedding. However, Lewis seemed to be less anxious about his possible sexual failure. He felt he should make some decision but seemed more to be asking whether or not continued interviews with the psychologist were necessary. He said he had thought once or twice about talking the whole situation over with his fiancée but had decided that it was really his problem and he should not worry her with it. He said that if the doctor would advise him not to get married he would delay the wedding now, but that it would really be difficult to do so. He was advised that he would have to make his own decision on this matter and that whatever he decided to do, he could depend upon the doctor to help in carrying out his decision. Lewis said that he felt that if he made the decision to get married that he felt that he should let the whole problem rest. The following week he left a message that he had decided to get married and would not return. The psychologist never learned whether or not Mr. C.'s impotence recurred. However, approximately a year later Mr. C. stopped the doctor on the street and introduced him to his wife. Mr. C. added mysteriously, "I want to thank you for all that you did for me."

Questions for Lewis C.

1. Under what conditions could Lewis maintain an erection and consummate the sexual act and under what conditions did he fail sexually?

2. How would you characterize the two sets of conditions listed in your answer to question 1 in terms of

    a. the social conditions surrounding the sexual act

    b. the emotions likely to be stimulated prior to and during the sexual act in Lewis

    c. the cultural connotations of the sex act under the different sets of conditions

3. If we view impotence as the result of an incompatible or conflictual sets of feeling states being elicited by the sexual situation, then what incompatible feeling states were most likely elicited by Lewis in the marital sexual situation?

4. Frequently a successful integration of sexual feelings into a love relationship is the end result of a long series of emotional conditioning in regard to sex. What sort of training did Lewis receive in regard to the expression of his sexual impulses and what effect did this training appear to have upon Lewis?

5. There are numerous theories which have been offered to explain sexual impotence in men. Four of the most popular are:

    a. latent homosexuality: that the individual is not genuinely interested in members of the opposite sex

    b. hostility-sexuality conflict: that sex is seen as a hostile act and the person cannot fuse the two impulses with a loved one

    c. sacred-profane theory of sex: sexual impulses are dirty and only appropriate to dirty ("bad") partners, while not appropriate to express with "good" women

    d. oedipal theory: a man with an unresolved oedipal conflict still fantasies his mother as a sexual object and when he performs the sexual act with a woman he loves these forbidden sexual fantasies are reactivated.

To what extent does each of these theories appear to shed some light on Lewis's condition? Defend your answer with evidence from the case.

6. In describing his early life numerous incidents occurred to Lewis which involved his father. What are these incidents and how might they be related to Lewis's sexual problem by *a.* a psychoanalyst *b.* a learning theorist?

7. Lewis's problem was specific, i.e. a sexual problem, and we see little evidence of a general disturbance of Lewis's personality. In other cases in this book we see instances in which conflict has affected all facets of the personality (i.e. self-esteem, anxiety level, social relations, and so forth). How, on a theoretical level, can you account for the fact that in some instances an emotional conflict can result in a relatively specific symptom while in other cases conflict affects all facets of the personality?

8. To understand the emotional meaning of events in a person's life it is often helpful to look at the sequence in which these events are told and the associations which are made as he links one event to the next. What might each of the following sequences in Lewis's story suggest about his sexual impotency?

   a. the incidents surrounding his tonsillectomy, the loss of his eye, and his imaginary appendectomy

   b. his concern over the virginity of his first wife, his father's attitudes about control of impulses, and his response when asked to describe his mother

References

FREUD, S. Contributions to the psychology of love: the most prevalent form of degradation in erotic life. In *Collected Papers of Sigmund Freud*, Vol. IV, chap. 12. London: Hogarth Press, 1953.

SENUSSI, A. E., COLEMAN, D. R., & TAUBER, A. Factors in male impotence. *Journal of Psychology*, 1959, **48:** 3–46.

THE CASE OF KITTY G.

Who'll Feed a Bad Girl?

After repeated warnings from the school nurse that her son, Pete, was becoming uncontrollably hyperactive in the classroom, Mrs. G. reluctantly brought him to the psychiatric clinic. At first Mrs. G. denied having any problems other than Pete. However, in the middle of the initial interview she broke down and wept, saying that she considered herself "hopeless" but that perhaps something could at least be done for her son. She readily admitted to being very depressed much of the time. During these periods of depression she felt helpless, alone, and unwanted. She brooded guiltily over her past, regarding her "sins" as unforgivable. She had frequent premonitions that God would punish her or that she might die. On several occasions she had seriously considered suicide, although she had made no actual attempts.

Despite being seventy pounds overweight, Mrs. G. was a pretty woman, with a fair complexion and light brown hair, and a childlike, winsome smile. Indeed, at times the interviewer thought that he was talking to a teenager rather than a 26-year-old housewife because of the glib manner in which she spoke and her girlish poses. She usually had on a well-worn, faded housedress, but she was neat, clean, and well-groomed. In between her occasional outbursts of tears and the depression which clouded her face, she often smiled and kidded in a flirtatious manner with the interviewer. She could discuss freely her current troubles, but after she began her general descriptions of her feelings of unworthiness and sin, Mrs. G. bit her lip and became silent. Finally she blurted out that she was afraid the interviewer would regard her as "a no-good tramp" and would have nothing more to do with her.

It seemed to Mrs. G. that she could remember very few happy periods in her life, but at least she had always managed to scrape by financially. For several years, Mr. G. had not been steadily employed, the family was deeply in debt, the rent was in arrears, and there was little food in the house. About three months ago, her husband deserted her, telling her that he was going to live with another woman with whom he had been consorting for the past year. They had a violent quarrel during which he struck her. Declaring that she was a "fat pig" for whom he had no further use, he stalked from the house. Mrs. G. ran after him but he drove off, leaving her screaming in the street. For several days, she sat immobilized in their tiny two-room apartment, moaning and crying. Pete, age eight, and his brother, Raymond, age six, who had been shut in their room, remained there, also crying, until finally overcome with hunger, they escaped to beg a meal from a neighbor. The neighbor fed and comforted the boys, but Mrs. G. rejected her further offers of help. Finally the neighbor was able to rouse Mrs. G. sufficiently to get her to obtain a food and rent allowance from the county welfare bureau. A warrant for failure to support was issued by the district attorney against her husband.

During the next three months Mrs. G. did little but sit around the house, care for her children, and eat. Considerably overweight when her husband left, she gained thirty additional pounds. Mr. G. began to visit the family about once a week. Sometimes he would bring a little money, but he always would demand sexual relations with Kitty. She usually complied with his demands, hoping to induce him to return. Mr. G. had made daily demands for sexual satisfaction throughout their marriage. Kitty had never been able to enjoy their sexual relations and now his advances revolted her. His visits often ended in screaming violent fights. Twice the neighbors called the police, although no arrests were made. After these quarrels Mrs. G. would sit for hours, staring into space, leaving the children to fend for themselves. Whenever the children made demands, she became irritable and she would strike out at them. Then, guilty over her outburst, she would weep with them. Pete, in particular, seemed to annoy her with every action. He always seemed to be the one who spilled his food, left his toys strewn about, refused to go to bed, or failed to come home promptly from school. In contrast, Raymond made extra efforts to please her, in effect telling his brother, "Look what a good boy I am." This served to enrage Pete, who would run out of the house and remain away for hours while Kitty roamed the streets looking for him.

Mrs. G.'s application for psychiatric help was also motivated, at least indirectly, by two other current situations. First, the county welfare department had threatened to terminate financial aid in order to force her to go to work. She argued that she was needed at home by her two boys, but the welfare office demanded that she accept their plan to have the boys cared for during the day at a public nursery. Kitty felt emotionally unable to work and hoped that the clinic would attest to this fact.

Second, about a week previously, Kitty had allowed a completely strange man to walk her home from the bus and to stay overnight with her. She continued to have sexual relations with him for the duration of the week; moreover, for the first time in her life sex was satisfying to her. She guessed that he was twenty years her senior, gray-haired, well-dressed and, in her opinion, handsome, although not exactly her romantic ideal. Most of all, she found him a kindly and reassuring person who was attentive to the boys. He bought them all food although he did not give her any money. Otherwise, she knew nothing about him, not even his last name! She appeared very guilty about this relationship and called herself "a prostitute," but she made no effort to send him away. In addition to this illicit relationship, she later revealed that several nights after her husband had left she had sexual relations with the husband of the neighbor who had helped her out initially. This incident made her feel even more guilty and it was soon after this that she began to have premonitions that she might die suddenly. Nominally a Catholic, she had not attended church for many years. On several occasions she had wanted very much to receive absolution through confession, but she could not bring herself to enter the confessional booth. Once she attended mass but halfway through the service, Kitty began to cry and ran from the church. She tried praying at home but found that she was unable to say her prayers.

Past History. Kitty G. was the fifth of nine children, born and reared in the slums of a metropolitan Atlantic seaport. She described her family as "shanty Irish." Her father was a chronic alcoholic who occasionally worked as a longshoreman, but during the depression of the 1930's, when she was a child, the family lived mainly on relief. Occasionally her mother was able to earn some extra money doing housework at various homes. Her mother cautioned the children not to talk about the mother's earnings for fear that the relief worker would find out and cut them off from welfare funds. They lived in a crowded, third-story, cold-water flat, which had no heat except the kitchen stove. The children slept in one room—she and her sisters crowded in one bed and her brothers shared another. The children were approximately two years apart; in Kitty's memory, her mother was always pregnant or just recovering from childbirth. Kitty regarded herself as her father's favorite, even though she was often ashamed of him when he appeared drunk in public, often in broad daylight. The other children teased and jeered at her. Late at night, if her father had not returned home, Kitty would usually volunteer to search for him and to persuade him to come home. Her mother continually upbraided her husband for his failure to support them. When she berated him for his alcoholism, he would retaliate by heading for the nearest bar. Kitty recalled that often she would find her mother crying while carrying out her household duties; other times, her mother would sit at the kitchen table with her head buried in her arms. Her mother was devoutly religious and insisted that the children attend mass regularly and learn their catechism. Kitty believed that her mother's religious faith and insistence upon moral standards in the home helped to keep them out of trouble. Kitty could not remember that any of her brothers and sisters were ever in trouble with the law, although many of the neighborhood children were delinquent.

When Kitty was approximately eleven, her father disappeared, and for the following three years, the two oldest sons supported the family until they married. It was during these years that Kitty became increasingly disobedient, both at home and at school. She became impudent to her mother, accusing her of being responsible for the father's desertion. When Kitty related this, she became tearful. She said that even as a child she had felt extremely guilty after her outbursts against her mother; she realized that her mother had made many sacrifices, not only for the family but for Kitty in particular. Her mother had often stinted on her own needs in order that Kitty could be well-dressed. Other times, although Kitty never knew of it until afterwards, her mother denied herself supper so that the children could eat.

Although she was uphappy, Kitty did not become a serious behavior problem until after her puberty. About the time of her twelfth birthday, she had her first menstrual period; she was quite frightened for all she knew about menstruation was that her older sister had suffered continual cramps. Her mother gave her no explanation other than how to care for herself hygienically, adding the cryptic warning that she should have nothing to do with boys. Kitty began to be increasingly truant from school. At the suggestion of a welfare worker she was placed in a home in a rural area outside the city. Here she was extremely lonely, wept frequently, and felt that her mother had rejected her completely. After approximately six weeks she ran away and found her way back home. Her mother was ill and did not force her return to the foster home. She continued to be truant at school and began to run around with an older group. She had her first heterosexual experience when she was thirteen when a friend of her older brother forced himself on her in the basement of their tenement. She was frightened, angry, and guilty. She would have liked to confess to someone but there was no one she felt she could turn to. Soon afterwards she began to submit regularly to the sexual demands of the older boys in the gang.

Kitty was sixteen when she met her husband, who was five years her senior. She said, without boasting, that at that time, she was still slim but "with a good figure," was a good dancer, and one of the more popular girls in her "gang." Ramon, a handsome, dark-complexioned Mexican, was especially attractive because he had the things "every girl wanted." He owned a "souped-up" car, was a "flashy dresser," and always seemed to have spending money. At the time she met him he had just been released from the state reformatory after serving a year's sentence for car theft. Three months after they started going together, she discovered that she was pregnant. When he refused to marry her she appealed to his mother, who forced him into the marriage. She described her mother-in-law as an extremely dominating person who attempted in every way possible to control Ramon's life. She was a widow, Ramon her only son. Kitty spoke no Spanish and her mother-in-law very little English. Consequently Kitty often felt left out when Ramon and his mother conversed. Increasingly Kitty became jealous and angry as her mother-in-law hovered over her husband, trying to control their every action.

At this time, Kitty's mother made the surprising announcement that she was planning to remarry. Concurrently, Kitty's father returned and tried to persuade Kitty to live with him and to take care of him. Her reaction to these various strains was very similar to her current behavior, i.e. she sat alone for hours, crying, and she stuffed herself with food. She believes that it was as a consequence of these stresses that she miscarried. Because of their religion the couple used no contraceptives; yet despite her husband's constant sexual demands, she did not immediately become pregnant again. During this time Ramon was often unemployed and the couple was supported by his mother, who was now living with them. Her mother-in-law made constant reference to the fact that Kitty was not yet pregnant; she intimated that this was God's punishment for Kitty's promiscuous behavior prior to her marriage. After they had been married for approximately two years, Ramon suddenly deserted Kitty and went to live with another woman.

Kitty then moved in with her father; at this time he was "on the wagon" through the help of Alcoholics Anonymous. Kitty considered the following two years as the only happy period in her entire life. Her father was able to work; he made a fair living and they had a decent place to live. They enjoyed going out together, and they even went to dances. However, her husband and mother-in-law tried to make her life miserable—chiefly by parading the husband's common-law wife and baby in front of her and by gossiping about her to all the neighbors. Apparently the common-law wife also found the mother-in-law difficult to live with for she disappeared one day, taking her child with her. Even before she left, Mr. G. occasionally visited Kitty and talked about a reconciliation. Finally, he came to live with her and her father. Fortunately, there was not enough room in the present apartment for the mother-in-law and the couple lived in relative peace until Pete was born. Subsequently, Kitty's father started to drink heavily again, and he and Mr. G. clashed frequently. Eventually, in an effort to separate from both sets of parents, the couple moved away to another large city. When the mother-in-law attempted again to move in with them, Kitty threatened to leave if Ramon would not send his mother away; on one occasion she grabbed her mother-in-law and might have strangled her had her husband not stopped her. She was pregnant with Raymond, and her husband, fearful that she might lose another child, convinced his mother to leave.

Kitty found that caring for two children was a constant chore. She received no help from Ramon; in fact he began to make many more demands upon her. He became exceedingly jealous of the time that she spent with the children. Many a quarrel ensued because he expected her to cater immediately to his demands, even if she happened to be caring for one of the children at the time. She usually acceded to his sexual demands, but still he complained that because she was merely submitting, she was not satisfying him. He often demanded intercourse during the daytime when the children were awake, but Kitty always was fearful that the children could hear and possibly observe them. He also insisted on increased sexual play, both before and after intercourse, and this Kitty regarded as perverse. She accused Ramon of seeing other women; he never denied this charge, but instead used it as a threat to compel her to accede to his demands. Although he was frequently unemployed, and they seldom had enough money for food or rent, he managed to be well-dressed and maintained a good car. It occurred to Kitty that he might be receiving income from some criminal activity, but she was afraid to mention her suspicions to him. Whenever she remarked on his clothes or his car, he became violently angry and threatened to leave. He constantly teased her about her increasing weight and taunted her that she was becoming ugly. His relationship with the children varied: at times he would boast about them to everyone; other times he would beat them for the slightest infraction. The boys became frightened of him; they would hide whenever he came home, but this only irritated him more. Often, Kitty wished that he would leave; yet at the same time she thought that if he did leave, then she would truly be left alone in the world. With the exception of one sister, who lived fifty miles away, her brothers and sisters were scattered across the country. Kitty had never had a close relationship with this sister and recently this sister had told Kitty that she would have nothing to do with her as long as she was living with Mr. G.

Course in Treatment. When Kitty told the welfare office that she was to be accepted for psychiatric treatment, the welfare worker telephoned the clinic and was advised that, although currently Kitty might not be able to find or maintain herself on a job, it was probably a good idea for the welfare office to continue to insist that economic independence be one of the ultimate aims for Kitty. The welfare office agreed not to remove Kitty from their rolls at this time. Peter was seen by another therapist in a playroom setting once a week. At the same time individual interviews were conducted with Kitty for approximately four months. Although she continued to have some crying spells, her depression lifted markedly. She became openly flirtatious with her therapist. She reported that although she had discontinued seeing the older stranger, she was becoming involved with another man whom she had met through one of her girl friends. She often requested extra interviews, but just as likely, she would fail to appear for her regular appointments. She showed little insight into her behavior and showed a tendency to blame everything on her husband. Because of her intense feelings of unworthiness and her feelings that no one would like her, it was decided that group psychotherapy might be the treatment of choice. The only group open to new members at that time in the clinic consisted of women, all older than Kitty, who also had problem children being treated at the clinic. Kitty was angry when she was moved from individual to group treatment, regarding this as another rejection. In the group she discussed little of her own problems, but made constant hints that she could tell the "ladies" things that would amaze them. Most of the older women came from middle-class backgrounds and were amazed when Kitty began to reveal her history of sexual promiscuity. She seemed to enjoy shocking them but she was mystified when, instead of rejecting her, they began to regard her with pity. In a maternal fashion they advised and scolded her. However, they never really rejected her and when she became increasingly guilty they supported her and pointed out that she probably was really punishing herself. After a year and a half of attending the group, Kitty suddenly announced that she had taken a factory job and would be unable to continue treatment. Some six months later she appeared at the clinic without an appointment to tell the therapist she was planning to marry again. She did not seem to have doubts about the marriage but merely wanted the therapist's congratulations. She had lost forty pounds, looked relaxed and happy, and reported that she was still employed in her factory job.

Questions for Kitty G.

1. When Kitty came to the clinic, she was under considerable external stress.

    a. Summarize and categorize her reactions to this stress.

    b. In what ways might these reactions be considered "normal," i.e. related realistically to her circumstances, and in what ways "neurotic," i.e. associated with personal, internal conflicts?

    c. What aspects of Kitty's past history facilitated the learning of these ways of reacting to stress?

    d. In particular, what other needs or drives appeared to have been reduced by overeating and indulging in sexual relations?

2. What socio-economic class does Kitty come from? In what ways was her behavior normative and in what ways deviant for that social class?

3. Describe Kitty's behavior as a mother. What factors in her early environment seemed to predispose her to react this way toward her children?

4. Kitty was quite promiscuous sexually, but claimed not to enjoy sexual relations at all. How can these apparently contradictory facts be reconciled? What might have been the reasons that Kitty later was able to enjoy sex with the older stranger?

5. Although a welfare bureau and a district attorney's office commonly are faced with cases similar to Kitty's, such cases are rarely referred to mental hygiene clinics or other sources of psychological treatment. Even when so referred, they are often regarded as unpromising.

    a. What might be some of the reasons such cases are not referred (aside from the unavailability of treatment facilities)?

    b. Why might psychotherapists regard such cases as difficult to treat?

    c. Hollingshead and Redlich argue that one of the reasons that persons from Kitty's socio-economic group are often not referred nor treated lies in the class differences between the patient and the professional worker. Which of the reasons you have listed in your answers *a* and *b* might be associated with such differences in social class attitudes? What other inter-class differences might be present in such cases?

d. What factors in Kitty's case made her *more* likely to be referred and accepted for treatment?

e. To what extent do you feel compassion for Kitty and a desire to help her out of her difficulties? To what extent did you find Kitty's situation foreign to you? Why do you think that you feel as you do?

6.   *a.* In addition to the personal problems represented in this case, what social problems do such persons present to the community?

b. In what ways are such social problems perpetuated from one generation to another in these families?

c. What facilities in the community might be utilized to *prevent* such problems?

d. What agencies, other than psychological treatment clinics, might be used in rehabilitation of such individuals and families? (In your answers to these questions cite examples from Kitty's case.)

References

BOWLBY, J. *Child care and the growth of love.* London: Pelican Books, 1953. Read the whole book if possible, but particularly Chaps. 2–6 and 7–9.

BAAM, I. Psychic factors in obesity; observations in over 1,000 cases, *Archives of Pediatrics,* 1950, **67**: 543–552.

ERIKSEN, E. H. Growth and crises of the "healthy personality." In *Personality in nature, society and culture,* Kluckhohn, Murray, and Schneider (Eds.) New York: Knopf, 1955.

GREEN, A. "The cult of personality" and sexual relations. In *The family,* Bell, N. W., and Vogel, E. (Eds.) Glencoe, Ill.: The Free Press, 1960.

HOLLINGSHEAD, A., & REDLICH, F. *Social class and mental illness,* New York: John Wiley, 1958. Chaps. 3, 4, 11, 12.

THE CASE OF JONATHAN B.

Cup of Failure

Mr. B. arrived at the sanatorium shortly after midnight, stuporously drunk. He was an extremely obese man, and the alcohol made his normally pudgy face even more puffy and reddened his pale complexion. The formal dress suit which he was wearing seemed too small for his elephantine figure, and it was disheveled and muddy. He collapsed in a chair, bent over with his face in his hands, breathing heavily and audibly, almost as if sobbing. When the psychiatrist approached him, Mr. B. indicated with a wave of his hand that the doctor should talk to his wife, who was standing beside him. Mrs. B. was a tall, slim, gray-haired woman, neatly but modestly dressed in a dark brown suit. She spoke softly but there was considerable tension in her voice and her face had a harried expression.

Mrs. B. explained that earlier in the afternoon her husband had telephoned to say that he would not be home for dinner but was joining some of his friends and would go directly on to work. A violinist, he had been playing at an afternoon tea and was scheduled to play in the symphony that evening. She was quite uneasy about his phone call as his enunciation was slurred and she feared he had been drinking; however, she did not mention her apprehension to her husband as he had repeatedly told her that the reason he got drunk was because she nagged him. Several hours later, one of his colleagues called to advise her that Mr. B. was too drunk to play with the symphony that night. Because she was engaged at that moment in preparing their two pre-school boys for bed, she tried to get her husband's friend to put him in a taxi and send him home, but the concert was about to start. Although she was reluctant to reveal the situation to her mother-in-law, she was forced to call upon her to care for the boys while she herself went after her husband. She found him pleading with the concert master to be permitted to join the orchestra and was very embarrassed by the concert master's gruff order to "get this drunk out of here." Mrs. B. began to cry as she reported this incident; then, drying her tears, she apologized for losing control of her emotions.

At first Mrs. B. said that her husband had been drinking to excess "for the past three or four months" but then immediately corrected herself: "for the past several years." Even before they were married, five years previously, she was disturbed by the frequency with which he seemed to "have to have a drink." Before they would leave on a date, he would have one or two "quick ones," another before dinner or a show, and after the show, he rushed to the nearest bar. On their dates, he seldom became completely inebriated, but at cocktail parties or other social gatherings he usually ended up stupefied and incoherent. Afterwards he would be most apologetic. Whenever she tried to get him to limit his drinking, he kidded her about the fact that she was a social worker and complained that she was "trying to reform him." Indeed, if she remonstrated, he seemed to drink even more desperately—as if to spite her.

After they were married, Mrs. B. was dismayed to discover that Jonathan often had a drink beside him during the day and constantly throughout the evening. She estimated that as long as she had known him he had consumed at least a pint of whiskey a day. Thus, she had consciously admitted, at least to herself, that her husband was already an alcoholic at age twenty-five, when she married him. Her immediate impulse to help him was frustrated by his adamant refusal to recognize that any problem existed. Aware that his alcoholism might continue unabated, and possibly increase in severity, she feared that if she made an issue of it, her marriage would be endangered. Not only was she deeply in love with her new husband but, as she described herself, she was a "plain Jane" who had always been a "wallflower" and who, at age thirty-five had despaired of marrying until she met Jonathan. Although this dilemma continued to disturb her for the ensuing five years of her marriage, it was abated at least on the surface by the fact that his excessive drinking did not markedly interfere with their home life or, until recently, with his job. Even when drunk, Jonathan was a most amiable, easygoing person, who "never" lost his temper nor let things upset him. She described him as an affectionate and understanding person who "always made me feel wonderful even if I were blue," and "I hated myself if I

were critical of him or angry at him." Everyone "loved" him and seldom did anyone remark on his drinking.

Up until about six months before, Jonathan had usually been able
to get to work, although at times considerably under the influence
of alcohol. With increasing frequency in the past few months, Mrs.
B. had been forced to call the orchestra or his other employers to
report that he was "sick." His colleagues were aware of his increasing
alcoholism, and Mrs. B. felt sure that when he was "sick" it was
common knowledge that he was really inebriated. The previous
summer the orchestra had made a tour to Europe, and Mrs. B. was
very apprehensive that while away from home he might drink even
more and possibly lose his position with the orchestra. However, his
colleagues protected him when he did become drunk, and he was
able to make the tour and return without incident. Upon the orchestra's return, one of his best friends came to him and advised him
to seek psychiatric help. Mr. B. angrily told his friend to mind his
own business and broke off the friendship. Mrs. B. had tried her best
to keep her husband's parents unaware of his condition because
"it would break his mother's heart." However, she was pretty sure
that they had some idea of the extent of his drinking even though
it was never openly discussed.

In subsequent interviews, Mrs. B. recalled that her husband began
drinking most heavily about two years ago shortly after the couple
had moved out of the home of her in-laws. She regarded her mother-
and father-in-law as "the most wonderful people in the world"; she
"really adored them" and had no complaints against them. Nevertheless, after residing in their home for the first three years of her marriage, she became increasingly determined to set up a home of their
own. For some time, she had urged her husband to find them separate
living quarters, pleading that she wished more independence and
privacy. Jonathan had agreed but had made no move toward leaving
his parents' home. When she insisted more strongly, he demurred
on the grounds that their income was not great enough to obtain
the kind of home he wanted for her. She saw that their older child,
then almost three, made her aging in-laws uncomfortable with his
hyperactivity and added this as ammunition in her arguments with
her husband. Their problem was aggravated by the fact that this
was just after World War II and housing was very scarce. Finally
she herself went out and rented an old but roomy apartment which

was priced above their limited budget. In contrast with their previous quarters with Mr. B.'s parents, the new apartment was physically less comfortable and more shabby, but Mrs. B. felt a lessening of emotional tension. She had long realized that her husband was very dependent upon and under the domination of his parents, and she had hoped that the move away from them might lessen this childhood bond and intensify their marital tie. Mr. B., however, continued to visit his parents at least daily, sometimes twice a day. Mrs. B. was quick to point out that she felt that her in-laws in no way attempted to interfere with their marriage or with her management of the children. She had hoped that, once they moved away from Mr. B.'s parents, her husband would be less restless and more inclined to spend some time with her and the children. However, he continued to be unable to sit down around the house, always seemed to have something he *had* to do, or to feel a need to be "on the go." She was puzzled by his restlessness and tension and even though they seldom quarreled, she wondered if there was something wrong with their marriage.

The increased rent was only part of a rapidly increasing cost of living which the B.'s had not faced before. They had made only token contributions toward the family budget while living with Mr. B.'s parents. Mrs. B. had her master's degree in social work and for the decade prior to her marriage had been employed full-time as a medical social worker. She would have preferred to have stayed home and cared for her family but the new financial burden forced her to find a part-time job and put the children in a nursery school for half a day. She admitted that once she was back at work she enjoyed her job and realized that she had been bored with housework and baby care. Mr. B.'s income from his position with the symphony had always had to be augmented by giving private music lessons or by playing at weddings and other social events. As is true with even the most accomplished musicians, he continued to practice many hours of the day and his income was further reduced by such expenses as the cost of music lessons for himself, union dues, the care of his formal clothes, and so forth. Mrs. B. felt she might have managed on their combined earnings, but Mr. B., without telling his wife, got an additional job selling vacuum cleaners from door to door. Their working schedules left absolutely no time for any social life and, indeed, precious little time for relaxing together at home. Mr. B. defended his drinking by saying that "his occasional drink with the boys" after a concert was his only form of relaxation. Mrs. B. privately felt hurt, jealous, and angry that Mr. B. should spend any spare hours away from her and the children. Once, when she could no longer control her feelings and mentioned them to her husband, he became silent and guilty-looking and spent the rest of the evening getting quietly drunk at home. She in turn felt quite guilty that she had made any demands upon him since she realized that he had so few pleasures of his own. She tried to make extra efforts to make life comfortable for him at home; she made sure that she was at home whenever he was free, and that he had no obligations or things to do around the house. She tried to wait on him hand and foot. She sought to cook his favorite dishes, but she was never much of a cook and had done none of the cooking while they were living with his mother. Mr. B. never criticized his wife's cooking and, indeed, was quite appreciative of it, but Mrs. B. regarded her cooking as quite inferior to that of her mother-in-law who was "a natural-born" cook.

Though the B.'s had never discussed their sexual relationship between themselves, they each separately admitted to the psychiatrist that they felt their sexual relations had not been as satisfactory to them as they had wished. Each felt guilty that they might not be sexually satisfying to their partner. Although the B.'s had had one or two mutually satisfactory sexual experiences prior to marriage, their sexual relationships after marriage were less frequent and less satisfactory than either wished. Mrs. B. regarded herself as not too physically attractive and possibly sexually inhibited. Prior to her marriage she had often felt that she might not be sexually attractive to men and wondered if she could satisfy her husband sexually. She had never had any prior sexual relationships and had always felt somewhat uneasy and guilty regarding the topic of sex. She found that she reached sexual climax much more slowly than her husband and consequently felt both unsatisfied and inadequate. Mr. B. likewise had no premarital sexual experience other than masturbation. Although intellectually he knew that masturbation was a "natural part of adolescence," he did feel increasingly uneasy when this "habit" did not entirely abate following his marriage. He felt disappointed about their heterosexual relationship, admitting sadly that it did not seem much different from his masturbation. Jonathan realized that his wife was seldom satisfied even though she had never mentioned it to him. Both of them admitted that they would rather the other take the initiative in love making, each saying that they did not feel right imposing their impulses on the other person. More often than not, it was Mrs. B. who was the sexual aggressor, which made her feel angry at her husband and guilty over her own aggression. While living under Mr. B.'s parental roof, each felt queasy about having sexual relations, as though his parents might be aware and disapproving—even though in discussing this point each admitted that such a feeling was irrational for married adults, especially as the elder B.'s had never been disapproving of anything. Furthermore, neither of them felt very inclined to have sexual relations during and immediately after Mrs. B.'s pregnancies which had occupied almost two of the five years of their marriage. During the year prior to Mr. B.'s hospitalization, their sexual relationship had dwindled to almost nothing. Mr. B. was often too tired or too drunk. Mrs. B. likewise was usually fatigued or too angry. She would lie awake beside her snoring hulk of a husband, feeling both frustrated and guilty. In the morning she would be tired and sleepy, using all of her energy to control her feelings of irritability. Mr. B. sensed his wife's frustration, felt inadequate in that he was not satisfying to her, but felt dominated by her and resentful over the guilt she aroused in him.

Prior History. Jonathan B., age thirty, was born and reared in the same Atlantic coast metropolis where he then resided, and where his parents and his grandparents had lived most of their lives. His great-grandfather had been a court musician and composer in two different German principalities in the early nineteenth century. His grandfather, who had emigrated from Germany to the United States as a boy, founded a music publishing house and was noted in the community as an outstanding cellist. Jonathan's own father was an internationally famous violin teacher who tutored several of the major concert violinists of his time as well as most of the violin section of the symphony orchestra of the city. The elder Mr. B. shared in the profits from the family publishing firm and his income from his teaching provided more than a comfortable living for the family during Jonathan's childhood years. Most of the other immediate relatives and friends were also musicians and the house was continually filled with music and with talk about music. Although Jonathan was never told that he was expected to become a musician, music for the B. family was an exclusive way of life. Furthermore, Jonathan was the only child of the eldest son, and for many years the only grandson. Therefore, he was not only the subject of considerable attention and expectation but also of multiple if gentle correction and admonition. His parents were in their early thirties when they married and it was ten years before he was born. His uncles and aunts likewise married later than usual. Jonathan at one point speculated why this might have been so; he thought it was perhaps because they spent so much time developing their careers as musicians, but later he recognized that his grandmother played the role of "queen mother" who dominated her husband and all her children and kept them tied to her as long as possible. Daily visits by his father to his grandmother were mandatory until the day of her death. Usually Jonathan and his mother accompanied his father on these visits; illness was the only excuse for absence. Jonathan sensed that perhaps his mother might have resented this bond between her husband and his mother for the relationship between Jonathan's mother and his paternal grandmother was always very cold and formal; but his mother never said anything in his presence to indicate her displeasure. Yet, he remembered hurried whispered discussions between his parents whenever it was necessary for him and his mother to remain at home.

Jonathan knew nothing of the conditions of his birth, for "my parents never discussed such things." However, he was a sickly child who as far back as he could remember, suffered from one minor illness after another. The family physician, a gruff old man, frequently told the parents in front of Jonathan that there was "nothing much wrong with the boy," prescribed a "hardier life," and accused Jonathan's mother of spoiling him. Jonathan's many colds, fevers, and asthmatic breathing were treated with a variety of home remedies prescribed by his grandmother and aunts. His earliest years were spent largely indoors, usually in his own or the parental bedroom, both because he had to stay out of the way of his father and his pupils and because the fireplace in his parent's bedroom was one of the warmer spots of the house. Propped up on pillows in his parents' bed, surrounded by toys and books, he was waited upon and fed by his mother. He had no playmates before he entered school, and, even after he began to go to school, he seldom invited another child to his own home. He was treated as an adult by nearly everyone and his conversation and attitudes were adult. A precocious child, he learned to read several years before he started school, both in English and German. He was reading music and playing the violin and piano by the time he was six, and was familiar with most of the major instruments of the orchestra by the time he was twelve. Although religion was seldom discussed in his home, his parents were fairly faithful Catholics; thus Jonathan was sent to a parochial boys' school. He was always a top scholar and was graduated from high school at the age of sixteen. He completed two years in a Catholic university and was encouraged by several of his professors to continue but by this time, music had become so important to him that he decided to discontinue further academic training and devote himself entirely to becoming a polished musician.

Jonathan was subject to the military draft on his eighteenth birthday in 1943. However, because of his obesity and his history of continuous illnesses, he was deferred. Although he had no desire to join the military service, he often felt uneasy because he was one of the few men of his age who remained a civilian. His deferment added to his impression that "I really never was like other men." His embarrassment over his failure to meet the military's physical standards was later enhanced by the fact that his wife had served for two years with the Women's Auxiliary Corps.

Jonathan regarded both of his parents as very kindly, generous, and affectionate people. He expressed deep reverence for his father whom he described as a tall, stately man of grave demeanor, who always appeared old to Jonathan since he was white-haired at the time of Jonathan's birth. Yet despite the bond of affection between Jonathan and his father, these characteristics of his father made it difficult for Jonathan ever to ask questions of him, to discuss much with him other than music, or, in Jonathan's teen-age years, to question or rebel against anything that his father said or did. Furthermore, his father never made any open demands upon Jonathan; rather Jonathan knew what was expected of him and what his father's opinions were without his father ever putting them in words. Jonathan's mother was fairly quiet and busied herself continually with waiting on her husband and her son. She took considerable pride in her immaculate house and in the largesse of rich foods which were served continuously throughout the day and evening. Because Jonathan was sickly and pale, extra food was constantly urged upon him and, as a consequence, he was always obese. If his mother was not stuffing him, his grandmother was. Beer or wine was always served to guests as they entered the house. Jonathan's father usually joined his guests in a drink, but Jonathan never saw his father overindulge. Indeed, his parents made discreet frowns of disapproval at anyone who showed even the slightest sign of being inebriated.

In the all-boy school which he attended as a teen-ager, Jonathan had no opportunity to meet the opposite sex. His companions often discussed their dates and talked about girls, but Jonathan was not "on the in" of any of the groups of boys in his class. He remembered being very curious about sex and listening to the conversation of other boys, but was too bashful to ask any direct questions. Indeed, even at the time of his hospitalization, he considered himself sexually naïve. Only after his marriage did he find out some of the "facts of life" in discussion with his wife or from some of the books which she had. The other boys at school teased him unmercifully about his obesity and always told him that no girl would ever take a second look at him because he was too fat. After he started college his grandmother and aunts began a campaign of finding girls for him, but he was always too shy and reserved and could not carry on any conversation after the introduction. He disliked the girls who were aggressive and telephoned him with invitation to parties which he rarely accepted. The others, he recalled, were either "unmitigated gigglers" or "were as shy as I was."

As had been true with nearly every girl he had ever met, his introduction to his wife was arranged by Jonathan's grandmother. The future Mrs. B. had been reared abroad, the daughter of Protestant missionaries who were old friends of Jonathan's grandmother. She had been returned to the United States to complete her college and professional training and then had come to work in a social agency in this city where she was born. Jonathan found his wife to be different from any of the other girls; she was self-assured but not openly aggressive. She was interested in him and his work but made no demands upon him. He recalled that he was surprised to find himself calling her for a dinner date after their first introduction and equally surprised to find that she accepted it. He liked and envied her independent way of life and her social graciousness. He felt relaxed with her as he did with no other person and increasingly sought her company. His grandmother let him know in no uncertain terms that she disapproved of his attention to a non-Catholic girl. On the other hand, he was very happy that his wife and mother struck it off excellently from the beginning. He felt his father also approved of their marriage. When he proposed to his wife, he had no idea of where or how they might live, but, he admitted, it had never occurred to him that he might live elsewhere than under his parental roof. He realized later that his wife had many times suggested that they make plans for finding their own apartment after their wedding, but he ignored these hints, giving his limited income as an excuse. He denied that he was conscious of any tension between him and his wife during the years they lived with his parents and did not really understand why she finally insisted they move.

Jonathan often played in quartets and small orchestral groups with his family and their adult friends even when he was a child. His career as a professional musician began shortly after he finished high school. He received his seat in the symphony on his twenty-first birthday as a birthday gift from the symphony conductor, an old friend of the family. By this time, he was devoting nearly every minute of his waking life to music, even more than many of his fellow orchestra members, and he rose rapidly in the hierarchy of the orchestra to the second highest position, i.e. next to the concert master himself. In discussing his music he said that he regarded himself as certainly technically above average and probably fairly talented but that he had always felt in his own mind that he lacked something that would otherwise make him a great musician. He regarded his own playing as being so technically perfect as to be lacking in feeling. He felt that many of his colleagues, especially those who were jealous of his position in the orchestra, held similar views of his playing. He explained that in a symphony orchestra, where every chair was another mark in the hierarchy of one's worth and status, there existed a tense and constant rivalry. He knew that many of his colleagues believed that he had reached his position largely through the influence of his father, and Jonathan himself wondered if this were not true. At times, he grew very weary of the constant bickering within the orchestra, of the drudgery of day-long rehearsals and the evening and Saturday and Sunday concerts, all for a paltry subsistence. He was disgusted because it was necessary to supplement his income by "fiddling" at social events or "by trying to force music down the throats of rich young brats." Increasingly, his professional life began to pall, and music no longer was the wonderfully exhilarating emotional experience of his childhood. Although he had few acquaintances outside the field of music, he occasionally met other adults who seemed to enjoy their work, and he felt envious of them. The idea that he might enjoy doing something else crept into his mind with increasing frequency. He became depressed whenever he thought of how very limited his existence was; yet he regarded himself not only as ill-prepared but probably inadequate to any other way of life. He had never before discussed these feelings with anyone else. To have even hinted at this subject with his parents would have been unthinkable and, he feared, would have hurt them deeply. He did not mention his self-doubts to his wife because to do so would have seemed an admission of weakness to her. He already felt that she was far more efficient and worldly-wise than he; she was not only able to manage their private affairs but as a professional social worker made a living at managing the affairs of others.

Course in Treatment. Mr. B. remained in the sanitarium only a few days following his hospitalization. He and his wife accepted the advice of the psychiatrist that he enter into psychotherapy twice weekly and that she attend a psychotherapeutic group consisting of women whose husbands were alcoholic. During the first several months of treatment, Mr. B. abstained from any use of alcohol. He came faithfully to his treatment hours and discussed much of his history and present situation with considerable feeling and seeming insight. He did this, however, with the air of a person making a confession, believing that once he had described all of his background he would be forgiven. When confronted with this behavior by his therapist, he was very puzzled and denied it, pointing out that he had done nothing for which he might feel guilty and need forgiveness. On the other hand, he agreed that he blamed no one other than himself for his situation. Under questioning he admitted he resented the psychiatrist's interpretation but immediately apologized, saying that he hoped the psychiatrist would not feel that he was ungrateful. More and more, it became clear that in some way he expected the doctor to "do something for him." Thereafter, without mentioning it to his doctor, he began to drink again. Several times his wife called the psychiatrist to report that her husband was inebriated and to ask that the doctor "do something." Mr. B. denied his drinking and complained with considerable anger that his wife was overly suspicious. Twice during the ensuing four months it was necessary to hospitalize him for several days. Each time he was depressed and remorseful. The psychiatric treatment rapidly drained the B.'s savings, and, although the fees were markedly reduced, they grew farther and farther behind in meeting their bills. The situation was discussed with the B.'s jointly and the possibility that they might continue in treatment with the same therapist in a public clinic was explored with them. However, before this plan could be instituted, Mr. B. disappeared. Mrs. B. continued in private treatment, paying her own way. She revealed that she had become more and more open in her disapproval of her husband's behavior and in expression of some of her feelings of frustration and hostility. She felt very guilty that she might have driven her husband away from her. He returned ill and out of funds approximately three months later. He rejected further psychiatric care but accepted the psychiatrist's prescription of antibuse, a drug which makes a person nauseous when they consume alcohol. Mrs. B. continued in group psychotherapy for another year.

At the conclusion of her treatment, she had resolved some of her own guilt about Jonathan's behavior; she no longer felt obligated to wait on him or cover up for him. She remained cautious about criticizing him but in general felt more free in expressing her feelings toward him. Their sexual relations became more enjoyable and more frequent. She discussed openly with him her need for a professional career of her own, and both of them seemed less guilty over the fact that she provided almost half of their income. He regained his seat with the orchestra and, continuing to use the antibuse, refrained entirely from alcohol. However, he often became much more openly irritable, depressed, and restless. Three years later, he suffered several coronary attacks, which finally resulted in his death at age thirty-five.

Questions for Jonathan B.

1. According to your textbook, what are the criteria for classifying a person as an alcoholic? Which of these behaviors does Jonathan manifest and which are not present?

2. How would you characterize Jonathan's attitude toward his drinking? What classic mechanisms of defense are implied in these attitudes?

3. Alcoholics Anonymous, a private organization for the treatment of alcoholism, requires that a person admit that he is an alcoholic before a group of members before they accept him for treatment. Can you see the rationale for this procedure from your answers to the previous questions?

4. Frequently a pattern of psychopathology becomes easier to understand when we look in detail at the matrix of interpersonal relationships in which it exists. Characterize in detail, the nature of Jonathan's current relationships with the following figures:

    a. his wife

    b. his mother

    c. his father

What common pattern exists in these relationships?

5. Attempt to describe how these relationships might have grown out of Jonathan's early family environment? In your answer, consider, among other things:

    a. the behavior which Jonathan's parents expected of him and rewarded him for

    b. the role of music in Jonathan's background and development

    c. the role of illnesses in Jonathan's early years

6. Some psychologists have emphasized the fact that healthy psychological development requires that an individual master a graded series of developmental tasks. What developmental tasks did Jonathan fail to master and why did this mastery fail to occur? What effects did these failures in mastery have upon Jonathan's

    a. interpersonal relationships

    b. ability to handle later stress, personal and professional

7. Jonathan obviously had a limited background in sexual matters. Do you see Jonathan's sexual problem as a separate conflict or does it appear to be another manifestation of some other core problem?

8. Can you understand, after exploring Jonathan's early history and interpersonal relationships, why his wife-to-be was particularly attractive to him? What aspects of his wife's behavior appeared not to threaten Jonathan and, in turn, fit in with his needs?

9. Can you raise some hypotheses indicating why Jonathan developed alcoholism rather than, say, a phobic reaction or obsessive neurosis? What relation might there be between Jonathan's alcoholism and his somatic symptoms, i.e. his childhood illnesses, his obesity, and his final coronary attack?

10. In psychoanalytic theory, Jonathan's personality would be classified as "oral." What evidence would support this classification? In what ways is such a classification scientifically helpful and in what ways is it of limited usefulness?

References

CONGER, J. J. The effect of alcohol on conflict behavior in the albino rat. *Quarterly Journal of Alcohol Studies*, 1951, **12**: Issue 1.

McCORD, W. Some current theories of alcoholism: a longitudinal evaluation. *Quarterly Journal of Alcohol Studies*, 1959, **20**: 727–749.

ROSEN, A. C. A comparative study of alcoholics and psychiatric patients with the MMPI. *Quarterly Journal of Alcohol Studies*, 1960, **21**: 253–266.

ZWERLING, I., & ROSEMBAUM, M. Alcoholic addiction and personality. ARIETI, S. (Ed.) *American handbook of psychiatry*, New York: Basic Books, 1959, Pp. 623–644.

THE CASE OF LESTER V.

A Marriage of Inconvenience

On the advice of his wife's psychotherapist, Mr. V., a salesman, called the clinic for an appointment to discuss his marital problems. A tall, raw-boned man of thirty-nine, Mr. V. was striking in appearance and behavior. He sprawled across the chair, dangling his limbs, and gesticulated all the while as he talked. A bald pate topped an egg-shaped head; numerous gold-capped teeth called attention to his wide mouth which was in constant motion. If not talking or smiling, he would be biting or pursing his lips, all the while managing to pull on a cigarette. An extensive vocabulary, combined with a flair for varying the volume and pitch of his voice, dramatized his changing moods.

In the initial interview, Mr. V. said that he had been married ten years, and it had been "one continual hell." He had hoped that psychotherapy for his wife would improve their relationship, but, after a year and a half of private treatment, which was rapidly draining their savings, Mr. V. could not see any marked change in her behavior. He was ready to "chuck the whole deal." At this point, Mr. V. burst into tears, admitting that the necessity of making such a decision was extremely difficult. This was the reason why he had finally decided to consult a psychologist.

After Mr. V. recovered his poise, he began a detailed account of his marital history. It seemed to him that he had always been at the mercy of his wife's every little whim, ever since their engagement. Their life together was a string of quarrels, violent and frequent. There was no particular pattern to the quarrels; often the cause was very trivial. The only recognized leitmotif was Mrs. V.'s complaint that her husband was constantly trying to dominate her. On the other hand, he regarded his wife, Frances, as highly illogical and emotional. He further maintained that the quarrels usually started because he wanted to "explain things sensibly" to her, a process his wife resisted. He denied that he ever lost his temper during these sessions. Instead he would endure his wife's screams and tears, at times even allowing her to pummel him, and, finally, having reached saturation, he would retreat to the neighborhood bar for a series of "double Scotches."

Mr. V. then launched into a tirade on his wife's friends, whom he considered "arty beatniks," or alcoholics. Although he professed to share his wife's interest in the arts, in actual practice, they spent very little of their time together in these pursuits. Both drank immoderately at home and socially. Yet, he did not regard either himself or his wife as alcoholics, claiming that they were seldom completely inebriated. He defended his own drinking as a necessary release from the tension of their marital battles.

Another of his grievances was that his wife grossly neglected the care of their home and their three boys. He felt that she did not bother to feed them properly, nor did she pay adequate attention to their physical needs. Most of her time she spent with an odd assortment of friends, relatives, and on her perpetual art lessons. Several times a week, on his arrival home (which might be as late as seven or eight in the evening), he would find a restless babysitter waiting for him, the children still unfed, and the house littered with toys and dirty clothing. There would be a note from his wife, asking him to put dinner on, and also to take the wash to the laundromat.

All three boys showed signs of emotional disturbances. Robert, the oldest, continued to wet his bed at age seven and a half and was a mild behavior problem at school. He was the mother's favorite, although Mr. V. considered him the biggest baby of the three. Timmie, age five, was Mr. V.'s favorite, the one whom he regarded as "all boy," but he admitted that Timmie was often aggressive and destructive, relished breaking things, and was continually hitting his brothers. Larry, age two, was a constant whiner, which exasperated his father.

At the time Mr. V. applied for psychotherapy he regarded sexual incompatibility as the crux of their marital disharmony. During the past year, after a psychotherapy session, his wife sometimes announced new "insights" about their marriage, which she would use as a weapon in their arguments. An example, and one with which he concurred, was the acknowledgment that many of their quarrels ensued after one or both of them had been sexually frustrated. Both, he claimed, were sexually passionate, although he was hesitant to go further in details of their sexual relationship, since he thought that "more normal people" might regard them as "sex maniacs" or "perverts." He felt the need of sexual gratification almost daily.

Mr. V. volunteered that he carried home many of his business worries and anxieties. At work he was well liked and the top salesman in his area for a wholesale distributor of large electrical appliances. The sales manager, his immediate superior, had recently been transferred from another branch. Mr. V.'s colleagues had assumed that he would eventually be given the promotion to sales manager, and, secretly, Mr. V. felt that he had earned it. However, he consoled them all by pointing out that it was not usual company policy to make such a promotion from the ranks of the salesmen. He did not feel that the new manager was thoroughly qualified, nor did he approve of many of his policies. He denied that there was open disruption between them but confessed that many a time he left the office feeling frustrated and angry. At the time Mr. V. was applying for treatment there was a general economic recession; many of his steady customers were curtailing their orders. The company was going through a period of marked competition and the salesmen were pressed to intensify their sales records.

Prior History. Lester was the youngest of four children born to a lower-middle-income couple living in the county seat of a rural region, where the family had been settled for generations. His father considered himself an intellectual, having attended several universities in the United States and in Europe, although he never completed his degree. He worked at different and sporadic jobs, but he disdained hard labor and during the depression years was more often unemployed.

The V. family considered Lester's father as a ne'er-do-well, particularly since he had rejected joining the family hardware firm. On the other hand, Lester's father considered himself unjustly "gypped" out of his family inheritance, and he blamed his father for their state of near poverty. Lester remembered that his father made frequent and fruitless trips to ask his grandfather for loans and outright gifts. A good deal of the family income was derived from a small grocery store operated chiefly by Lester's mother, usually with the unwilling help of the children.

Using the excuse that he was seeking work, Lester's father began to be away from home for increasingly longer periods. Soon he was absent for as long as a year at a time; during such intervals, he seldom sent money home. Despite the fact that he knew his father was a poor provider, Lester regarded him with admiration, envying his intellectual acumen and encyclopedic knowledge. When his father was home he often spent the evenings reading aloud to the children and helping them with their homework. He insisted on a high level of performance at school, and was quite harsh with the children if they brought home less than A grades. Lester described his father as a physically large man with very powerful hands, who loved to demonstrate his prowess in feats of strength such as bending an iron bar or crushing a wood block with his fist.

His mother was the exact opposite of his father, both in appearance and in temperament. A woman of slight build, she was as a rule silent and dour. Lester depicted her as a hard worker, very efficient and swift. It was she who carried out the day-to-day discipline of the children; Lester remembered that the entire family, the father included, tried to keep out of her way as much as possible. She never said much, but she made her disapproval known. Although his father's occasional rages were feared, it was the mother who disciplined the children.

As far back as Lester could remember, there was constant disharmony between his parents. His father loved to state his opinions at length and in argumentative fashion. His mother's disagreement was expressed at most in a shrug, but her silence usually infuriated Lester's father; he would continue to argue even though there was no reply. Lester could remember many nights that his father would continue to bellow at his mother long after the children were in bed. He would lie there frightened, thinking that his father might physically attack his mother, because the only thing that he could remember her saying was, "Hit me if you dare. You're too big of a coward." After a long period of silence, there would be sounds, which, Lester thought signified physical struggle but which, on later reflection, he realized might possibly have meant that they were having sexual intercourse.

Lester's sister, Lenore, ten years his senior, frequently was left in charge of him and the other children while his mother was at the store. Lenore dominated them by threatening to tell their mother if they got into any trouble, but they soon learned that this meant merely that they were not to bother her. His older brother Robert had a special war on with Lenore, and delighted in teasing her. Lester remembered that Robert would often inveigle him into doing something that would annoy Lenore, who would then blame Lester, and report it to their mother. In particular, he could remember peeking through the keyhole at Lenore while she was in the bathroom, or when she was dressing. He was probably six or seven at that time, and he believed that it must have been Robert's sexual curiosity that instigated the spying. He also remembered that Robert taught him to masturbate, and how he constantly excited him with sexual facts and fantasies.

When Lester was about eleven or twelve he had his first heterosexual experience with his sister Mildred, who was two years older. Robert had surprised Mildred while she was dressing, and while he held her, he taunted Lester into attacking her. Lester was surprised to find that Mildred did not resist him, and later, throughout his teen-age years, they had intercourse intermittently. He became increasingly guilty about this, wondering if there could be anything wrong with being sexually attracted to his sister. Lester was very embarrassed while discussing this with his therapist, but he felt that possibly the sexual play between brother and sister was important to his current marital problems. In retrospect, he blamed his parents for this particular introduction to sex, believing that it could not have happened if they had supervised the children more strictly.

Lester was very bright and the work at school came quite easily to him. He was also an outstanding athlete, first in baseball and later in basketball. When he was fourteen and in junior high, he reached his present height of six feet, three inches, and he starred on the basketball team. Though he was very popular with his teachers and fellow students, Lester did not feel socially successful in high school because he was so bashful with the girls. Although he was often invited to parties and dances, he seldom sought a date on his own and never had a steady girl in high school. Also, he had neither the money nor a car for dates. By the time he was in high school his older brother and sisters had left home, and his mother exerted considerable pressure on him to help out at the family store. When he was sixteen his father left home permanently, and during his last two years in high school Lester and his mother lived alone, operating the store together. During this period his mother was depressed and angry, and Lester listened to endless accusations against his father. He felt uncomfortable when he tried to comfort his mother, particularly since he did not feel altogether sympathetic. He felt it his duty to take care of her, and was angry at his father for having left him this obligation.

Unlike his father who had been very proud of Lester's scholastic and athletic accomplishments, Lester's mother was totally indifferent. Lester wanted to go on to college, but received no encouragement from his mother. At the last minute, his paternal grandmother surprised him by promising to support him through university. His mother's only response to this offer was to remark sardonically that that was the first time that her husband's parents had ever done anything for them. During the intervening months between high school graduation and the university his mother grew even more silent; sometimes she would not speak to him for days. This made Lester increasingly guilty about leaving her. He would have periods when he found himself in a rage without knowing why.

His college years Lester remembered as the most enjoyable. The allowance from his grandmother was sufficient to permit him to live at a fraternity house and to own a car. At the beginning, he found himself a "naïve country boy," but, with the help of his fraternity brothers, he "learned a lot about life." He continued to maintain a high scholastic average and to participate in athletics. He went to parties and dated more frequently than he had in high school, although he still did not have a steady girl. In company with his fraternity brothers he had several sexual experiences, mostly with prostitutes.

At the beginning of his senior year in college he started to go steady with a girl with whom subsequently he had several sexual experiences. Shortly before graduation he was invited by the girl to visit her parents, who were the financial and social leaders of a nearby small community. At the Sunday morning breakfast, much to his amazement, the girl's mother announced to the assembled crowd that Lester and her daughter were to be married. He discovered that the wedding plans were all set and he was too shocked to refute the whole announcement. Three weeks later he went through the wedding ceremony, but immediately afterwards returned to his fraternity house. He refused to answer the phone or to have any contact with his new bride. Later, when he learned from his wife that she was pregnant, he went to see her. At this time an annulment of the marriage was agreed upon, and it was effected a few months after the birth of the child. He has never seen either of them since that time.

After his graduation from college in 1942 Lester, who was then twenty-two, was very much at loose ends. He was relieved to be out of the marriage but he was soured on women. He did not know what he wanted to do with himself vocationally. War had been declared, and he knew that it was very likely that he would be drafted. He received a letter from his mother, saying that she was ill and depressed, so he decided to return home for the summer, the first time in several years. Enroute he met his present wife, who was the hostess on the airline. They shared a taxi from the airport and, as he put it, she "seduced him" into staying with her at her hotel instead of going on to his mother's home. He found himself entranced with Frances, not only because of her beauty and seductiveness but also because of her "high spirits and intelligence." He saw her several times during the summer, whenever she was in town. At the end of the summer, still awaiting a draft call, he returned to the university to begin his graduate studies in business administration. Shortly after he returned to school Frances appeared and they took an apartment together, where they continued to live for the following three or four months. When Lester received his draft notice, early in 1943, he and Frances decided to get married. He left for the service a week later, and she returned to her work as an airline hostess; however, since the hostesses had to be single she retained her maiden name. Whenever Lester wrote he had to be careful to use her maiden name. Only rarely did he hear from her, and then it would be a very casual note, with little or no reference to what she was doing.

After a brief period of military training Lester found himself at the front in the Italian campaign. He sloughed through a winter of bitter fighting, in constant combat, including the prolonged nightmare of the Battle of Cassino, where he was wounded. Struck by a piece of shrapnel, he remained in a mudhole for many hours and finally was taken to a hospital. During the first few weeks of hospitalization he was feverish, and had many confused "dreams," involving visions of his father. He remembers calling out loud for help from his mother. He also had the inexplicable feeling that he had done something awful and that he was being punished. He was seen by a psychiatrist and was given some psychological tests. Later, at another hospital away from the front, he was informed that he was considered to be "psychotic" and would not be returned to active duty. When he asked for an explanation of the diagnosis he was told that the psychiatrist had been transferred. Other medical officers shrugged off his questions, and he was discharged from the service with a medical disability. When he received his papers, there was no mention of any mental or emotional disorder. Even after the shrapnel wound healed, he continued to suffer from pains in his back. Also, for a while after his discharge, he had more nightmares, reliving the battle period when he was wounded. Immediately on his discharge he wired Frances to meet him at the airport. He received no word from her, and it was several days before she appeared at their apartment. When she finally appeared, she explained casually that she had been away on vacation. This particular incident, Lester considered as a prime illustration of his wife's general neglect of his needs.

The couple returned to the same life they had had prior to his service: Frances continued to work as an airline hostess, and he returned to graduate school. She earned the living, while he kept house and did the cooking and housework. He had high hopes of completing his master's degree in business administration. Through his contacts with his fraternity brothers, he planned to secure an executive position in a reliable firm. Both their idyllic honeymoon and his education plans were interrupted when Frances became pregnant. She was the more distressed of the two because she wanted to continue with her work. Lester became angry with her when she complained that her pregnancy was ruining her figure, and also because she made no attempt to take over the housekeeping.

At this point he was forced to quit school, and he found a job as a salesman with the company with which he was still employed. Soon afterwards he was required to sell "on the road"; to his surprise, he found that he enjoyed it. Frances complained bitterly at being left alone. It was during this period that their marital battles really began. After the baby was born Frances was entirely occupied with the infant; even when Lester was home she paid him little attention. During the next few years of their married life they were shifted sev-

eral times across the country, working out of different headquarters
for the company. Although Lester had not previously met his wife's
family, he soon discovered that she was very attached to her mother,
although the relationship was an ambivalent one. Frances complained of the fact that they were not living in the same town with
the rest of her family. Under her pressure he requested assignment
to the city where her family, and, incidentally his, were living.

Shortly before they returned to Frances's home town, their second
son was born. Frances was even more resentful about the second unplanned pregnancy. She insisted that Lester had deliberately made
her pregnant in order to force her to continue in the marriage. She
declared even before Timmie was born that this was his child, and
she would have nothing to do with him. From the beginning, Lester
felt a strong attachment and identification with the child, and a
growing repugnance with the older boy, Robert—who, Mr. V. explained, was named after Frances's brother, not his. Shortly after
they returned to her hometown, her father, a well-known attorney,
died suddenly of a heart attack. Frances was considerably depressed,
as she had been his favorite child. She felt that she had not really
lived the kind of life that her father had wanted. She would become
guilty and enraged; she blamed Lester for leading her astray, particularly for separating her from the Catholic Church, which had
been her family's religion. Lester, himself, had no religious ties and
was unaware before this time that Frances had been Catholic. Lester
tried to reassure her and comfort her, but to no avail.

To avoid her rage, Lester often spent extra hours away from home,
burying himself in his sales work. Twice his wife threatened to leave
him, but she never actually made the move. More often, she tried to
get him to move from the house, and once went to the extent of
swearing out a warrant to force him to leave, but did not have this
warrant served on him. She spent many hours with her family, especially with her mother. Whenever her mother appeared at the house
Frances would make every effort to try to straighten up the place, as
her mother was hypercritical of her housekeeping. At the same time,
she would berate Lester in front of her mother in order to gain her
mother's approval. Lester felt frightened by his mother-in-law, a
stern, silent woman who reminded him a great deal of his own
mother. Again, it was just about the time when the couple had
agreed to separate that their youngest boy, Larry, was born. Shortly

after Larry's birth Frances became so depressed that psychiatric care was recommended, and she began her psychoanalysis.

Course in Treatment. An avid reader, Lester was familiar with many of the writings and theories of psychoanalysis. He, therefore, conceived of psychotherapy chiefly as digging up as fast as possible many of his memories of his childhood and early life. Although he declared repeatedly that his marital problems arose in part from his behavior and were related to his background, he spent an increasing amount of time in his psychotherapeutic hours in reciting the latest attack on him by his wife and reviewing her problems and the problems that she caused him. At that time under the pressure of the marital situation, it seemed unlikely that he could look objectively at the part that he played in his marriage. Therefore, in addition to the individual interview, he was placed in psychotherapeutic group, along with other men who also had marital problems. After approximately nine months' treatment his marital relations did seem to be going a little more smoothly. He seemed to have gained some slight insight into the role he played in relation to his wife and children. At this point his psychotherapist was transferred from the clinic. He recommended that Mr. V. seek psychoanalysis. Arrangements were made to help Mr. V. receive psychoanalysis at lowered cost, through the clinic of the Psychoanalytic Institute. Two years later Mr. V. called the clinic again, asking for advice. He had not followed through the previous advice of the clinic for psychoanalysis, and, in the meantime, his wife had recently separated from him, and the separation looked as though it would result in a divorce. He was advised again to seek either psychoanalysis or intensive psychotherapy. Shortly thereafter, a letter was received from the Psychoanalytic Institute, requesting a report from the clinic, and indicating that Mr. V. had been accepted as a candidate for psychoanalysis.

Questions for Lester V.

1. Lester recognized that some of his behavior as well as his wife's behavior incited and aggravated their marked marital discord. What kinds of behavior, other than those patterns that he recognized consciously, may he have persisted in and thus annoyed his wife?

2. Considering both his relationship with his wife and his earlier life history, summarize what you regard to be the underlying traits in this man's personality; state how these traits are interrelated.

3. What appear to be the main sources of these traits in Lester's childhood?

4. What aspects of Lester's relationships with each of his parents might be reflected in his marital maladjustment?

5. Considering the above answers, how might you account for the fact that:

    a. Lester evidently "backed" into marriage on two occasions

    b. Lester continued his second marriage even after it was so patently difficult. What did this second marriage offer him?

    c. Lester never really had a satisfactory relationship with a woman since reaching adulthood

6. At the time that Lester applied for treatment at the clinic, he was diagnosed as a *character disorder.*

    a. What is the formal definition of a *character disorder?*

    b. How is this different from a neurosis?

    c. In what ways does this case fit the formal definition of *character disorder?*

    d. Why might the army psychiatrist have regarded Lester as psychotic at one time?

7. Often it appears to be the case that when two people with neurotic conflicts marry, the marriage provides a fertile ground for unconscious gratification of each person's neurotic needs. In what ways were neurotic needs being gratified for Lester and Frances in their marriage?

8. What changes occurred in the family dynamics and structure over the years which interfered with these neurotic forms of gratification?

References

EISENSTEIN, V. (Ed.) *Neurotic interaction in marriage*, New York: Basic Books, 1956.

THE CASE OF SALLY D.*

The Fight for Life

Sally D. was a markedly overweight woman whose face, although rather plain, seemed somewhat younger than that of a person of fifty-six, perhaps because of her close-cropped, sandy-colored hair. She frequently appeared in a black, cotton, semi-sack style dress and her attire in general was loose, scanty, and careless if not sloppy. Out of doors she wore sandals and at home went barefoot.

She gave the impression of being constantly active, either moving about the room or accompanying her rapid speech with a variety of gestures. Her voice was memorable because of its peculiarly penetrating quality, particularly when she laughed, which was often.

As she related her history Sally constantly submitted detailed descriptions of situations, lost track of topics she had just initiated, and was carried away in tirades against doctors, former acquaintances, and other figures from her past life against whom she apparently still held painful grudges. Photograph albums were brought out to illustrate and clarify many of the events which were related. Sally had been in psychotherapy for over a year at the time this history was accumulated, having originally requested treatment because she had contemplated suicide.

Childhood. Sally's childhood was spent in a large house in a small western town where her father was a wealthy lumber baron. Her grandparents were all native Americans and, on the father's side, extremely wealthy. Her father's father owned several banks and a

---

* Unlike many of the cases in this book, Sally D.'s case history was not taken in a clinical setting but emerged in the course of a laboratory exercise in psychological testing by one of our students. Thus, why psychotherapy was terminated is not known.

lumber company and was "worth several millions." Sally's father managed to retain a good deal of this wealth and, although he later suffered several financial reverses, at the time of her birth "had almost a million."

Sally was preceded by three sisters four, six, and seven years older. Her birth in 1898 was accompanied by that of a twin brother. Sally described her father as "a short man . . . quiet most of the time, but he had a *terrific* temper. He ran everything and mother did everything to suit him." Her mother was a "wonderful person, very athletic, and with an exaggerated sense of duty. She never did what she wanted to do, but always did what was proper. She never had a chance to think about herself. She was short too, on the squatty side, and very loud like I am."

Sally could remember nothing of her childhood before the age of eight. At that time she was an active athletic youngster who "went around more with boys than with girls; I suppose because of my twin brother . . . I don't know." Her recollections of this period begin with memories of sex-play with her brother and numerous neighborhood children: "they liked to use me because I enjoyed it so much." Her sisters, however, did not participate in these games. At about this time Sally's uncle, who had been having marital difficulties, began to seduce her regularly . . . "and from then on I had quite a sex life." In regard to more formal sex education Sally stated, "We didn't know too much . . . you mentioned somebody having a baby and you got slapped, so I couldn't ask my mother questions. I had to have other ways of finding out things."

Although she was very much attached to her sisters and especially to her twin brother, often they would not play with her. Sometimes her mother would intervene, but "I was always a nuisance. My brother would say: 'Does she always have to follow me around everywhere?' . . . The poor guy." He preferred the company of the next oldest sister who was "something of a tomboy." Nevertheless, she frequently comforted her brother against his fear of the dark. Her siblings were all successful in school and skipped grades, however, Sally passed only "because the teachers couldn't control me." At that time Sally was "always naughty . . . had a vivid imagination and used to tell horrible tales; I don't remember what they were . . . about things happening at home. I usually got half-killed, beaten up every day by mother." Sally also suffered from asthma and hives: "sometimes my feet would swell up so badly that my brother would have to bring me home from school on a sled." Her asthma continued to afflict her seasonally until she moved to California in 1925. On the other hand she had no serious illnesses and thought of the hives and asthma as "just annoying things." She described herself during this phase (about age 12) as "an athlete, scraggly, scrawny, no-account, no-good kid." Although she "can never remember having had affection from anyone in the family," some of her happiest memories were of the outdoor life in a remote, wooded, lakeside area where her father owned a large, rustic, vacation house. Here she went sailing, canoeing, swimming, and horseback riding. She recalled with great pleasure that every evening the whole family would gather on the porch overlooking the lake and watch the sunset.

Adolescence. Sally's adolescence was "nothing but one orgy of sex . . . that's the horrible part of it . . . I had intercourse with practically every boy or man I knew." She also maintained her interest in outdoor sports throughout this period. However, from the age of fourteen to twenty-two one of Sally's major interests was a Jewish boy, Lawrence. At the age of sixteen she became pregnant by him and wanted to get married. Unfortunately, her father, who was rabidly anti-Semitic, objected, and when he found out that Sally was pregnant he insisted that she have an abortion . . . "I would have had twins." The father also went to Lawrence's parents and threatened them with a pistol. Sally believed that he must have been drunk at the time. After that scene, marriage seemed out of the question, but the relationship with Lawrence continued in a sporadic and clandestine manner for about six years. Sally never stopped thinking of Lawrence with affection and always felt that her life would have been totally different had she been permitted to marry him and give birth to the twins.

Sally's twin brother was shot and killed in a hunting accident on his seventeenth birthday. He had been determined to join the army but his parents had refused to permit it. Sally felt that in some obscure way her parents were responsible for his death, and also that he had abandoned her: "He died just when I needed him most."

At seventeen, during the First World War, Sally worked for a while as a nurse, having obtained this position by falsifying her age and qualifications. Later in the year her family sent her to a private girls' school in New York. The school did not grant a high school diploma, a situation which has "stymied me ever since," and for which she blamed her parents throughout her life.

At eighteen Sally again became pregnant by Lawrence and again had an abortion. This was followed by a "nervous breakdown." "I was terribly upset because I couldn't get married . . . I wanted babies terribly; as far as I was concerned, all women were for was to have babies." Following her breakdown Sally's mother refused to let her stay at home. Sally wanted to go back to New York, so her father supplied the money for the trip. While living there her roommate introduced her to Phil, and although she hadn't wanted to go out with anybody, she saw Phil frequently and soon became pregnant again. Another abortion was carried out followed by another "nervous breakdown." At this point Sally began treatment with a psychiatrist "who had studied under Freud." This doctor, "thought I was bad all the way through," and advised a hysterectomy to reduce Sally's sexual drive. When she rejected the operation the doctor advised that she be placed in a sanatorium. Both Sally and her family were opposed to this, but a compromise was agreed upon and she was sent to an Episcopalian retreat in New Jersey. Here she lived for several months among the nuns in an environment without mirrors. Her sister "just about died" when she visited Sally. "It was a horrible place, but a gorgeous place."

Adulthood. Following her stay at the retreat, Sally did considerable traveling between her home and New York. She spent several semesters at a junior college and resumed her affair with Lawrence. In 1920 she again moved to New York, where she began seeing Jack, "an old friend who knew all about me." Although she wasn't in love with him they were married and moved to Nevada, where Jack had a position as a mining engineer. Unfortunately, Jack became seriously ill shortly after their arrival at the small mining town where he was to work and had to be hospitalized. Sally lived all alone in a little shack. She recalls the bedroom being full of snow so that she almost froze to death, and that she let in all the stray dogs and cats in the neighborhood to help keep her warm. Jack's recovery was followed by a series of strikes at the mine. Their financial situation deteriorated still further and Jack began to drink heavily. Sally's weight had increased to three hundred pounds in spite of their lack of funds for food. Jack continued to drink heavily and at one point had an attack of delerium tremens. The couple next moved to Montana, but Jack's illness returned and became worse so they returned to the Far West to live near Sally's family.

During the summer following their return Sally worked as a lifeguard. While on this job she met Bill, also a lifeguard, with whom she engaged in an affair because "Jack never did me any good sexually." During a trip to Chicago with Bill, Sally had intercourse with several of Bill's friends, and another pregnancy resulted. This time no abortion was performed and Sally's first child, Keith, was born. A year or so later, another child was born, Laura, who could definitely be attributed to Bill. By this time Sally's relationship with her husband had become quite stormy. When Jack threatened to shoot both Sally and himself she left him, taking the five-month-old Laura and Keith with her. Since she had no job she soon had to place the children with a community shelter. After several months she was able to secure a good paying job through her father's influence, but had again become pregnant. At this point her father visited her and decided to take her and her children back home with him. Another abortion was performed, but it was only partially successful; Sally had been pregnant with twins again. A tubal pregnancy occurred and Sally had to undergo several operations.

In 1925, Sally's divorce from Jack was final. The following year her father gave her $1000 so that she could move to California. There she quickly secured a job as a swimming instructor at a private club. While working there she formed an attachment to Phil, a young man who had never held a steady job and who was unemployed at the time. After a pregnancy, an abortion, and another pregnancy Sally and Phil decided to get married. Phil had promised to get a job before the marriage, but it was over a year before he was able to do so. Meanwhile a third child, Tim, was born. Following Tim's birth Sally "had one abortion after another . . . I aborted four pairs of twins altogether." Phil didn't want any more babies because Sally was "horrible to live with when pregnant." They had been living on money sent by Sally's father until 1933 when financial reverses forced him to discontinue his support. Bills mounted up quickly and the couple had to borrow a considerable sum. One day Phil told her that they were "all through . . . he no longer wanted to live with a fat old woman with three kids." Sally "couldn't get over him" and "wept for a year," but nevertheless got into her car with the children and drove across the country to Michigan.

During the trip Keith became ill with appendicitis, Laura's stomach was upset, and Tim had tonsillitis. Sally, in desperation, went to the police in an effort to locate Phil's brother, whom she had never met, but with whom she had corresponded. With the police's help she located her brother-in-law's house. When he arrived home from work he found her there with her three sick children. He and his pregnant wife were "wonderful" to Sally although they had never met her; she stayed with them for several months.

In the ensuing period Sally made many trips, but couldn't be happy anywhere. She made attempts to reconcile with Phil, "but it didn't work out." Returning to California with her children, she found a place with two teen-age boys. Although she slept on the floor and the house had no lights, gas, or hot water, she regards this as a happy period. "We had lots of fun; we even had a sailboat that one of the boys found." She managed to make some money by taking in washing for truck drivers, collected food that had been discarded by wholesalers and cooked it in the fireplace.

Then, just as she had acquired some furniture and rented an apartment with all the usual conveniences, her son Keith came down with polio. Sally's description of this period was related angrily. She refused to permit the doctor to take Keith to the county hospital because "conditions were horrible there, he would never have lived . . . the doctors were all sick . . . they tied kids to the beds." In the period of deprivation that followed Sally contacted a number of welfare agencies and once sat in a welfare office until the police came, because they wouldn't give her a job.

However, by the time the children were out of grade school, Sally had again been able to improve her status and was living in a large house in a good neighborhood. Since then she had had a variety of jobs: taught swimming and managed the laundry at a dude ranch, done practical nursing, supervised a girl scout troop, worked at various aircraft plants, was a telephone operator, and drove a school bus. She had maintained her interest in travel and took trips all over the country with her children.

Sally remained sexually active throughout her life. Her partners in the latter period were usually younger men, although she had several lesbian experiences which left her unsatisfied. She estimated she had had eighteen abortions. She stated that within the last three or four years she had become increasingly "depressed, tired of fighting," and had attempted suicide. The attempt followed the conclusion of an affair with a young medical student. She then entered psychoanalysis because her father's will was being settled and "if I died my children would not receive any money and that's all I'll have to give them." She hoped also that analysis would solve her weight problem which she felt to be psychogenic.

Asked to describe herself at the time the history was taken, Sally said: "I'm a fat, blowsy blonde covered with blubber. A loud, brash sort of creature . . . I'm everything I would like not to be. I'd like to be a nice, quiet, intellectual. Instead I'm a boob . . . my own worst enemy."

Epilogue. Several months after relating her history Sally's father's will was settled and Sally was able to see that the money was distributed between her three children. After this matter was disposed of, Sally found herself becoming progressively more despondent. Her life seemed to have little meaning any more and she felt that she was rapidly losing her ability to snap back from each adversity of her life. One day, after her children had been placed with a baby-sitter for the weekend, Sally drove to an isolated mountain area where she rented a cabin. That evening, Sally filled the bathtub with water, climbed into it, and swallowed fifty barbiturate pills. She was found the next morning floating in the tub, dead.

Questions for Sally D.

1. From the brief description of Sally's early life, what hypotheses can you raise about which of Sally's basic needs were not satisfied in her early family relationships? List the need or needs which you feel were not adequately gratified and describe the reason for the failure of gratification (overindulgence, deprivation, traumatic training, and so forth).

2. What modes of behavior did Sally adopt in her interpersonal re-

lationships to compensate for her frustrated needs? Are these behaviors covered by some of the conventional terms used to describe psychological defense mechanisms? If so, what are some of the terms that describe Sally's reaction patterns?

3. In your estimation, does your answer to question 2 explain Sally's pattern of sexual behavior? In what way does it provide an explanation? What other hypotheses do you find necessary to explain Sally's sexual pattern?

4. Evidently it was terribly important to Sally to have children. How can you account for the intensity of this need?

5. Sally evidently had a tendency toward overeating and obesity. What hypotheses can you raise which might provide an explanation for *both* Sally's sexual promiscuity and her overeating? (*Hint:* Assume the operation of a single need system with different manifestations and see how far this takes you.)

6. Sally evidently had a large reservoir of energy to resist repeated psychological and physical stress. What clinical disorder, in its acute state, is characterized by high energy, loudness, overeating, and a flight of ideas? Does Sally manifest a mild form of this clinical disorder or do you see her as manifesting a totally different reaction pattern? Justify your answer.

7. What role did Sally's energy and high activity appear to play in keeping Sally's anxiety level within livable bounds?

8. Describe the events which were going on in Sally's life at the time that she committed suicide. Contrast these events with the state of Sally's life over the previous twenty years. What hypotheses can you raise to account for the fact that Sally committed suicide when events were as they were?

9. It is frequently argued that a profound mood of depression coupled with intense guilt feelings predisposes a person to consider suicide as a solution to her problems.

　　a. Do we see any suggestions of consciously experienced depression in Sally at the time that she committed suicide?

　　b. Do we see any indications of long-term defenses against depression which were beginning to fail at the time of the suicide?

10. The reading list below includes a number of theories of suicide. Do any of these theories seem to cover Sally's situation? If so, which one does seem to fit?

References

BRUCH, H. Psychiatric aspects of obesity. *Psychiatry*, 1947, **10**: 273–281.

FARBEROW, N. L. Personality patterns of suicidal mental patients. *Genetic Psychology Monographs*, 1950, **42**: 3–79.

FARBEROW, N. L., & SHNEIDMAN, E. *The cry for help*. New York: McGraw-Hill, 1961. Of particular interest in understanding the present case: Chap. 5, The assessment of self-destructive potentiality, and Chaps. 12–19, in which various experts, representing different psychological points of view, attempt a theoretical explanation of suicide.

HENDIN, H. Psychodynamic and motivational factors in suicide. *Psychiatric Quarterly*, 1951, **25**: 672–678.

THE CASE OF PHILIP H.

The Bottom of the Stairs

Philip H. appeared at a psychological clinic in the spring of the year expressing a desperate need for help with his problem. He was at forty-five, a man with little or no purpose in life, bright and well-educated—yet marked by a severe sexual deviancy. Philip was a child molester who had spent most of his adult years deriving his primary sexual gratification from relations with young adolescent boys. Although Philip had followed this practice for over twenty-five years, his first conflict with law enforcement authorities occurred only two years previously when he was arrested for molesting a young boy in a movie theater. Following this arrest, Philip was committed to a state hospital for sexual deviants where he received group therapy as well as various forms of occupational therapy. At the time of his discharge, Philip was considered to have been a model patient—bright, insightful, and co-operative, and one who had apparently conquered his problem. It was obvious from talking to Philip that this hospitalization had had a profound and shocking effect upon him. For many years Philip had been able to maintain the fiction that there was nothing wrong in his sexual behavior. Indeed, he had built up a complex set of rationalizations for his behavior, built upon the premise that he was actually providing needed love and affection for the boys. His encounter with the judicial and hospital system seriously challenged this distorted self-conception.

Philip arrived at the clinic a frightened man, on the surface superficially eager to be co-operative, but still reserving judgment about whether or not he wanted to change his ways. In appearance, he was of average height, thin and tense looking, and dressed quite shabbily. Yet he affected an air of dignity and intelligence which was hard to reconcile with his appearance. He stated at the outset, with apparent pride, that he was a "sexual psychopath." However, as he spoke these words, the sense of shame which he felt about coming to a clinic was more evident than this superficial bravado. As he talked, it became obvious that Philip was a well-educated person who was pedantic in his speech and placed a great value upon his intellectual achievements. An underlying mood of tension and hostility also was present in Philip's behavior. He fidgeted a great deal during the interview and mentioned that he was struggling against a blinding headache which started that morning.

Background and Early History. Philip was born in a large metropolitan area on the eastern seaboard of the United States, the next to youngest in a family of four children, all girls but himself. His father was a large vigorous man who ran a tavern. Philip admired him but had little contact with him. His father was away much of the time and when he was home there were many family problems which kept him busy. Philip recalled that when he was young, he was thin and scrawny and wished that he was larger and more like his father in physique. He was unable to remember anything about his mother. She died in childbirth with his younger sister when Philip was only four years old. Philip did recall his mother's death and the drastic effects which followed with considerable emotion. Following her death Philip was cared for by a series of foster parents whose modes of discipline and affection varied widely. After two years, Philip's father remarried and he was taken back into his father's home. Although he was apprehensive about this move, his fears were quickly dispelled when he met his stepmother, Rosemary. Rosemary a warm, affectionate person made efforts to make Philip and his sisters feel that they had a real home once again. Philip recalled the next two years as the happiest of his life. The family was again a unit and although Philip still was unable to get as close to his father as he would have liked, he was happy with Rosemary. This idyllic period ended dramatically and drastically when Rosemary suddenly became ill and died. Following this second devasting experience, Philip was sent to live with an aunt and uncle on a farm in New England. He stated that his aunt and uncle were very kind to him and made every effort to raise him as their own child. He was raised with a cousin who was close to him in age. Philip found the small-town life very pleasant and friendly. He attended grade school there between his eighth and tenth years and was a very good student. During this period, he recalled the beginning of his interest in sex, and also recalled that when he was ten, he and his cousin would spend many hours playing in the barn and the hayloft. During one of these periods the boys talked of sex and exhibited themselves to each other. Philip found himself very excited during the experience and pressed his cousin to let him fondle his sexual organs. His cousin reluctantly agreed and Philip found the experience very pleasurable. On a number of different occasions following this experience Philip tried to have sexual experiences with his cousin, but the cousin became more and more reluctant to participate until finally he refused altogether.

When Philip was ten, his father remarried once again and asked that Philip return home. Philip left his aunt and uncle reluctantly to face a new stepmother and a father whom he had seen only infrequently during the previous three years. Unlike Rosemary, Sally G., his new stepmother, was a cold, ambitious woman whom Philip disliked intensely from their first meeting. Philip found himself in constant conflict with her. She insisted that Philip wear fancy clothes so that he frequently was more elaborately dressed than the other boys, which made it difficult for him to make friends. Sally also was very strict with Philip. Whenever anything was missing or broken about the house, Philip was automatically accused and punished. Although Philip pleaded with his father to intervene with Sally, his father expressed a sense of helplessness in dealing with her. Sally had very strict rules about studying and insisted that Philip return home immediately after school to do his lessons. Many afternoons Philip passed other boys playing in the street and longed to play with them, but Sally insisted that weekday afternoons were for studying and not for play.

During this period, Philip's father began to drink heavily. While he previously had a reputation for consuming his own product at work, he gradually began to drink more and more at home. Philip recalled that on numerous occasions, his father drank himself into a stupor by early afternoon. When Philip was fourteen, his father became quite ill with liver trouble and was confined to bed. The illness took a progressively downward course and within six months he was dead. Philip recalled his father's death as a tremendous blow. Since the family was Catholic, a priest was called in to administer the last rites. After the rites were administered, Philip asked the priest if his father was going to heaven, and the priest replied that his father had not been a good man and would probably end in Hell. Philip was furious at the priest for this and vowed that from that day onward that he would have nothing further to do with the Church, a vow which he assiduously kept over the years.

Following his father's death Philip continued to live with his stepmother and an uncle who moved in with them. The uncle evidently took over the financial responsibility for Philip, and was reluctant to spend money on him. Philip remembered the next three years as very bitter ones in which he felt alone in a hostile home. He felt that he was a financial burden on the family and that they were basically not interested in him. Throughout this time, there was constant pressure on him to leave school and go to work, pressure which he successfully resisted until he graduated from high school.

It was during his last year of high school that Philip met Elizabeth, a girl who lived nearby who was very attractive but who walked with a slight limp. Philip fell madly in love with Elizabeth and felt that possibly her deformity might make her more likely to be interested in a man like himself. He mentally put Elizabeth on a pedestal, worshiped her, and never dared to approach her sexually, feeling that this might destroy the relationship. Shortly before graduating from high school, Philip asked Elizabeth to marry him. She refused on the basis that they were too young to marry, and Philip felt crushed. He recalled thinking at the time that this was the last time that he was going to have anything to do with women. From this point on, Philip turned progressively to homosexual outlets for sexual gratification.

It was the middle of the depression of the 'thirties when Philip left high school and he found it impossible to get a job. He left the big city and roamed from town to town as an itinerant construction worker. He evidently picked up some surveying knowledge and was able to get work. Philip mentioned that he rarely stayed for very long on any one job despite the fact that his bosses were always satisfied with him and wanted him to stay. He mentioned that once a job was going well, he felt an unexplainable need to leave. Philip felt that he was always looking for something and felt that it lay just around the next bend. But, just what he was looking for was hard to say. All he could verbalize was that once his part on a job was completed and he no longer felt essential, he had to leave.

This pattern of drifting from job to job continued throughout the depression and until the beginning of World War II. At this time, Philip was drafted into the army as a private and within a few months of basic training was shipped overseas and stationed in Hawaii. Philip rose rapidly in army ranks and was evidently a very successful soldier, so successful that by the end of the war he had reached the rank of first lieutenant. Philip was evidently quite happy during this period and did not often engage in homosexual activity. From time to time, when tension built up, he sought relief with a young boy, but these occasions were rarer than they had been in civilian life.

It was during this period that Philip met the woman who was later to become his wife. Each Sunday he visited the home of a local woman, considerably older than himself, who invited him and his buddy over for dinner. Philip spent most of his time with the older woman while his friend dated the woman's younger friend, Evelyn. Philip mentioned that he enjoyed his relations with this older woman as it provided him with feminine companionship without any possibility of sexual relations. It was during this period that Philip was surprised to receive a letter from Elizabeth. In the letter, Elizabeth indicated that she expected him to marry her when he returned from the war. He found this implication very disturbing and resented the fact that Elizabeth was proposing to him instead of him to her. In a moment of combined rage and panic, Philip called Evelyn, the buddy's girl friend with whom he had had little contact and asked her to marry him. Much to his surprise and chagrin, Evelyn accepted and they were married two days later. Philip left for the battle area shortly thereafter and saw little of Evelyn except for a few brief furloughs. However, during these furloughs, they engaged in sexual relations and Evelyn became pregnant and over the subsequent two years bore two children.

Following the war, Philip returned to the United States where he enrolled in college under the G.I. Bill. He reluctantly brought Evelyn to the mainland and they set up house. From the outset the marriage was not a happy one. Philip did not want to be married and the constant threat of heterosexual relations stood over him. He tried to avoid sexual relations as much as possible and responded only to her direct requests for intercourse. This he found disturbing also, as he felt that he should be the aggressor and not the passive member of the family. Philip resented any requests that Evelyn made on him to do anything around the house and constantly tried to teach her to be self-reliant and to fix things herself. During this period he engaged in frequent sex play with young boys, and gradually his wife became aware from some campus gossip that something was wrong.

Despite the disordered marital relationship, Philip had phenomenal success in his academic work. He was a straight A student and was well-regarded by all his professors. Evidently, he was successful in keeping his sexual deviancy from the attention of his teachers and fellow students. At the time of graduation, he accepted a good job with an advertising agency in a large western city. He went ahead to make plans for housing, and planned to have his family follow him west. However within two days after arriving in the new city, he received a letter from Evelyn's lawyer indicating that a suit for divorce had been filed. He wrote a letter to Evelyn asking what was behind this action, but when no reply was received he decided that possibly it was all for the best and dropped the matter. It was around this time that Philip started frequenting certain movie houses in town which were rumored to be hangouts for homosexuals. It was in one of these movie houses that he was arrested for engaging in sexual relations with a sixteen-year-old boy.

Although throughout his life, Philip had had sexual relations with boys, he was not attracted to all types of boys or boys of all ages. The boys had to be of "good build" and smaller than Philip, usually between twelve and sixteen years of age. There were some adult men that he found sexually attractive, usually Mexican or Negro of slight build, whom he felt were inferior to him. In all his sexual contacts, he felt it necessary to feel superior to his partner. He never felt attracted to white adult males. At various times, in an effort to break out of his antisocial action, Philip tried consciously to become a true homosexual who focused exclusively upon adults. He found these attempts futile as he did not know how to approach adult homosexuals and often felt rejected by them. Also, sexual relations with an adult male did not satisfy him in the way contact with younger males did. In describing his sexual contacts, Philip emphasized time and again his desire not to harm the boys in any way. He approached them cautiously, never forcing his attention, and trying desperately to get some sign of willingness from the boy before making any approach. He also emphasized how important it was to him not to be rejected by his prospective sex partner. He had to be sure that the boy was interested in him sexually; he developed a complex set of maneuvers desiged to avoid rejection and at the same time to test the potential partner's interest in him.

In describing his relations with the boys, Philip emphasized the tender feelings he felt for them during and after the sex act. He wanted to do something for them and frequently bought them clothes and books. He hated furtive, one-time relations and frequently would try to establish a long-term relationship with a boy. Interestingly, after such a relationship was established, he lost interest in the sexual side and found it fully satisfying just to spend time with the boy and to take him places.

From time to time, Philip would attempt to tell the interviewer how he felt while having sexual relations with a boy. He described a sensation almost mystical in quality, of fusing with the young boy in the midst of sexual relations. He stated that when he was holding a young boy he felt a sense of identity with him and could not distinguish between himself as a person and the boy as a person and frequently felt that he was the boy, and his own personality failed to exist. The interviewer who saw Philip could not help but feel as he heard these descriptions, despite the repugnance of the act, a pathetic, love-starved quality about Philip as he talked of these contacts.

Course in Treatment. Philip was accepted into psychotherapy with misgivings on the part of the clinic staff. His age and general lack of insight argued against a successful outcome. Philip was seen on a once-a-week basis. Initially, he was very defensive, talked pedantically about himself and his past, and typically tried to present the picture of a perfectly co-operative patient. After a while, he began to manifest various signs of dependence upon the therapist and was continually concerned as to whether the therapist would be present for the next meeting. Philip gradually became less defensive and as he did so, he became more willing to explore his past, particularly as it bore upon his sexual deviancy. It was obvious from reports that Philip brought in that his behavior with others, particularly on his job, was undergoing a marked change for the better. However, he reported little or no change in the intensity of his sexual desires for young boys. At one critical point, Philip indicated that he would like to give up his perverted way of expressing his sexual desires, but one thing made it difficult for him to do so. From his vantage point, these sexual experiences were the only pleasures he experienced in his life and he seriously challenged the therapist to guarantee him that some other substitute source of pleasure would be available to him if he gave up his perversion. Time and again, he said to the therapist, "You're trying to take away from me the only pleasure I've ever had in life. Can you guarantee that some other pleasure will exist for me, after I give this one up?" At the height of dealing with Philip's feelings about giving up his perversion, a most unfortunate experience occurred; Philip's therapist was forced to leave the city because of serious illness in his family and it was necessary for him to suspend therapy for a month. This matter was discussed with Philip and he showed no particular concern about it and a date was set five weeks later for the next appointment. Philip kept that appointment but expressed his intention to terminate his therapy. When pressed for his reasons he said that during the period that his therapist was gone, he noticed a subtle change in his ability to control his sexual experiences. While previously he felt that these impulses were under his control, he now experienced them as obsessive thoughts totally outside the range of conscious control. He found that he could think of nothing else but finding young boys and was so pre-occupied that he could do little else. This shift in the way that he experienced his sexual impulses frightened Philip intensely and was the major reason that he reported wanting to leave therapy. His therapist tried to explain to Philip the implications of his actions —that another contact with the law was inevitable, this time with a longer sentence. Philip agreed that this was a horrible, yet likely, prospect, but was so disturbed that "anything is better than this hell of therapy." Before leaving, Philip mentioned a dream which he had the night before. In this dream, a recurring one which dated back to childhood, he was about to be hung. However, in the past he was always able to slip out of the rope before the trap door was sprung. Now, however, his therapist was the hangman and Philip had the feeling that he was no longer able to slip out of the noose; he was terrified as he stood at the top of the stairs and when the trap door was sprung he fell down to the bottom of the stairs. As he was falling he thought in his dream, "I don't care if I die, but I hope I don't hurt myself when I hit the bottom of the stairs."

All further efforts by the therapist were futile. Philip left the clinic and never returned. To this day nothing is known of his sexual adjustment.

Questions for Philip H.

1. Describe the experiences which Philip had with his mother and mother figures prior to reaching adulthood.
2. What common core do you see in all or most of these relationships in terms of
   a. their duration
   b. their emotional quality
   c. their mode of cessation
3. What basic needs were frustrated in most of these relationships and what effect did this frustration appear to have upon
   a. Philip's self-concept
   b. Philip's attitudes toward women
   c. Philip's general comfort with other people, regardless of their sex
4. From the brief description given in the case concerning Philip's relationship with his father, what inferences can you draw about the following:
   a. Philip's closeness with his father
   b. Philip's sense of adequacy as a man as compared with his father
5. Summarize from your previous answers:
   a. Philip's attitudes toward women
   b. Philip's attitude toward men
   c. Philip's attitudes toward himself
6. Does this summary in question 5 aid in explaining the following events in Philip's later life? If so, how can they account for them?
   a. Philip's preference for boys between fourteen and sixteen years of age who had to be smaller than himself
   b. Philip's anxiety when Elizabeth intimated that they might marry when he returned from the war
   c. Philip's attitude toward his wife
7. Philip tells us two interesting things about his job behavior prior to World War II. First, that he moved from job to job as soon as he felt that his job was accomplished. Second, that he constantly felt

that he was looking for something which might turn up in the next city.

    a. What motivation or motivations appear to underly this restless, longing behavior?

    b. Do you see any relationship between this motivation and Philip's sexual behavior? If so, what sort of relationship do you see?

8. *a.* What hypotheses can you raise to account for the fact that Philip, despite numerous conscious attempts to focus on adult males as the source of sexual gratification, was unable to achieve the same gratification with older men? (*Hint:* This question might be best answered in reverse. First, try to understand which of Philip's needs were met with young boys and then attempt to understand why grown men could not meet these needs.) Reread Philip's description of how he felt during sexual relations with his adolescent partners before answering this question.

    b. What psychological mechanisms, which you may have read or heard about, are useful in understanding Philip's attraction to adolescent boys? In what way are these mechanisms helpful in understanding this case?

9. Philip never returned to therapy after his therapist was unavoidably called out of town. From your understanding of Philip, how do you account for this reaction?

10. What are some theories which have been offered to explain the etiology of homosexuality? Do any of these theories apply to Philip?

References

BRANCALE, R., ELLIS, A., & DOORBAR, RUTH. Psychiatric and psychological investigations of convicted sex offenders: a summary report. *American Journal of Psychiatry*, 1952, **109**: 17–21.

FREUD, S. Instincts and their vicissitudes. In *Collected papers of Sigmund Freud.* Vol. 4. New York: Basic Books, 1959. Pp. 60–83.

GREENSPAN, H., & CAMPBELL, J. D. The homosexual as a personality type. *American Journal of Psychiatry*, 1945. **101**: 682–689.

HARLOW, H. F. The nature of love. *American Psychologist*, 1958, **13**: 673–685.

KARPMAN, B. *The sexual offender and his offenses.* New York: Julian Press, 1954. Pp. 104–106.

THE CASE OF ALBERT I.

A Place in Society

Albert I., age thirty-one years, was confined to an army disciplinary barracks, serving a five-year general court-martial sentence for frequent absence from duty without official leave (AWOL), striking a noncommissioned officer, and two charges of failing to obey direct orders. This severe sentence was imposed because this was Albert's fifth court-martial. Albert offered the following explanation of his behavior: One evening, about six months previously, he left camp between guard shifts, with the unofficial permission of the guard sergeant, to see his wife off at the bus station. Although Albert was not required to be on duty at that time, the sergeant not only failed to cover for him but actually reported Albert's absence to the authorities. When Albert returned to camp and discovered this betrayal, he beat up the sergeant and left the camp without permission for two days, in his words, "To think things over." At the end of this period, he returned voluntarily to the camp to face the consequences of his actions. Following Albert's court-martial, his wife threatened to divorce him for nonsupport, and accused him of "loving the stockade more than he did her." Subsequently they became somewhat reconciled, although Albert admitted that he had genuine doubts as to whether his wife would wait for his eventual release.

During the first few weeks of his sentence, Albert appeared bitter, almost to the point of being paranoid. He recited, over and over, a tirade against the service, protesting that his sentence was unusually severe, repeatedly requesting to be assigned to a salvage unit, and claiming that his health was in need of immediate attention. Gradually Albert cooled down and conformed to prison rules. His work record was consistently excellent, although his supervisor noted that he preferred solitary duties to group work. Albert did not belong to any of the prison "gangs," excused himself from sports because of a "bum leg," and spent most of his leisure time in the library, working out crossword puzzles. After three months, Albert was designated by the officer in charge of his unit as a possible candidate for the barracks special rehabilitation unit, and an evaluation of his intellectual potentialities was requested from the psychological unit.

During the ensuing interviews and tests, Albert tried to affect a relaxed posture, although obviously tense and guarded. A short, stocky Negro with broad shoulders and well-developed muscles, his posture was stooped and he walked with a slight shuffle. However, his movements were well co-ordinated, with no noticeable tremors or hesitancies. He spoke in a soft, deep voice, occasionally slurring his words. Throughout his contacts with the psychologist, Albert was ingratiatingly polite and good-natured.

Past History. Albert was the third of four living children who were born and reared in a very poor section of a large eastern industrial city. Albert claimed that this was not exclusively a Negro section, that all nationalities lived in the area. Albert's father, a veteran of World War I, died when Albert was still an infant. His mother remarried shortly thereafter to a baker who was often unemployed and was an alcoholic. Albert's mother was usually employed away from home as a housekeeper, leaving him in the care of his older sister. The family was poverty-stricken and often on relief. School reports indicated that the children were frequently truant because of a lack of proper clothing, and when they did come to school they had had no breakfast and were unable to afford lunch.

There were large gaps in age between Albert and his siblings, several intervening children having died in infancy. Albert was the surviving member of a twin birth. Albert's oldest brother, fifteen years his senior, was reported to be in a state hospital for the criminally insane as a result of an extensive history of petty crimes and alcoholism. Albert avoided speaking of this brother at first, though later he mentioned him as an additional source of grief to his mother. Albert's oldest sister, Shirley, of whom he spoke in greater detail and with greater affection, ran away from home to get married at sixteen. After two years she returned home with her two children when her husband deserted her. Prior to Albert's court-martial, his younger brother, Jack, had returned from combat service with the Marines with an honorable discharge and was a hero to his family. Albert claimed that there was no rivalry between him and Jack when they were young, and, in fact, they played very little with each other because of the marked age difference. Albert and Jack had been separated since Albert was fifteen, when Jack was sent to live with some relatives.

Albert pictured his mother as the main source of affection in the family, although she was not openly demonstrative. She administered most of the minor discipline, but attempted to intercede for the boys when the stepfather beat them. Albert claimed that his mother set "practical ambitions" for her children and always urged them to get as much education as possible, although she was uneducated herself. She evidently had musical training as she occasionally earned extra money by giving piano lessons to neighbor children. She was quite unsuccessful, however, in interesting her own children in playing a musical instrument. Albert's mother suffered continuously from multiple illnesses which at one time were believed to be diabetic in origin. Since Albert entered the service, she had become practically invalided with a type of cardiac problem. During Albert's early years, his mother was fanatically devoted to her religion and attempted, through frequent references to Hell and other severe punishments for transgressions, to instill a "fear of God" in her children. Albert claimed that despite his early training he attended church rarely, but he appeared very familiar with the Bible and quoted readily and accurately from it during his interviews with the psychologist. On one of the occasions that Albert's mother sought welfare aid for her family, she was described by a social worker* as being antagonistic in her racial attitudes and "fiercely proud of being a Negro." When Albert was asked about this he vigorously denied that she ever concerned herself with racial matters or talked about this problem at home.

From Albert's comments it was apparent that his stepfather played no direct role in caring for the children. Albert remembers that he slept during the day, worked or went out drinking at night, and thus had little time for the family. Albert could not remember his stepfather ever buying a gift for any of the children. His stepfather had a

---

* In addition to the history which Albert related, a social work report on his family and his wife was obtained through the Red Cross. His civilian and military police records were also on file at the prison.

violent temper which was easily aroused; and although Albert's mother did not refer discipline to him, he frequently administered punishment by harsh beatings. In spite of all this, Albert spoke of his stepfather with considerable affection. For a long time, Albert fancied following his stepfather's trade, but gave up the idea only because the stepfather complained of the low wages, poor working conditions, and frequent unemployment in the baker's trade.

Albert began school at age six. He was frequently truant but nevertheless maintained fair grades. His mother punished Albert for his truancy but to little avail. Albert did not get along well with his teachers and was frequently a disciplinary problem. His school and home situation reached a climax in an incident which occurred when he was in the sixth grade. Sent to the principal's office for discipline, he ran off, fearing a beating and stayed truant for three months. Truant officers were unable to contact the parents during the day, and Albert destroyed the notices they left. When the authorities finally contacted the stepfather and threatened him with arrest, he became enraged. The boy was ordered to strip for a beating but he escaped down the street with the entire neighborhood after him. When he was finally captured, he was tied and beaten until almost unconscious. When relating this incident, Albert pictured his stepfather as the hero and himself as the culprit; he went into great detail, emphasizing the righteous anger of his stepfather, almost relishing the recall of his cruelty. School authorities assigned Albert to a trade school, which he attended until age sixteen, learning a little baking and later some auto mechanics.

Albert spent most of his youth on the streets. Even as a young child, he associated with a group of other Negro children known to the police for delinquency. He denied that he ran around with any one gang, but occasionally participated in gang activities, such as petty thefts and property destruction. He describes himself as more of a "lone wolf," especially with the girls. He obtained his sex information from the streets, as the subject was taboo in his home. His first heterosexual experience was at age thirteen with a girl his own age. He had been sexually promiscuous ever since.

When Albert was sixteen, the family home burned down; he went to live with family friends, and from then on was on his own. He quarreled with these people and was arrested for disturbing the peace. (Police records show Albert was charged with attempted arson, but he denied this.) He was unemployed, left school, and "played around with the idea" of taking up boxing as a career. He had been practicing in a neighborhood gym and later he hung around an "uptown" professional gym, acting as a sparring partner for professional boxers. He finally gave up boxing when his mother convinced him that he might become physically disfigured. Although Albert's health was always good, he had an intense fear of physical injury.

Homeless, he moved out on the city dump, in the "jungles of shack-town," where he eked out a living selling "pickings." Apparently he had had frequent contact with salvaging before; he had been arrested for selling stolen auto parts to the junk man when age thirteen and sentenced to Juvenile Hall for thirty days. His first full-time job was assisting a junk-man in street collections. After a year he found a job in an auto "cemetery," where he learned the salvage business and became fairly skilled. The only employee at first, he became friendly with this employer. Albert described his boss as "a Jew, tight-fisted like all Jews, but really a good Jew." He also frequently quarreled with his boss, usually over petty money matters; he would quit in a huff, retreat to his shack on the city dump, until the boss would come down and cajole him back to work—"like the prodigal son." They often drank together, although Albert denied that he himself was a heavy drinker. Occasionally he would take the boss to find some "high-yellow" prostitute. However, he himself did not have anything to do "with that class of people."

He was arrested again, at age twenty-three, for reckless driving, although he claims he was actually parked by the curb all along. He said something the policeman didn't like—explaining that he was "some smarty" at that age—and ended up serving ten days in jail for this offense. A year later he was convicted of a larceny charge and sentenced to a year in the state penitentiary. His version of this incident was that he had sold the stolen goods, but pleaded guilty to the theft to protect his friends who committed the actual theft. He explained that the others had previous prison records and would have been subject to more severe sentences than he. Although he probably would have received a lighter sentence had he pleaded guilty only to the sale of stolen goods, he decided to help his friends because they had families who would suffer from the longer sentences.

After serving most of this prison sentence, he returned to his old job where he was put in charge of the wrecking department. He hired several of his friends and taught them the work. He was making about $55 a week, and started "living high." He had a "big car," fancy clothes, and moved away from the dump to a nice uptown apartment. Over the next three-year period, he had three common-law wives—the last bore him a son. Although they were separated just before he was drafted, and despite the fact that both have since remarried, Albert expressed a hope to get his son back, saying, "A man should raise his own son."

Drafted into the army in early 1942, his attitude toward the service lacked any elements of patriotism or even ambition. He was shifted about from camp to camp, in racially segregated units, without any real training for combat or any specific duty. He was finally assigned as a guard—a routine and seemingly meaningless task. He was a frequent visitor to sick-call for various minor complaints: a sore back, weak legs, headaches, and stomach trouble. Examinations revealed no organic findings. He was hospitalized once for a stomach complaint but when he admitted malingering to avoid proposed surgery he was released. Albert confessed freely that most of his complaints were malingering but excused himself on the grounds that this was a common and accepted practice by many soldiers. "I know now that those docs aren't so easy to fool, and I'm sorry I was so ignorant as to try." For the first year of service, his disciplinary record was fairly clean, with only one or two "company punishments" for being late to "formations."

In June 1943 he married a Southern Negro girl, several years his junior, whom he had known for a very short time. His wife, an only child, came from a middle-class, economically stable family, and Albert felt that she was somewhat spoiled by her father. She had always been rather sickly, and her health grew worse after marriage; she usually became violently ill whenever they had sexual relations. Albert's first AWOL involved a trip to the doctor for his wife. He claimed that he left camp only after permission had been refused him for an emergency leave. A second court-martial grew out of an assault on a Negro noncommissioned officer who "cussed" Albert out. Subsequently, he was court-martialed two more times for short AWOL's when he left camp to take care of his wife.

During the interviews with Albert an attempt was made to explore his feelings about being a member of a racial minority group. In these interviews, Albert continually denied that race prejudice or even membership in an out-group had affected him seriously or directly. He admitted that race relations were a problem in some parts of the country, but he felt that he had encountered little difficulty. When stationed in the South, he had no trouble with or feelings of antagonism against the Southern white man. When forced to stay on one side of town or on one side of the street or to face up to restricted eating places, he accepted these restrictions as necessary evils, but denied that they disturbed him particularly. During his stay in the disciplinary barracks, Albert avoided being identified with the Negro group. He claimed that he did this to avoid the trouble and violence which frequently arose along racial lines in the barracks. Albert expressed the opinion that the main reason Negroes are restricted was their lack of "education." When questioned as to why this lack of education existed, Albert claimed that the Negro's own laziness and lack of ambition led better schools to believe that they could not afford to waste time and money on Negroes. Albert contended that a Negro who wanted an education could find someplace to get it. Albert's general disparagement of Negroes was epitomized in the following story which he recited spontaneously: A Southern white army officer assumed command of the Negro guard unit in which Albert served. At the first formal meeting of the unit, the officer remarked, "You're all a bunch of worthless niggers." Albert commented that the officer was entirely right in making this remark. "There wasn't any one of them worth anything; none of them was educated." When asked how he believed that the Negro could achieve greater respect in the general community, Albert claimed that first the Negro had to learn his "place." Only after a period of learning to behave according to white group standards, and with more adequate schooling, could the Negro become an acceptable citizen. Albert deplored any attempts to achieve equal rights for the Negro even by legal or non-violent methods until this type of upgrading of the race had occurred.

Subsequent Military History. Albert was seen by the clinical psychologist for a total of ten hours, during which he was interviewed and received an intensive battery of tests. On measures of intellectual functioning, Albert showed an average learning ability and a fair command of language. Considering his limited educational experiences, it was felt by the psychologist that Albert's optimal level of intellectual functioning was somewhat higher than average. This hypothesis was somewhat supported by Albert's interest in crossword puzzles, which he carried around constantly during free periods, dictionary in hand, checking his answers. On the psychologist's recommendation, Albert was assigned for three hours daily to the prison school; his teacher subsequently reported that he was doing about eighth grade work successfully.

In various staff conferences, Albert's potentialities for adjustment to army and later civilian life were thoroughly discussed. It was felt that Albert's good behavior in the disciplinary barracks indicated a desire to conform to social standards in order to achieve a short sentence. If his frustrations in the barracks remained moderate, it was predicted that Albert could probably continue his acceptable behavior until discharged. However, whether he could ever make a socially useful adjustment to civilian life remained doubtful. Job adjustment would be difficult with a dishonorable discharge behind him, and Albert's limited vocational, social, and psychological resources severely limited the possibility of his avoiding future social difficulties as a civilian. With this guarded prognosis, the review board recommended that Albert be placed in a special "good soldiers unit," where, in addition to the educational program, he participated in one of the earliest attempts to use group psychotherapy in prisons. Six months later, Albert was released to military duty, with the specification that if he continued to conform to military regulations for a year, his dishonorable discharge would be revoked. At that time, after the conclusion of World War II, many military prisoners were released without serving the balance of their sentences; thus, Albert probably was discharged from the army soon after release from the disciplinary barracks. His subsequent career is unknown.

Questions for Albert I.

1. Read through the case and list each instance in which Albert came into conflict with some representative of society (authority figure).

2. Classify these instances you have listed above into one of two categories:

   a. planned attempt to circumvent the rules of a social group
   b. impulsive actions, largely unplanned, which violated the
   rules of a social group.
On the average, which category appears more characteristic of
Albert?
3. From what you have read in your textbook and other sources on
personality development, what early experiences are necessary to
establish an inner control system (call it conscience, superego, or
what you will) more or less congruent with social mores?
4. Which of these experiences did Albert experience and which of
these learning conditions were absent? (In your answer, attempt to
distinguish between two phases of this social learning process, direct
verbal teaching by parental figures of right and wrong, and identifying or modeling of behavior after that illustrated by parental
figures.)
5. To what extent did Albert experience a family constellation different from the statistically average lower-class Negro home? Consider
the following in your answer:
   a. stability of marital relationship of parents
   b. absence of father from home
   c. deprivation of physical dependency needs (food, shelter,
   clothing, and so forth);
   d. educational background and experience
6. Despite the fact that we know little concerning Albert's brother,
Jack, how can you, on a theoretical basis, account for an Albert and
a Jack developing in a similar home environment?
7. What means of coping with anxiety does Albert manifest throughout his adult life?
   a. What general diagnostic classification is usually used with
   people who manifest these means of coping with anxiety?
   b. How can this clinical group, as exemplified by Albert, be dis-
   tinguished from the neurotic group as exemplified by an obsessive compulsive neurotic? (Hint: What does it take to develop a neurosis as compared to Albert's reaction pattern?)
8. How would you characterize Albert's methods of resolving his
role as a member of a racial minority group? What technical term is
used for that pattern of reaction? What does it mean?
9. To what extent does this way of handling membership in a
minority group shed light on the following:

a. The fact that two of Albert's offenses in the Army were committed against Negro personnel

b. The fact that Albert preferred not to associate with other Negro prisoners and remained a lone wolf

c. His relationship with his stepfather

References

DAI, B. Some problems of personality development among Negro children. In *Personality in nature, society and culture.* KLUCKHOHN, C., MURRAY, H. A., SCHNEIDER, D. M. (Eds.) New York: Alfred A. Knopf, 1955. Pp. 545–566.

HAVIGHURST, R., & DAVIS, ALLISON. Social class and color differences in child rearing. *American Sociological Review,* 1946, **11:** 698–710.

HAVIGHURST, R., & DAVIS, ALLISON. A comparison of the Chicago and Harvard studies of several class differences in child rearing. *American Sociological Review,* 1955, **20:** 438–442.

MACCOBY, ELEANOR, & GIBBS, P. K. Methods of child rearing in two social classes. In *Readings in child development,* MARTIN, W. E. & STENDLER, C. B. (Eds.) New York: Harcourt, Brace, 1954.

POWDERMAKER, HORTENSE. The channeling of Negro aggression by the cultural process. *American Journal of Sociology,* 1943, **48:** 750–758. (Also reprinted in Kluckhohn, Murray, and Schneider, pp. 597-608.)

PART III EMOTIONAL DISTURBANCES OF CHILDREN

THE CASE OF THE T. FAMILY

"Eat, My Children!"

Initially, Mr. and Mrs. T. came to the clinic for help with their daughter Sharon, age nine. They were troubled by the fact that Sharon could not be separated from her mother even for a short while. If Mrs. T. had to leave the house to run an errand, Sharon had to be taken along. Sharon refused to go to school unless her mother accompanied her every morning; even then, she was likely to raise a fuss about entering the classroom. She would hang on to her mother and beg to return home. Mrs. T. had to arrange her daily schedule in order to pick up her daughter after school.

Although the I.Q. tests showed that Sharon had superior intelligence, she was inattentive and unco-operative in the classroom and consequently made mediocre grades. At school and at home Sharon was a very demanding child; if she did not immediately get her own way she would throw a screaming tantrum.

During the interview with Sharon, she stated that her main problem was her brother Jerry, who was almost thirteen. According to Sharon, Jerry always got everything he wanted; yet whenever she asked for anything, her parents would say no. Her brother also teased her constantly, particularly about her weight, and he was always doing things just to annoy her. Jerry, in turn, had almost identical complaints against his sister. She was always into his things, she was a big cry-baby, and she was always getting him in trouble by "tattling." Both parents said that Jerry was also a discipline problem although in a different manner. Jerry procrastinated; he would forget to do things they wanted him to do, and in general, passively resisted their authority. For example, he would forget to bring his homework from school or he would forget when he had a music lesson or when it was time to go for his religious training. Jerry complained that his mother was always after him for something, "She'll jump down your throat before you have a chance to open your mouth."

Mr. and Mrs. T. had many complaints against one another, particularly in regard to rearing their children. Sylvia T., age thirty-two, said that since her household was in such a constant turmoil of bickering, it was no wonder that she had frequent headaches. She felt that her husband did not appreciate the immense amount of responsibility and pressure he left to her. She made bitter complaints that he made no attempt to discipline the children. For example, the children could be screaming and pommeling one another and he would ignore it completely, "once he gets his nose in the newspaper." Sidney T., age forty, retorted that his wife "makes a mountain out of everything." He said that Sylvia was a constant worrier and that he felt the children were merely resisting her "nudging." Mrs. T. responded that if Sid were ever home he would see what she was up against. She explained that Sid was a salesman who was frequently "on the road" and even when in town he seldom came home until late in the evenings. In addition, he was very active in community and church affairs and was currently the treasurer of the synagogue, which he had helped to found. He also "had to" have his night a week with the "boys" bowling. On top of everything, Sylvia worried over the fact that Sid had suffered a coronary attack three years before. After the attack he had been unable to work for almost six months. His physician had advised that he cut down on all activities except work and had put him on a strict dietary regimen.

All four members of this family were obese. Sharon, tall for her age, was almost thirty pounds overweight. In appearance, she seemed to be bursting out of her clothes, her face was pudgy, and she wore a constant pouting expression. Jerry was always getting into scrapes at school over the nickname "Tubby." He had always been at least fifteen to twenty pounds overweight. Sidney usually weighed about 225 pounds although he was only five feet, nine inches tall. After his coronary he lost seventy-five pounds, and he stayed on his diet for about two years; however, during the past year he had gradually started gaining, so that he now hovered around 200 pounds. Sylvia, who was only five feet, one inch, weighed 170 pounds. Even before Sid's coronary, the entire family had tried various diets, but without noticeable results. Sylvia complained that the children used their allowances to buy candy. Sid pointed out that his

wife bought herself sweets which she hid in the top kitchen cupboards, but the children knew of this and helped themselves. He
agreed that he was not consistent about keeping to his own diet, but
he shrugged his shoulders and said that "life wouldn't be worth living if you couldn't eat."

It was really Sylvia who seemed to feel the most miserable. In addition to her frequent headaches, she suffered from periods of excessive fatigue and occasionally had to take to her bed for twenty-
four-hour periods. On these occasions, she always felt guilty, because "there are so many things to be done." From her husband's
description and her own account, Sylvia must have been a meticu-
lous housekeeper. Sid joked that you could scarcely finish eating
before she had the table cleared. She was always nagging the children to pick up their things. Daily she vacuumed the entire house
and scrubbed her kitchen. She kept a strictly kosher house, which
meant extra cooking and special sets of containers and dishes. She
did all her own laundry and ironing and even the major part of the
gardening. Her main complaint was not about the amount of housework, only that she got absolutely no co-operation from her children
or husband. They never put anything away and they seemed to ignore her efforts to keep an immaculate house. Sylvia tried to get Sid
to supervise Jerry and take over the heavy work of the gardening,
but Sid always seemed to be busy with something else. Jerry was
pretty fair about keeping his room reasonably neat, but Sharon's
room was always in shambles. Sylvia readily agreed with her husband that she was fast becoming a "nag," but she argued that if she
weren't, the children would never learn to take care of themselves.
It was true that she seldom left anything for the children to do; it
always seemed easier for her to go ahead and do the necessary chore.
She worried a great deal about whether or not she was a good
mother, and she always felt guilty after she had scolded her children. Because of her husband's heart condition, she tried to shield
him from the minor household worries, but as a result she felt resentful and neglected.

Sylvia also was left with the responsibility of managing the complicated family finances. Sid was given an expense account, but there
were always items on the monthly sheet for which he was not compensated by his company. Sylvia felt that Sid had no conception of
the household budget; for example, they were already in debt, yet

in the past year Sid traded in his two-year-old car for a new one, and bought an expensive air conditioning set for their home. On the other hand, she felt that her weekly food budget was much too low. She mentioned that she had had no new clothes other than what her mother had bought for her the previous summer. She also made Sharon's clothes, but Sharon outgrew them so fast that it was discouraging. Besides, Sharon was very careless with her clothes. Although Sid had encouraged his wife to join him at the church in his activities, or in bowling, Sylvia often felt too tired. Moreover, if she did leave the children at home, Sharon was likely to raise a fuss, or the two children would start a fight, so that Sylvia would find it necessary to return home. The few times that she went to the synagogue with her husband, she received constant phone calls from home; one time, Sharon even appeared at the synagogue in her pyjamas, weeping loudly and greatly embarrassing her parents.

A typical day at the T. family home began at six in the morning when Sid would arise as "I have done all my life every day of the week whether I was working or not." Sylvia, on the other hand, always had great difficulty in waking up and would have liked to stay in bed half the morning but felt terribly guilty in doing so. In recent years Sid had tried to reassure her by getting his own breakfast, particularly mornings when Sylvia wasn't feeling well. He was frequently joined by Jerry, who seemed to enjoy a few minutes with his father before the women appeared. Sylvia, from her room, would worry whether or not they were getting the proper breakfast, and she would become even more upset if she should hear any word of dissension between them. Since this was one of the few moments that Sid and Jerry had together, Sid would attempt to inquire about Jerry's progress at school or his social life, and there were times he would preach at his son. Jerry would become sulky and sometimes he would talk back. By this time, Sylvia would be up, fussing over Jerry's lunch, his homework, and criticizing his attire, all of which would irritate her husband so that he would slam out of the house.

Ordinarily, Sharon would not arise until just before Jerry left for school, but even during this short interval, the two managed to argue over trifles. Then there was a daily fuss over Sharon's breakfast. Getting Sharon dressed was also a constant struggle, during which Sylvia felt she had to return to Sharon's room every few minutes to make sure she had pulled on the other sock, buttoned her dress cor-

rectly, combed her hair, and so forth. Before they started off for
school Sharon had to be reassured that she would be picked up at
noon and brought home for lunch. Sylvia then returned home exhausted, attempting, however, to get her house cleaned before lunch.
The whole problem with Sharon was repeated at lunch time, sometimes so unsuccessfully that both became exhausted and spent the
afternoon sick in bed. On the days Sharon returned to school, Sylvia
would try to get her daily shopping done before school was out so
that she would not have Sharon dogging her heels in the market.
Very often, however, Sylvia's routine was interrupted by some other
business or a caller and she could not always accomplish everything
on schedule. Whenever possible, she tried to be home at the time the
children got home from school to prevent another fight over the
afternoon snack. Then there would be laundry and gardening and
the attempts to get the children to help her. Jerry was not so much
of a problem after school as he had his religious training three times
a week and was involved in after-school sports, and, for a while, also
had a paper route. Sharon, though, had absolutely nothing to occupy
her time. She had no friends; she would not leave the house to go
play with any of the children on the block, and when any of the
neighbor children came over to play she was so possessive with her
toys and so resentful of any demands that they might make that she
soon drove them away. Thus Sylvia was left with the chore of keeping Sharon entertained; Sharon would whine for the rest of the afternoon that she was bored. Sometimes she begged to watch television,
but Sylvia tried to limit this.

By the time Sid came home from work it was usually past six-
thirty. Sylvia had spent the last hour before her husband's arrival
arbitrating between Sharon and Jerry over which TV program, if
any, they were allowed to watch. Both children would immediately
demand some attention from their father, often by creating a fuss
which Sylvia would then turn over to him to settle. Sid considered
the evening meal a family gathering and would not brook his wife's
suggestion that the children have an earlier dinner by themselves.
Here at the dinner table, all the problems of the day would reappear
with Sid trying to play the role of judge and lecturer. Very often
Sylvia would become so upset that she was unable to eat dinner; as
a result she would raid the icebox later. After dinner, there were the
children's homework and more TV programs to arbitrate. Getting

the children off to bed was the final battle. Even after Sylvia finally got the children off to bed, she continued with the housework, catching up on her ironing, mending, or sewing. Many of the evenings, Sid would go out after dinner, leaving Sylvia feeling rejected and lonely.

Their sexual life was also a matter of dissension. Sylvia was often too tired and irritable to have sexual relations with her husband. Although she might be quite tired, unable to sleep, often she would get up from bed to read for another hour in the living room. Sid had long felt frustrated by his wife's denial of his sexual needs and from time to time tried to make some demands on her but to no avail. Only rarely did they desire sexual relations simultaneously or find any satisfaction. Sylvia admitted that she had long been sexually inhibited, but defended herself by pointing out that her husband had a need for a great deal of sexual play prior to intercourse, which disgusted her. Furthermore, she argued that in view of his heart condition, she was afraid that the strain and excitement of sexual intercourse might be dangerous.

In addition to their immediate family problems both Sylvia and Sid had extrafamilial stresses. Sylvia, who had always been exceedingly attached to her parents, worried a great deal about them and her siblings, none of whom lived close to her. She wrote daily to her mother; if she so much as missed one day, her mother would telephone. She was particularly worried about her father who had had a coronary about the same time as her husband. She heard frequently from her brothers, mainly about their marital problems and their problems with their children. She had no immediate relatives where she was living and felt quite homesick. Because of their many debts and Sid's illnesses, it had been necessary for the T.'s to borrow several times from Sylvia's parents. Although the money they received from Sylvia's parents was technically a loan, they were never pressed for repayment. Sylvia was determined to repay her parents in monthly payments, but Sid regarded this as unnecessary. On the other hand, Sid's mother was always writing to ask for money. His brothers and sisters also wrote to Sid, criticizing him for not contributing to his mother's support. Sylvia was disgusted; she felt her mother-in-law did not really need the support from them. She pointed out that the elder Mrs. T. had all the necessities provided by the older bachelor brother, whose home she was sharing. Moreover, Sid's mother was an inveterate gambler; hence the constant requests for money. Sid felt guilty about the situation; from time to time, he would resolve that he was going to "do something" for his mother, but he seldom even wrote to her.

Sid's personal worries were chiefly occasioned by his job. He had worked for the past five years for the same company selling plumbing supplies to retailers. He earned a good base salary, and his commissions were above average. His company had been most considerate of his illness, keeping him on salary during the entire period, despite the fact that they had no definite sick-leave plan. Nevertheless, Sid knew that if he were to have another attack it was unlikely that the company would be so generous again. Lately, he had begun to feel very discontent with his job; in his eyes he was "getting nowhere." It was a very conservative company which had not turned out any new products, and Sid knew that salesmen from more progressive companies were making sales where he was not. He considered his company very tight-fisted with their expense account. He wished that he had make a shift to another company when he had first felt dissatisfied with his present job. However, Sylvia was opposed to his changing jobs because she feared that he might lose out, particularly if he had another heart attack. More and more Sid found himself idling time away rather than pushing his sales.

In addition to this daytime stress, Sid found his position as treasurer of the synagogue a strenuous one. It provided him with considerable social status, but it demanded a great deal of time and energy. He was responsible for the fund-raising affairs of the synagogue as well as keeping the accounts. His phone, both at home and at the office, constantly rang with calls regarding the synagogue's business.

He was very concerned that Jerry get a complete religious training, which was an additional financial burden. The family was currently trying to scrape up enough money for Jerry's Bar Mitzvah, which was planned for the coming summer. It was hoped that both Sid's and Sylvia's parents would come from New York to California, since Jerry was the oldest grandson. Sid openly voiced the hope that his parents-in-law would make a sizeable contribution toward the cost of Jerry's Bar Mitzvah because a large catered party was planned, but Sylvia was set against asking her parents for any more money, especially for this event. She pointed out that the Bar

Mitzvah symbolized the relationship between father and son, and therefore Sid should stand the major cost.

Past History. Sylvia was born and reared in Brooklyn, New York. Her father was owner of a small dressmaking factory, which he had inherited from his father. He always made a fair living, even during the depression years. Sylvia had two older brothers, three and five years her senior. The family lived in a spacious, old-fashioned flat in an older part of the city. In an upstairs flat lived Sylvia's maternal grandmother and uncle. Sylvia described her family as a very tight-knit group in which everyone was concerned with everyone's else business. Sylvia was always extremely attached to her mother. As she began to talk about Sharon's school problems, she remembered that her behavior in grade school was almost identical. She cried desperately when she was taken to kindergarten, and her mother stayed with her in the classroom for many weeks. She always hated to go to school and was otherwise afraid to leave her mother. She described her mother as "the most wonderful person in the world," who "always did almost too much for everyone." She described how her mother was almost a martyr-like slave to her father and brothers, and how she tended to their every need, even to the extent of polishing their shoes. She could not remember that her mother ever scolded her for anything, or that she had been denied anything. "I guess I was dreadfully spoiled." She described her father as a very kindly man, whom she adored. At the same time, she admitted that he was a quite tyrannical disciplinarian with his sons and that the only time she saw any dissension between her parents was when her mother occasionally tried to interfere with her father's domination of her brothers. In general, however, Sylvia's mother was able to keep peace in the family. She was always a little over-anxious that Sylvia and her brothers had the proper food or that they were warmly dressed. The boys teased her affectionately about her overprotection, and they nicknamed her "Queeny," a name that was soon adopted by everyone. Even as an adult, Sylvia alternately referred to her mother as "Queeny" or "Mommy." Although Sylvia did not regard her mother as dominating or overprotective, she openly was critical of her grandmother for being excessively dominating. Her maternal grandmother ran her mother's life and would have dominated her father had he permitted it. She depicted her maternal uncle as being so cowed that he had no life of his own; even as an adult he was unable to function without his mother telling him every step to take.

The weight problem was an early one for Sylvia. Periodically she was overweight; yet other times she could actually be underweight. She was frequently told that she was prematurely born and considered a feeding problem as an infant. The family tried special formulas and special foods which were either prescribed by the pediatrician or based on the folklore of her maternal grandmother. "If any problem occurred, my grandmother had some old remedy for it, usually something to eat. *'Kinder ess!'* was her motto." By the time Sylvia started school, she was tubby. Then came alternating periods of dieting and stuffing. When Sylvia turned thirteen and her menses and secondary sexual characteristics began to appear, she suddenly became conscious of and concerned with her weight. She went on a very strict diet, starving herself so that she rapidly lost a considerable amount of weight. Afterwards she could no longer eat regularly and she suffered such a loss of appetite that her weight fell far below normal. She was hospitalized for a short time at age fourteen when it was considered that her life was in danger because of her loss of weight. She was force-fed for a brief period and then placed under the care of a psychiatrist. She remembered very little about the nature of this psychiatric treatment except that she talked to the doctor. Her appetite returned and she regained weight, but she remained slim throughout the rest of her adolescence.

At school Sylvia was an above-average student. She had many playmates but preferred to have them come to her house; rarely did she go to their houses. During adolescence she became more and more socially isolated. She did not learn to dance nor did she enjoy parties where there were boys. She never accepted a date. Her mother and grandmother began to worry about her and tried to encourage her to take some interest in boys, but whenever they started on the subject Sylvia would burst into tears and run to her own room. While relating her adolescent fear of boys and sex, Sylvia remembered that as a growing child she had somehow gained the impression from her grandmother and mother that sex was extremely painful, and possibly even dangerous. She was aware that her mother had become pregnant when Sylvia was about ten and had had an illegal abortion. The abortion left her mother quite ill for some time, and disrupted the entire household. When Sylvia had her first menstrual period, her grandmother slapped her face, which greatly frightened the child. Her mother explained that this was an "old country" custom, considered necessary in order to restore color to the girl's face because of the loss of blood. Thus, Sylvia understood her menstruation in terms of "the curse," a painful and embarrassing period to be endured. No other explanation regarding sex was ever given her, and she recognized the topic was entirely taboo in her family. One time when her father discovered that her older brother had a collection of pictures of nude women, he upbraided him for hours, and her brother had to destroy the pictures in the fireplace in front of the family.

Sylvia was nineteen and had finished high school and one year of business college when she met her husband. Her family had known Sid's family for many years but regarded the T.'s as beneath them socially. Sylvia met her husband through a girl friend who was going with Sid's younger brother. Sylvia's family was torn about the possibility of Sylvia and Sid getting married. Her grandmother and mother were very eager that she should marry, but they wanted the marriage to be a "good one." They disapproved of Sid because he was older and had been previously married and divorced, and also because his family had no social status. On the other hand, it was considered in his favor that Sid was presently making a good living. Sylvia, herself, did not know at the time what she actually wanted to do. The whole possibility of their getting married was discussed for many weeks by her parents and brothers and grandmother, shortly after Sylvia and Sid met, and long before Sid gave any indication that he was interested in marrying Sylvia. Finally her mother and grandmother decided that this could be a good marriage, and, thereafter, they encouraged Sid. Sid, in reporting his version of their courtship, laughed, saying he knew very well that he was being pulled into the marriage by Sylvia's mother and grandmother, but he enjoyed it as he was very much in love with Sylvia and liked Sylvia's mother. "It probably was really Sylvia's mother I was in love with, as she is a wonderful warm-hearted person and a topnotch cook." Sid would have preferred to have a quiet, civil ceremony, but his in-laws would have none of it, and planned an elaborate social wedding. Sid had made arrangements to rent an apartment, but on their wedding day Sylvia broke down in tears and confessed that she would be unable to leave her mother's home. Sid was almost ready to drop the whole marriage, but he was persuaded by Sylvia's mother to try the arrangement for a short while. For the next year-and-a-half Sid and Sylvia lived with her parents, using the bedroom Sylvia had as a child.

From the very start the couple had considerable difficulty sexually. Sylvia had had no sexual instruction or experience whatever; she reported that she does not believe that she even masturbated, although she later did remember that she was very much afraid that she might be caught masturbating. On the other hand, Sid readily admitted that he had had considerable sexual experience from the time of early adolescence and, of course, there was his previous marriage. He said that one of the most difficult problems of the first months of their marriage was that he could not really initiate his wife into such relations because of the lack of privacy in his mother-in-law's home. Not only was he afraid that they might be overheard, but he also knew that Sylvia would run and report everything to Queeny. He acknowledged that he always got along well with Queeny and with his father-in-law, but gradually, he began to feel that his in-laws were dominating his entire marital life. They inquired kindly but firmly about his business affairs and about personal expenses. Many times Sidney urged Sylvia to move into separate living quarters, but Sylvia would stubbornly refuse. The usual result was that she would become tearful and develop a headache. Despite their sexual difficulties Sylvia became pregnant approximately three months after their marriage, a pregnancy which resulted in Jerry's birth. Shortly after Jerry's birth Sid decided that once and for all they must make the break with Sylvia's parents, so he rented a separate apartment. With the help of his father-in-law he moved Sylvia's furniture into the new apartment. Sylvia was led by her mother from her home to the new apartment, both of them weeping all the while. Even after the couple was settled in the new apartment, Queeny continued to visit Sylvia daily; she helped to take care of the baby and did most of the housework. The hours that Sylvia's mother was not at her home, Sylvia was back at her parents' house. Sid found the situation intolerable but did not really know how to free her and himself from his in-laws. This situation continued for four more years until Sharon's birth.

Formerly, Sid had scarcely qualified as a social drinker, but now he started the habit of stopping in at the neighborhood bar after work. It was at the bar that he met a woman who confided to him that she was unhappy with her marriage, and coincidentally, she also lived in the same apartment house. Shortly after they began an affair, Sylvia learned of it from the neighbors. Indeed, neither Sid nor the other woman made any effort to cover up the relationship. Sylvia was extremely angry and depressed and threatened to return to her mother. Sid became contrite and guilt-ridden. Finally he convinced Sylvia that he had been unfaithful only in desperation and that he really wanted to continue with their marriage. Their rabbi advised Sylvia to forgive her husband and he supported Sidney in his determination to leave New York City to get away from Sylvia's parents. Very reluctantly Sylvia agreed, and the couple and their two children used the last of their savings to make the move to California. Almost immediately Sid found his present job, and soon he was earning enough for them to live quite comfortably. They bought a new development home and furnished it in the standard style. For a year or two they were busy and happy, although Sylvia remained depressed about the separation from her mother. New problems arose concerning the children and the extra demands of Sid's jobs. The final crisis in their family life was Sid's heart attack which threatened Sylvia extremely. She became very apprehensive that she might be left with two children to support, and she had no idea how she could ever manage to earn an income.

Sid was also born and reared in Brooklyn, also the youngest of three children, all boys. He remembered practically nothing of his early childhood. He had very little memory of his father, who died of tuberculosis when Sid was six. The family lived in extreme poverty, subsisting on government relief and also help from friends, neighbors, and the temple. His mother worked as a seamstress in one of the nearby clothing factories. Sid could not remember a period when he was not attempting to supplement the family income. He shined shoes, sold newspapers, ran errands, at times he even stole. He was often absent from school; by the time he was thirteen he had already made several appearances in juvenile court for being truant or for disobeying the curfew. At one time, he was convicted of petty theft in company with a gang of boys but was given in probation to the youth director of the neighborhood youth house. Both of his older brothers also had police records for minor delinquencies. "How we ever grew up without permanently becoming criminals I don't know." For the most part, Sid and his brothers were left to shift for themselves, for his mother was not home to cook meals or take care of the house. By the time she returned home late in the evening she was often too tired to do anything. She began to gamble with friends and often spent her weekends at the racetrack. She frequently came out ahead in her gambling, and on these occasions the family would be able to have extra clothing or have a small celebration. Otherwise Sidney had very little family life.

Sidney began having heterosexual relationships at a very early age, first with the neighborhood girls and later with prostitutes. He married a neighborhood girl when he was eighteen and left high school to get a job. Shortly thereafter, he was drafted into the army, just before the beginning of World War II. It was while he was overseas that his first wife wrote him that she was obtaining a divorce in order to marry someone else. Sid was embittered and, upon his return to civilian life, resolved to have nothing more to do with women. He went to night school and completed his high school education. Through some army buddies he obtained a fairly good job as a salesman in the plumbing business. He was thus earning a fair living at the time he met Sylvia. Although he was determined to remain single, he found that he was very attracted to Sylvia. He was very lonely and was happy to be welcomed into her home, which he readily admitted was the kind of family he had always dreamed of having. Regarding his own overweight, he reported that he had been excessively thin as a child and was extremely underweight when he went into the military service. He gained a considerable amount of weight in the service; "It was the first time I had good food and regular hours." He continued to gain weight on Queeny's and Sylvia's cooking.

Course in Treatment. Although the focal point of the T. family's complaints was Sharon, both Sylvia and Sid readily admitted that they themselves needed direct help with their own problems. They half-recognized that their own obvious anxieties were a strain on the children. At first Sid and Sylvia were treated by separate psychotherapists. In his treatment Sid began by trying to maintain that his behavior needed very little change, but that his wife was the one who was really "neurotic." However, in his behavior toward his therapist he was very much like a little boy, constantly asking for advice and making extravagant promises. As he described first his marital history and then his childhood, he began to understand how he was using his wife and family to satisfy some of his own emotional needs, without providing anything in return.

Sylvia spent most of her initial treatment hours reciting her complaints against her husband and children. Gradually, however, she began to realize that she was repeating much of the pattern with them that she had experienced in her own childhood. She denied vigorously that she had any resentment toward her mother for her overprotection, but then she remembered nightmares where she had dreamed of her mother's death, which had always made her feel guilty. Furthermore, when she recalled her grandmother's extreme overprotection of her uncle and her mother, she began to feel that perhaps in some way her mother's overprotection might have not been the "wonderful" thing that she really longed for. She began to admit that she had considerable hostility toward Sharon and she wished at times, secretly, that she had never had Sharon. At one point while she was admitting this, she wondered whether her mother had felt this way when she was born. Shortly after the time that she began to recognize some of these factors, she became quite resistant to treatment but was able to overcome her resistance, with some support. She recognized that there was a realistic problem of finances in the family and on her own initiative took the step of finding a job in a nearby manufacturing plant—the first time in her life she had worked outside her home. Her children were left a little more on their own and the housework seemed less important to her. She also began to share the responsibility of determining the budget with her husband; much to her surprise he proved very adequate to the job.

Sharon's psychotherapy was most stormy. She resented having to come at all. She refused to talk to her therapist, and at first it was even difficult to get her to enter the playroom. She played by herself in the corner, ignoring the doctor, spending considerable time with doll play. She spent many hours rearranging the doll furniture and taking care of the baby doll. When the therapist noticed that Sharon made use of the baby, father, and boy doll but no use of the mother doll, Sharon became very angry and said that she could not come back for further treatment. Later, Sharon picked up the mother doll and tried to drown it in the sink. She dropped it on the floor and "accidently" stepped on it. One day after "accidently" kicking the mother doll across the room she began to weep and then built an elaborate mausoleum in which to bury the mother doll. Sharon gradually began to talk to her doctor; she raised many side questions which indicated that she had an intense sexual curiosity. Sylvia was then encouraged to discuss some sexual matters with Sharon which Sylvia had ignored previously. Sylvia was made very anxious by this and was helped only by further discussion of her own sexual fears. At the end of the first year of treatment Sharon went on a voluntary diet and lost about fifteen pounds. Sylvia, remembering her own diet as a child, became fearful for Sharon, but she helped to support Sharon and watched closely the nature of the diet. Sid also returned to the diet prescribed for him. Sharon's school reported improvement in her behavior. At the end of the year of treatment Sharon's doctor left the clinic. Although Sharon's behavior had not altered to the point that her parents were completely satisfied, it was decided not to continue further treatment at that time. For the following year Sid and Sylvia were seen jointly by the same therapist as a means of permitting them to work out some of their common problems. At the end of this year, much of their marital tension had abated and both of the children seemed to be adjusting at home and school without any serious difficulties. Sylvia calculated that the four of them had successfully lost a total of one hundred pounds in weight, without discomfort.

Questions for the T. Family

1. Make a list on a sheet of paper with two headings, one for Sidney and one for Sylvia as follows:

Sidney T.   Sylvia T.

Under each heading list the treatment experienced by each individual during their early home environment with regard to:

    a. gratification and frustration of dependency needs

    b. handling of aggressive expression

    c. training and introduction to sex

2. Which needs or drives appear to you to have been excessively

gratified for each individual and which appear to have been frustrated and associated with anxiety? Can you, from your answer, explain the eating behavior of the T. family?

3. If we look exclusively at the area of dependency (i.e. satisfaction of the need for help and support while young), what contrast do we see between Sidney and Sylvia?

4. How did these contrasting experiences shape the personalities of each individual? (*Hint:* Seek out material in your text or in the research literature which contrasts the effects of excessive dependency gratification with the effects of deprivation of dependency needs on personality development.)

5. Looking at their marital relationships, in what way could you say that these contrasting childhood environments provided a crucial source of conflict for Sylvia and Sidney?

6. In what ways might Sidney's and Sylvia's conflicts have influenced their treatment of Jerry and Sharon?

7. From your reading in the text or in other sources, what three hypotheses can you raise about the basis for maternal overprotection? (See Levy's article "Maternal Overprotection" for a good summary of the basis for maternal overprotection.) Which of these hypotheses best accounts for Sylvia's treatment of Sharon?

8. How can you account for the fact that Sylvia and her daughter demonstrated similar behavior patterns when they were young?

9. From the brief descriptions of Sylvia's and Sharon's psychotherapy as well as the background history, what hypotheses can you raise to account for Sharon's school phobia?

10. When attempting to understand the dynamics of family relationships, it is helpful to spell out the needs of each individual and the degree to which they are gratified by the significant individuals in their family. In an attempt to integrate all of your previous answers, fill in the blank in the following pairs of incomplete sentences. When you finish, if done correctly, the incompatibility in need-gratification within the T. family should be clear. Feel free to use more than single word answers in doing your completions.

1.   *a.* Sylvia desired .... from her mother.
    b. Sylvia received .... from her mother.

2.   *a.* Sidney desired .... from his mother.
    b. Sidney received .... from his mother.

3. *a.* Sylvia desired .... from Sidney.
    b. Sylvia received .... from Sidney.

4. *a.* Sidney desired .... from Sylvia.
    b. Sidney received .... from Sylvia.

5. *a.* Sharon desired .... from her mother.
    b. Sharon received .... from her mother.

6. *a.* Sharon desired .... from her father.
    b. Sharon received .... from her father.

11. In psychoanalytic theory, the T. family would be considered "oral" personalities.

    a. List the behavior of each of the T.'s (in addition to excessive food consumption) which might be classified as "oral."

    b. What factors in each of their lives led them to "regress to oral" behavior in the face of stress?

    c. What aspects of their culture promote use of this defense?

12. Although this report dealt almost exclusively with the conflicts *within* the T. family, it is very likely that their anxieties impinged on their relationships outside their home. Imagine, if you will, how each of the following might have reacted to the T.'s. What might these other persons do to exacerbate or ameliorate the T.'s anxieties, within the limits of their respective social roles?

    a. Sid's employer

    b. the T. family's rabbi (at present)

    c. Sid's physician

    d. Sharon's schoolteacher

References

BAAM, I. Psychic factors in obesity: observations in over 1000 cases. *Archives of Pediatrics,* 1950, **67**: 543–552.

BOWEN, M. The family as the unit of study and treatment: I. Family psychotherapy. *American Journal of Orthopsychiatry,* 1961, **31**: 40–60.

LEVY, D. *Maternal overprotection.* New York: Columbia Univer. Press, 1943.

PARLOFF, M. The family in psychotherapy. *Archives of General Psychiatry,* 1961, **4**: 445–451.

THE CASE OF RANDY S.

Nobody Plays Fair

At first glance, Randy did not appear markedly different from most nine-year-old boys. He was slim but not underweight, and his height was average for his age. His sandy hair was clipped short in a "crewcut," which seemed to emphasize his large round head and protruding ears. His arms and face, particularly his upturned nose, were heavily freckled. His behavior as he sat in the waiting room *did* seem out of the ordinary. His eyes continually searched the room when his face was otherwise still, which was not often. Even during these moments of inaction, Randy's lips betrayed a slight sneering smile. Generally, Randy's face was distorted into a variety of grimaces that were accompanied by intermittent hooting, clucking, or some other kind of noise. The rest of his body was also in constant motion; his hands rubbed, touched, or tapped something; his legs swung or kicked something. He wiggled over and across the chair and finally he began to wander restlessly about the room and down the hall, peeking into offices until hauled back to his seat by his father.

Although his parents disputed openly about the causes and even the necessity for bringing Randy to the guidance clinic, both parents expressed intense frustration in their attempts to discipline Randy. Mr. S. complained that if he told Randy to do something, Randy would burst into tears and run to his mother. He accused his wife of overprotecting Randy so often that Randy had come to believe that he did not have to do what his father demanded. In rebuttal, Mrs. S. claimed that Mr. S. commanded Randy like a sergeant in the army. Mrs. S. denied that she had ever told Randy not to obey his father. She claimed that she had simply tried to reassure Randy when he expressed fears of his father. Mrs. S. complained that her husband was unduly harsh with Randy and that far too often he enforced his discipline by spanking the child. Mrs. S. believed that Randy was afraid of his father. She had noted that Randy always entered the room by the door farthest away from his father and circled the room by a route obviously calculated to keep him as far as possible from Mr. S. Mr. S. confessed regretfully that he "might have" driven Randy away from him, but defended himself again by complaining that Mrs. S. left all the punishment to him, with the result that in Randy's eyes, Mr. S. was the "bad" parent and Mrs. S. the "loving" parent.

Both parents complained also that they were unsure of when Randy was telling the truth. When they asked him anything, even in a casual tone, his response was usually vague and evasive. If he seemed angry or upset, it was impossible for them to find out from him what disturbed him. Unlike the other children, he never volunteered anything about his school work or play. When they did corner him and drag an answer from him, they suspected he was lying. Their suspicions were affirmed when they caught him in baldface falsehoods. Asked for an example of such "lies," Mrs. S. cited the following incident: Randy had been asked to clean his room, but when his mother returned, the room was just as she had left it; yet Randy maintained furiously that he had cleaned it.

The parents were particularly annoyed by Randy's mannerisms, his funny noises and faces, because he seemed to be mocking adults. Not only were they angry when he aped their voices and gestures, but they were embarrassed when he made fun of other adults. When questioned about these mannerisms, Randy denied any purpose in them. Sometimes Mrs. S. found Randy so annoying that she locked him out of the house. Mr. S. agreed that the grimaces and noises were irritating but pointed out to his wife that they occurred less frequently in his presence, especially when Randy was with his father and other men at the boys' club. Mr. S. noted that Randy's sneering attitude was not limited to adults. He also frequently derided his peers with a disdainful "yeh-yeh" in response to their statements. For this reason Randy had few friends at school or at the boys' club. Other children in the neighborhood refused to play with Randy and he frequently fought with them. Randy continually squabbled with his sister Emily, two years his junior, or with his twin siblings Robert and Roberta, age four. Mrs. S. said sadly that she was afraid that Randy was growing up to be a mean and cruel child, recalling that only last week she had found him standing over their six-month-old baby dropping blocks on him. Yet both parents admitted that their other children blamed everything on Randy and always accused him of teasing them or starting a fight, even though they equally often interfered with his activities.

Another item in the S.'s list of Randy's annoying actions was his "sneakiness." He seemed to enjoy hiding behind furniture and doors and eavesdropping on adult conversations. Mrs. S. had to check her room before she changed her clothes because she had discovered Randy under the bed or in the closet while she was dressing. Randy spent "hours" locked in the bathroom until Mr. S. pounded on the door threatening severe punishment. Once they awoke in the middle of the night to discover Randy standing at the foot of their bed. Several mornings they found food out on the table or other evidence that Randy had been up in the night; but they never apprehended him and he evaded their inquiries. In similar fashion, Randy prowled through neighbors' yards and even into their homes. When the neighbors angrily complained and threatened to call the police, Mr. S. was again embarrassed and furious at Randy.

At school Randy's behavior was no better. Although on educational achievement tests and I.Q. tests, he performed at above-average level, his school work had been barely passing. Randy had been promoted each time from the first to the third grade, but his third grade teacher had currently advised his parents that he seldom did his school work and was so far behind that he would not be promoted at the end of the spring semester. Moreover, he was such a behavioral problem that the school was considering the possibility of placing him in a special class for emotionally disturbed children. In the classroom he was hyperactive, often on his feet without permission, constantly talking with the other children, and generally disconcerting the classroom. He seemed particularly adept at getting other children to misbehave, or to send them into gales of laughter with his "faces." He seldom seemed to pay attention and often gave nonsense answers, which the teacher felt were intended to amuse the class. The other children considered him at best a clown but more often a nuisance. Although very good at athletics, Randy was a poor sport, always the first to cry unfair at any little incident and usually the last chosen on a team. If there was a fight on the school ground, Randy was always in the midst of it. He was frequently "on the bench" in the school yard for infractions of the playground rules or in the principal's office when the teacher could no longer endure his upsetting behavior. Mrs. S. had been called to the school for conferences with his teachers several times a semester for the past four years. She was embarrassed by having to come to the school and had tried her best to talk with Randy about his school difficulties, but he always "clammed up" and shrugged his shoulders, and seemed unable to discuss any of it. Mr. S. had threatened and punished, but to no avail. Mr. S. was of the opinion that Randy's behavior at school was occasioned by the fact that he had had only women teachers and that he was reacting to them in the same way that he reacted to his mother. He argued that Randy would behave at school if he had a male teacher.

The incident which had finally convinced Randy's parents that he should be brought to the guidance center was the fact that Randy had been apprehended by the teacher in the act of going through her purse. Moreover, several children accused Randy of stealing things from their desks and lockers, but the school authorities admitted that they had no proof that Randy was the culprit. Later Mrs. S. had realized that Randy had a pen which she knew did not belong to him and which the teacher had reported was stolen. Mrs. S. further admitted that she had missed money from her purse from time to time; secretly she searched Randy's room and clothes and uncovered several caches of change. When she faced Randy with her evidence," he argued that he'd been saving his allowance and was furious that she had invaded his privacy. Mr. S. had tried to talk to Randy about these thefts, but Randy had stoutly denied all allegations and maintained that the teacher had misinterpreted his behavior, that he had only picked up the purse from off the floor where he had found it when he had returned to the empty classroom.

During Randy's first contact with the psychologist he systematically explored the playroom cupboard, looking over the toys and equipment, examining each object but making no effort to play with anything. Asked why he had been brought to the clinic, he shrugged his shoulders and said, "It was my mother's big idea." Asked what he thought the reason might be that his mother brought him, he denied having any idea and turned his back to the psychologist while he continued to examine the playroom. When told that the guidance center was interested in boys and the kinds of things that made them happy or unhappy or the kinds of things that created problems for them, he retorted that nothing made him unhappy and he had no problems. Finally he rolled some clay into little balls and idly threw them at the punching bag doll. Casually he volunteered that he did have two problems: his sister was a "pest" who was constantly causing him "trouble," and his parents believed his sister and not him. The psychologist agreed that this could be a serious problem and asked him to tell more about it, but he retorted, "What's to tell!" His second problem was that a neighbor had threatened to call the police if Randy's dog was not shut up in the yard. Randy hated this neighbor and wished he could kill him. He was quite fierce in this statement and began to throw the clay balls even harder at the punching doll. Asked what made him happy, Randy scowled and said, "Nothing." When the psychologist expressed surprise, Randy said, "Well, I do have fun at ball games but nobody plays fair." He then brought out a packet of baseball picture cards showing the various players of the major league teams and began to discuss baseball, a subject on which he seemed well informed. Asked his three wishes, he said his first wish was that he had a gun so that he could kill the neighbor who wanted his dog locked up. His second wish was that he could be grown up so that he wouldn't have to do what anybody told him. It seemed to Randy that whenever his parents, teachers, and other adults spoke to him, they were always telling him "what to do"—"especially my father." He complained that his father told him two or three things to do all at once so he couldn't remember anything his father had ordered. And his mother changed her mind so many times that he didn't know what she wanted either. His teachers were all "old crabs," and none of the other kids liked them either.

His third wish was that he were the only person in the world. "There's too many people everywhere always in my hair." He explained that his class at school seemed too large, that he never got a chance to ask the teacher a question when he didn't understand something, and that he had to wait too long for his turn to come up either in the class or the play yard. (His parents later agreed that he had originally been in a kindergarten class of sixty children and that in the following three years, his classroom had never held less than forty children.) Asked who his best friend was, he replied, "My dog." As to the other children in the neighborhood, "Well some of them are all right but you can't really trust them." When the psychologist wondered if he also felt there were too many kids at home, his face lit up and he said, "Yeah! How did you know?" Asked if he really wished he were the only child in the family, he replied, "That's my first wish." He had to share a room with his sister, and although his father had recently built a set of shelves separating the room in half, his sister had to exit through his half of the room. He had little privacy from the twins who loved to get into his play things and destroyed his models and other things he was working on. About the baby—"You know how babies are; they're always crying." He proceeded to imitate the baby's crying in a mocking voice.

Randy's Development. Mrs. S. said that her pregnancy with Randy was largely uneventful; she had been in good health and for the most part had looked forward with joyful expectation to her first child. Later she admitted that "perhaps" she was a bit young, only nineteen, and that at times she had wished that she had had a little more time to become adjusted to her husband, as they had been married less than a year at the time she became pregnant. Furthermore, there were several situations in Mrs. S.'s life during her pregnancy with Randy which, although they may not have directly affected her pregnancy, may have colored her emotional attitudes toward it. Her mother had died the previous year and she had barely recovered from her grief over her mother's death. Her father also was aging and ill, and she would have liked to have been close to him and cared for him, but they lived at opposite ends of the country. During much of her pregnancy her husband was occupied in attempting to build up his business and was away from home both day and night, sometimes for several days at a stretch. Thus, she found herself sitting around their apartment, lonely and depressed. Although in the past she had had trouble keeping her weight down, she began to eat quite heavily, and gained far more weight than her obstetrician thought good for her health. She had never really lost the weight she gained during her pregnancy with Randy, and continued to have problems with overweight. Despite these emotional and physical pressures, she gave birth to Randy with little difficulty; her labor was brief, only a local anesthetic was used, and delivery was normal.

Randy's birth weight and size were normal. He took his first breath easily and seemed a healthy baby. He nursed readily, but after the first several days of breast-feeding her lactation failed and Randy was put on a formula. She was more awkward in handling Randy than with her subsequent children. He seemed to be a restless baby, wiggly and difficult to hold. "He has been on the move ever since birth." He was colicky during his first few months of life, crying, coughing, spitting, irritable. She had read in books that a child should be on a schedule, but found it difficult to apply. Randy developed rapidly, however, gaining in weight and size, and began to sit up, explore his crib, and stand; and he was walking by the time he was ten months old. Mr. S. participated little in Randy's care, but was very proud of his accomplishments, taking him everywhere and showing him off. Randy was making efforts to talk at approximately twelve to thirteen months, according to her baby book, and was speaking his first words fairly clearly by the time he was a year and a half. She began to make efforts to toilet-train him at this time, but she was pregnant with her second child, Emily, and was unable to carry through with the toilet-training. She was acutely ill during her pregnancy with Emily, and went to the hospital several times with labor pains before giving birth. Rather weak after bearing Emily, she remained in the hospital several days longer than she had with Randy.

During this time, Mr. S. was left with the care of Randy, since there were no grandparents about, nor were they able to afford to hire help. Mr. S. was disgusted with the fact that Randy was still in diapers and began a rigorous program of toilet-training, climaxed by putting Randy under the bathtub tap and running cold water over him. Mr. S. boasted that this "shock treatment" worked immediately, and from then on Randy did not soil himself. On the excuse that his wife was still physically weak, and had the care of the new baby, Mr. S. continued to assume the major care of Randy. He admitted also that he felt that his wife had not been very effective in Randy's training and that he wanted to show her how a child really should be disciplined. He therefore began teaching Randy to feed and dress himself and take his bath. Mr. S. even went to the extent of leaving notes, instructing his wife how to handle Randy while he was at work. At first, Mr. S.'s successes continued. Randy seemed to enjoy his father's attention, and he learned very rapidly to care for himself much better than have the younger children. By the time Randy was a little over two, he was completely toilet-trained, could feed himself almost independently, and took his own bath, with only minimal supervision. He was "all boy," imitating his father in many ways, such that friends and relatives remarked on how much alike they looked and acted. However, Mr. S. began to expect more of Randy than Randy was able to accomplish. Particularly, Mr. S. demanded exact manners at the table and kept after Randy for every little mistake or failure to behave exactly as Mr. S. expected. Often Mr. S. would expect Randy to perform with objects or tools which Randy could not lift or manipulate. Randy would burst into tears and have minor tempor tantrums, throwing himself on the floor and screaming. Mr. S. would become more desperate and harsh, scolding Randy unmercifully. When Mrs. S. attempted to intervene or mollify her husband, Mr. S. would protest that she was being a molly-coddle and interfering in his efforts to discipline Randy. He felt that if he allowed his wife to have her way, Randy would be a baby or a sissy. Randy began to avoid his father and run and hide when his father came home. He no longer responded to his father's directions, and Mr. S. began to withdraw from the situation, blaming his wife. In contrast, Emily proved to be a placid and lovable child, who sought affection from her father as well as from her mother. From the time that she could crawl she was pulling herself into her father's lap. In turn, Randy turned more and more to his mother for affection and comfort. He became particularly dependent upon her during a mild but prolonged bronchial infection when he was about four and a half. He recovered just in time to start kindergarten at age five. Simultaneously, his mother was enduring her most difficult pregnancy with the twins.

The family had just purchased a home in a new suburb where there was no school. Randy was placed in an overcrowded school some distance from home. At first he seemed to enjoy kindergarten, but because of the size of the class, he received very little personal attention. Left much to his own devices, Randy became the terror of the kindergarten class. He paid no attention to the instructions of the teacher, seemed to enjoy interrupting and destroying the work of other children, and made no effort at co-operative work or play. Mrs. S. was disturbed by the notes and the phone calls she received from the school, but, preoccupied with her new babies, she was unable to visit the school and respond to the complaints. The school's complaints continued when Randy was in first grade, and both Mrs. S. and Mr. S. made periodic visits to the teacher and principal. Mrs. S. tried to drill Randy in learning to read at home, believing that the school's complaints regarded Randy's schoolwork rather than his classroom behavior. Even prior to this time Randy had amused his parents and others by imitating their voices and facial expression, but by the time he was six he had developed this technique into a method of mocking and irritating others which drove his parents and teachers wild. Often he did not have to say anything, but by just beginning to make his faces he made others uncomfortable. One thing that particularly annoyed both his father and the teacher was that he seemed always to have something in his hand to throw: a little mud at some prettily dressed girl at school, a pebble against a window, or a ball in the living room. Mr. S. reported wearily that he seemed to be always saying to Randy, "Stop it" or "Drop it." Randy's behavior, at home and school, continued to grow increasingly difficult for the adults to control. Several times the school urged the S.'s to visit the child guidance clinic, but Mr. S. huffily disregarded these suggestions, saying that no one was going to tell him how to rear his children.

Randy had been quite aware of his mother's most recent pregnancy, and asked many questions about it. He was told that the baby was "in mommy's tummy," but when he wanted to know how the baby would come out, his mother did not know how to answer him, and she became even more embarrassed when he asked how the baby got in there. She told him to ask his father about these things, but Randy never did, and Mr. S. did not seem aware of Randy's curiosity. Mrs. S. remembered with considerable embarrassment, how Randy began to talk about "when the baby would pop out." Although Mrs. S. did not associate the following incident with Randy's curiosity about her pregnancy, she later recalled that it was approximately during this period that she received a note from the school, complaining that Randy kept entering the girls' toilet. He was marched into the living room late one afternoon by a neighbor, who reported to the parents that she had caught him attempting to undress her five-year-old girl. The parents were ashamed, and Mr. S. proceeded to spank Randy and send him to his room. It seemed to Mrs. S. that during her most recent pregnancy, Randy was more difficult than ever. He seemed always in the way, always to be asking questions, always to be doing something naughty. It seemed that every reaction between Randy and his parents was one of defiance and punishment. While Mrs. S. was in the hospital giving birth, Randy took off one night after a particular fuss with his father, and was gone from home for almost ten hours. His father was frantic. He searched the streets for him and finally called the police, to discover that he was at the police station. As usual he was scolded and spanked. It was shortly after this that the parents conferred with their pediatrician, who advised against frequent physical punishment; the parents then began to resort to depriving Randy or sending him to his room. After the report from the school that Randy was stealing things from other children, and the incident with the teacher's purse, Randy was given a long lecture and deprived of TV for two weeks and, as usual, sent to his room. An hour later, when she thought Mr. S. was not watching, Mrs. S. went to see Randy and found him in his closet, standing on a chair with a rope thrown over the closet bar. She became alarmed and asked him what he was doing, and he said casually that he was playing cowboy. She wondered if this was a possible suicidal attempt, but said nothing to Mr. S.

Parents' Background. Randy's mother was the oldest of five girls, born and reared in a semi-rural area in the Midwest. Her father scraped a bare living off the farm, and the family rarely knew more than the bare necessities of life. Mrs. S. had considerable responsibility for the care of her siblings and for the housework in general. She maintained that her relationship with her parents was always an affectionate one. However, she described her father as a harsh disciplinarian who, although rejecting physical punishment, kept the girls in awe of him by his general demeanor. Mrs. S. was an above average student in school, and at the time of high school graduation longed to attend college. However, family finances were so stringent that she felt forced to leave her home town and seek a job in a nearby city. Prior to leaving home, Mrs. S. had had little social life, only a few dates, and no steady boy friends. Her husband, whom she met at her job in the factory, was her first boy friend and they were married shortly after they became acquainted.

Mr. S. came from a very different background. He was the only son of a professor of engineering who was quite successful professionally and economically. The way Mr. S. talked about his father suggested that he regarded him as a godlike figure, omnipotent and unapproachable. In discussing his efforts to discipline and rear Randy, it was evident that Mr. S. attempted to follow his father's model, hoping, however, to achieve a closer relationship with his son than he had experienced with his father. Due to Mr. S.'s father's many activities outside the home, most of the discipline in his family had been administered by his mother, who, he said, was quite insistent upon self-control and good manners. Mr. S.'s mother emphasized that he should not in any way embarrass his father by "childish" behavior.

Mr. S.'s three older sisters were all outstanding students, but Mr. S. never made better than average grades. He disappointed his father and mother by not achieving a sufficiently high grade point average to enter the university where his father taught. His embarrassment was further accentuated during World War II when his father received the rating of colonel while Mr. S. remained a corporal throughout his three years of army service.

Although never able to complete an engineering course, Mr. S. gathered a good background in electronics and specialized in television repair after the war. He had a number of well-paying and interesting jobs but was never able to achieve the management-level position which he desired. Mr. S. continued to be dissatisfied with his achievement and had moved several times to different cities in the hope of attaining a position above a technician's level. Despite several increases in his rate of pay, Mr. S.'s income never seemed to stretch to meet the demands of his burgeoning family and the rising cost of living. Once he had signed up for a payroll deduction for government bonds, hoping to save toward Randy's college education, but had been forced to cancel it when Mrs. S. was pregnant with the twins. He had also let his life insurance drop, although he kept this fact from Mrs. S. Already their new home was proving too small for their family. Mr. S. had borrowed the down payment from his father, and now his mother was hinting strongly in her letters that he should begin repayment of his loan. He remembered with longing the spacious home and comfortable mode of living of his childhood—and felt guilty and inadequate because he could not match it for his own children. In his spare time, he made attempts to improve his house, building cupboards and closets and a room-divider, and he planned to add another room. However, he admitted that he never really completed anything; his construction jobs remained unfinished and he never had the time to do what he wanted.

Mr. S. had made a number of attempts to get close to Randy; he joined a boys' club as a parent-supervisor and tried to include Randy in his woodworking hobby. Mrs. S. contended that in all these activities, Mr. S. became so involved with his own needs that he lost sight of Randy's interests and expected too much of him. Most woodworking projects ended with Mr. S. doing the project by himself while castigating Randy for failing to do things his way.

Course in Treatment. In the conference following the initial "intake" interviews with Randy and his parents, the guidance clinic staff discussed at length the possible approaches to treating Randy. Although these interviews provided considerable data about the nature and sources of Randy's anxieties, the staff realized that there were still gaps in their information, particularly regarding the S.'s marital relationship. Both Mr. and Mrs. S. seemed to avoid the topic. The staff wondered if the S.'s had more conflicts than they voiced. The psychiatrist who had interviewed Randy's father was of the opinion that Mr. S. was far more anxious than he appeared on the surface, and the doctor doubted that Mr. S. could endure much more extensive exploration of his anxieties. The social worker reported that despite Mrs. S.'s complaints about her husband's treatment of Randy, Mrs. S. was also quite cautious in expressing any of her own opinions or discussing her own feelings. The staff decided that the psychologist should continue in his approach to Randy in the playroom and that in the interviews with the parents, the psychiatrist and social worker should concentrate on the relationship of each of the parents with Randy, avoiding for the moment, the parents' other anxieties.

Unfortunately, these well-laid treatment plans were soon disrupted. Mr. S., although he overtly accepted the psychiatrist's offer of continued intreviews regarding Randy, soon excused himself from regular appointments, because his "important" job at the plant suddenly demanded irregular overtime. All in all, he appeared only three more times at the clinic. During these three hours, however, he talked almost exclusively about his own disappointments in life, his failure to meet his educational and vocational goals, and his feelings of inadequacy as a father and husband. All of these feelings he poured out in breathless desperation. At the end of each hour, he recovered sufficiently to relate a joke about psychiatrists or to tell of some friend who had been made worse by psychotherapy. Shortly after Mr. S.'s last contact with the clinic, Mrs. S. informed the social worker that Mr. S. had decided that he should not have to depend on a psychiatrist to tell him how to manage his life or rear his children. Only with considerable argument did she gain his grudging permission to continue in treatment with Randy.

Mrs. S.'s defensiveness also melted quickly. In tears, she confided that her marriage was very unhappy and was, she feared, near the breaking point. Not only did she resent her husband's oppressive domination over the whole family, but there was also an intense conflict between them over their sexual relationship. She revealed that she had many fears about sex, left over from childhood, which so inhibited her that she was almost frigid. Mr. S., on the other hand, pressed her daily for sexual intercourse. Rejecting him or acceding to his demands had become her only weapon over him. Despite considerable support from the social worker, a skilled and experienced therapist, Mrs. S. became increasingly depressed. After six months, she reached a state where she remained in bed most of the day, weeping, unable to care for her home and family, and the social worker came to see Mrs. S. in her home. On the social worker's advice, Mrs. S. was voluntarily admitted to a nearby state hospital, where she remained for three months. How Mr. S. and his family fared was unknown, for he continued to reject any contact with the clinic. However, much to the staff's amazement, he continued to bring Randy to the clinic, waiting outside in the car until Randy's hour was over.

Randy's response to psychotherapy was equally stormy but not as disastrous and, indeed, partially gratifying. He tried out all of his aggressive and defensive maneuvers on the psychologist, and, when his therapist indicated that he was aware that Randy was trying to cover his anxieties, Randy at first only intensified his efforts. Unlike his parents, Randy had little choice about coming to the clinic; despite his feelings on a particular day he was, in effect, pushed into the psychologist's playroom twice a week. It was when the psychologist recognized this fact with Randy that Randy lessened his resistance and gradually began forming a close and confiding relationship with his doctor. When Mr. S. decided to terminate his contacts with the clinic, Randy renewed his resistance; for two succeeding visits he refused to leave the waiting room. Randy blamed the clinic for his mother's hospitalization, refused again to talk with his therapist, and proclaimed he was going to kill the social worker. Later he admitted that his father had voiced similar threats at home. As far as could be ascertained, before Mrs. S.'s hospitalization Randy's behavior at home showed no change. However, at school he appeared to settle down remarkably and at the end of a semester was allowed to continue with his class. Randy proundly displayed his report card with passing grades to his doctor.

When Mrs. S. returned home from the hospital, she visited the clinic once more. Although less agitated in her depression, she remained listless and apathetic, evidently not interested in continuing treatment at the clinic. She reported that Randy's behavior at home as well as at school did seem improved but regarded his co-operative attitude as a kind of "truce," much as she had obtained from her husband on her return home. The following week, Randy excitedly informed his doctor that Mr. S. was taking the family on a long vacation to visit Mr. S.'s parents. Randy made the psychologist promise that treatment could be resumed at the end of summer. However, the S. family never contacted the clinic again. Their telephone remained disconnected and the clinic's letters were unanswered.

Questions for Randy S.

1. List the difficulties Randy was manifesting which eventually prompted his parents to bring him to the clinic. What emotions or drives appear to be expressed by these behaviors?

2. What appear to be the stimuli in Randy's environment which were eliciting these emotions or drives? Classify these stimuli according to the people responsible for them (i.e. father, mother, siblings, teacher, and so forth.

3. What behavior had Randy developed that appears to be designed to reduce his anxiety level?

4. Attempt to integrate your answer to questions 1-3 by drawing a diagram representing the sequence of events in Randy's life, using the following schema:

Patterns of parental control ———→ Drives or behaviors rewarded or punished ———→ Randy's reaction to this parental treatment ———→ The effect of Randy's reactions on his parents, friends, and teachers ———→ Randy's counter-reaction to this treatment from parents, friends, and teachers

5. In particular, how might one explain:
   a. Randy's stealing
   b. his "sneakiness"
(Hint to question a, review Randy's relationship with his siblings. Hint to question b, review the incidents cited by his parents as evidence of his "sneakiness.")

6. How would you characterize the relationship between Randy's mother and father, particularly as it related to Randy's discipline? How did this relationship appear to affect Randy's behavior?

7. What sorts of emotional problems did Randy's father appear to have? How did these problems affect Randy's psychological growth and development?

8. How can we account for the fact that Randy appeared so disturbed while his siblings appeared quite normal?

9. If Randy had never had any psychological treatment, what sort of behavior might you expect from him ten years later? On what evidence did you make this prediction? Cite whatever bits of Randy's behavior that you use for prediction as well as any text material or research literature that leads you to your prediction.

10. What resources or agencies, other than guidance clinics, might a community have or develop which could be used to prevent or ameliorate situations similar to those presented in this case?

References

ACKERMAN, N. *The psychodynamics of family life.* New York: Basic Books, 1958. Read Chaps. 11 and 12 particularly, but whole book is of value.

MURPHY, L. B. Preventive implications of development in the pre-school years. In CAPLAN, G. (Ed.) *Prevention of mental disorders in children.* New York: Basic Books, 1961.

THE CASE OF PAULA O.

What's in a Name?

When Paula O., a sixteen-year-old high school student, confessed to her teacher that she intended to commit suicide, her parents decided to bring her directly to the hospital that evening, without waiting for an appointment. However, this decision was reached only after intense discussion. Her father, Mr. O., scornfully skeptical, believed that the school was exaggerating the situation. Mrs. O. was more obviously concerned for her daughter, particularly since this was not Paula's first suicidal threat. The parents' confusion and ambivalence made the situation a difficult one to assess. Paula, white-faced and tense, sat silent and refused to answer any questions. The admitting psychiatrist advised that a brief period of immediate hospitalization was warranted because of the danger of further suicidal attempts. Mr. O. protested vigorously that the doctor was making far too much of Paula's threats. In response, the psychiatrist pointed out that Mr. O.'s inability to recognize the seriousness of the situation was probably part of the problem, and that if Mr. O. refused to follow his advice, then neither he nor the hospital could assume any responsibility in the eventuality of Paula's death. The father continued to argue with the psychiatrist. Mrs. O. broke into tears at this point and hurriedly left the office with the two younger children. The psychiatrist walked out and Paula followed him. Finally, after several minutes, Mr. O. came out and joined his family.

Paula's over-all appearance suggested a child closer to ten years of age than an alolescent. She wore no make-up and her dark hair hung in twin braids down her back. Her chubby figure was exaggerated by a simple, childlike frock closed at the collar. At the time of arrival, Paula carried with her three worn pocket books: Plato's *Dialogues,* Dostoevsky's *Crime and Punishment,* and a biography of Mozart. It was impossible to interview her. She sat rigidly upright in the chair, staring at the interviewer. When she did answer, it was mostly in monosyllables and frequently in a manner which made it difficult to assess whether or not she comprehended the question. Paula's face was generally expressionless, but on occasion her eyes would narrow and she would quickly look away. Whenever the interviewer made a particularly strong effort to get her to discuss what had happened, Paula would fidget in her chair and pull at her dress.

In the interview with the mother, she stated that Paula had been unusually upset two months ago, when she brought home a report card with a B in Science, instead of the A she had been striving for. During the following months, Paula became listless and careless with her homework, although up until then she had been a straight A student. At home, it was noticeable that she paid little attention to the family conversation, and she was very slow to respond to any question or request. In subsequent interviews the parents dated the onset of Paula's difficulties to approximately three years before, when she was thirteen. At that time, Paula began to withdraw more and more into herself; isolated in her room, she would either read or listen to music. The only activity that brought her out of her room was her piano practice. At the time, her parents saw nothing unusual in this behavior pattern, since they themselves enjoyed all three of these activities. However, it gradually dawned on them that Paula had no close friends. In fact, their daughter avoided her peer group entirely.

Currently, Paula spent all of her spare time behind the locked door of her room. When her father ordered her to leave her door unlocked, an angry tearful scene ensued. Mr. O. was astounded, for Paula had always been respectful of his wishes. Her father, in going over her school work, which he was in the habit of doing rigorously, discovered that the margins of her books and papers were filled with bizarre and morbid notes which he could not comprehend. When Paula sloughed off his questions about these notes, he decided she was deeply involved in her studies and decided to ignore them. The psychiatrist recognized that these notes contained broad hints of suicide.

In the middle of March the school guidance counselor called Mrs. O. to report that she was disturbed by Paula's behavior; particularly, she was uneasy about the essay on suicide that Paula had written for her English class. Although excellently composed, with many scientific references, it impressed the teacher as exceedingly morbid. The teacher also had noticed that Paula had no associations with any of her classmates, but sat silently by herself in the classroom during period when the class was not in session. Previously, Paula had recited easily, often volunteering material, but during the past month and a half she had been almost completely silent during class periods. When Paula went to this same teacher to discuss the easiest way to commit suicide, the school authorities finally demanded that the parents remove Paula from school and seek psychiatric help. Mr. O. admitted that two weeks earlier, he had been looking for Paula to call her to dinner and discovered her in his workshop over the garage. She was standing on a chair, with a noosed rope flung over the rafters. He asked what she was doing; when she replied, "Nothing," he responded, "Well, then, come in to dinner." Mr. O. denied that he saw anything of import in this incident and maintained that his off-hand response to her at that time was appropriate, since he considered that nothing was amiss; the whole thing was probably "a childish fantasy."

Family Background and History. The O. family consisted of Mr. O., age forty-two, Mrs. O., thirty-eight, Paula, sixteen, Karen, twelve, and Paul, three. They lived in an upper-middle-class district of an urban community. Their spacious but older house sat isolated on a knoll above the new homes of a recently built-up community. Each child had his own room, and in addition to the usual living quarters there was a library and music room. The O.'s had very little association outside of their own family. They did not belong to any club, they did not attend PTA, and they had few friends and no relatives in the community. Only on rare occasions did Mr. O.'s business require him to be away from home other than during working hours. Mrs. O. did not enjoy shopping; she seldom left the home except for direct purchases, and even these errands she tried to save for Saturday morning when she could be accompanied by her husband. Thus, there was always someone home during the day, and during the evening the entire family were always together.

THE FATHER: Mr. O. was assistant director of a large, commercial, scientific laboratory. He immediately informed the interviewer that, despite limitations in his education, he was enjoying a very responsible position in the laboratory, directing the activities of scientists with doctoral degrees. The elder son of a small town New England judge, he was brought up in an environment in which conformity to "proper" standards of behavior was emphatically enforced. Although not generally a superior student, he obtained outstanding marks in science courses in high school.

Throughout his childhood, he had yielded unquestioningly to the autocratic domination with which his father ruled the family. However, in his late teens he became more sullen and finally rebelled by refusing to attend college as his father demanded. Instead, he left home and obtained a job in a chemical laboratory. All during high school, he had had very little social life. It was on his first date, away from home, that Mr. O. met his wife-to-be. They were married two months later. The United States had just entered World War II and almost immediately Mr. O. was inducted into military service and shipped overseas, where he remained for two and a half years without furlough. On the basis of his civilian interest and employment, Mr. O. was assigned to a chemical warfare unit, where he received a commission and was assigned administrative duties. Thus, upon discharge from the army, despite his lack of a college education, he was able to obtain a managerial position in an industrial firm. In appearance Mr. O. was a tall, lean, rangy man, casual but not untidy in his dress. He loved to talk and to argue; he admitted he often took the opposite position at any point "just for the fun of it." A chain smoker, he never seemed to relax, and always gave the impression of being in a hurry.

THE MOTHER: Mrs. O. was born and reared in a rural New England community, the only daughter of the owner of a small restaurant. She had always been a very timid person who was dominated by her complaining and overbearing mother. She could not remember her father well since he died at sea when she was still very young. During her early childhood, she spent many long hours alone in the apartment behind the restaurant while her mother waited on customers. Mrs. O.'s attempts at courtship were strongly resisted by the mother, who had constantly warned her daughter about the unreliability of men. Mrs. O. continued to live with her mother after her husband went overseas. Soon after her husband left for overseas, Mrs. O. discovered that she was pregnant with Paula. Friction with her mother increased during her pregnancy and continued after

Paula's birth. However, Mrs. O.'s mother found Paula such a charming baby that she changed her attitude, and she gradually began to show off the infant to her customers.

On Mr. O.'s return, the postwar housing shortage made it difficult for him to find a place of their own. Thus, the following year was one of mounting hostility between Mrs. O.'s mother and her husband. Each made constant demands upon her and each blamed the other when she failed to live up to their demands. Mr. O. began to put pressures on his wife to move away from her mother. This prospect frightened her, as she had never been separated from her mother even overnight, except for the time she spent in the hospital giving birth to Paula. Mr. O. was finally able to find a flat nearby and insisted that his wife move away from her mother. About the same time as this move was made their second child, Karen, was born. The new home was unsatisfactory, and Mrs. O.'s mother continued to interfere in their marriage. It was partly for these reasons that the couple moved to the Pacific coast.

On the surface, the balance of the O.'s marriage was most peaceful—chiefly because Mrs. O. deferred to her husband's every wish and opinion. During her therapy she admitted that she was always tense whenever her husband became amorous, even though this was infrequent. Having been brought up in a home where the "dangers" of sex were frequently emphasized, she had no sexual experience prior to marriage and was always frightened by it afterwards.

When first seen in the clinic, Mrs. O. gave a rather dowdy appearance. She was dressed in an unassuming tweed suit with white lace blouse buttoned up to the collar; she wore no make-up, and her dark, graying hair was tied up in a low bun at the nape of her neck. With her lips pursed and her hands folded in her lap, she usually sat rigidly upright at the edge of the chair, staring straight ahead, very much like a frightened animal. Often she had to clear her throat several times before speaking and then her voice was so low as to be nearly inaudible. At times, however, when tense or excited, her voice broke into a high pitch. She seldom volunteered anything except when questioned, and her answers tended to trail off into generalities. "Oh, you know," was one of her favorite responses.

PAULA: At birth, Paula seemed in every way a normal infant. Her mother's pregnancy had lasted almost exactly nine months and despite a prolonged labor, there had been no difficulty at her birth. Her weight and length were fairly average. She breathed immediately and fed at the breast readily and without difficulty. Mrs. O. was able to continue breast-feeding of Paula for over three months, at which time she gradually shifted Paula onto a formula in the bottle. Paula's development during the first year of life was fairly regular and uneventful. She grew rapidly and, if anything, was somewhat precocious in the development of her motor and social functioning. She was sitting up before age three months, standing in the crib by five months, and was taking her first steps before she was a year old. Mrs. O. had nothing to do but care for Paula and poured a great deal of affection and attention upon her during these first three years of her life. Paula began to speak her first words shortly after her first birthday; she never talked any baby-talk and was combining words into two- or three-word combinations and sentences by the time she was eighteen months old. Mrs. O. reported that Paula "almost toilet-trained herself." Paula's development continued uneventfully until her father's return three years later. At their reunion, Mr. O. grabbed her and overwhelmed her with a "bear-hug." Paula was terrified and for the first two weeks after his return ran screaming from the room at his appearance. His pride was injured and he kept making remarks about the fact that he had hoped for a boy, and "What did you expect from girls anyhow." Soon afterwards, however, Paula and her father made up, and very quickly she became known as "daddy's little girl."

During Mrs. O.'s pregnancy with their second daughter, Karen, Mr. O. cared for Paula in many little ways, brushing her hair, toileting her, and putting her to bed. His attentions to her continued unabated even after the birth of the younger sister. Paula was obviously very bright, and her father was able to teach her to read and write before she started school. He let everyone know how proud he was of her intellectual development. Paula read everything she could lay her hands on, started playing the piano as soon as she could sit up to it, and by the time she was eight she had helped her father build a ham-radio set, which they both operated. She seldom participated in any of the housework but was always there ready to help her father with the gardening.

Paula appeared to have little in common with Karen; they shared no friends and usually played separately. Although they were disdainful of one another's opinions and sarcastic toward one another, they seldom openly quarreled, as this was forbidden sternly by their parents. At school, Paula made excellent progress, usually had all outstanding or A grades and was twice given a double promotion. She had no intimate friends and even her casual acquaintances seldom numbered more than two or three. She did not seem to be interested in little girls' games, and her friends were uninterested in her scientific prowess. Thus her friends seldom returned to her home after one visit and she seldom visited them. She had no interest in sports and several times the teachers reported to the parents that Paula was reading instead of playing on the playground during recess. Since the school was nearby, Paula usually came home for lunch.

Paula began to take on some weight and the secondary sexual characteristics of womanhood at about age twelve and had her first menstrual period the week of her thirteenth birthday. Her mother had been completely unable to give her any sex instruction, but her father was doggedly determined that she should be informed and the year before had given her books, chiefly medical, regarding the facts of life, and had discussed them with her, including the fact of her onset of menses. He even provided her with her first supply of sanitary napkins! In junior high, Paula withdrew more and more from her classmates. She had several admirers among the boys but kept them at a distance. Her intellectual interests and her formal manners and speech tended further to isolate her from the other children. In contrast, her teachers praised her intellectual achievement and her creative writing. She was fascinated by the prospect of her brother Paul's birth and offered to care for him at every opportunity. However, she proved to be quite clumsy with the baby, almost dropping him several times, and was never really able to dress him or feed him properly. Her father was quite upset by her inability to care for her brother and made remarks about how unfeminine she was.

KAREN: Little was known of Karen other than the behavior mentioned above. She apparently was of no general problem to the family other than that she adopted typical teen-age ways which were disapproved by her father. She was more able to ignore her father's disapproval than Paula, who became tearful whenever her father glowered. Karen enjoyed helping her mother and made fun of Paula when she did not join in the housework. She rivaled with Paula for the attention of their father, but maintained more of a teasing, provoking relationship with her father, while Paula tended to treat her father with deference. Whereas Paula failed in her attempt to help her mother with the new baby, caring for an infant came rather naturally to Karen, who had always "played house" with dolls much more than had Paula.

PAUL: Little data were obtained regarding Paul's development and insofar as Paul was discussed with the parents, both described him in idealistic terms as the "perfect baby," who gave them no trouble. Mr. O. was obviously delighted to have a son. During the one occasion when Paul accompanied his parents to the clinic, he constantly interrupted them, ran noisely up and down the hall, and grabbed at any thing he wanted! Mr. O. smiled benignly and made no effort to control him; Mrs. O. was manifestly uncomfortable, looked pleadingly at her husband, but said nothing.

When queried why they had decided to name the baby *Paul* when they had already named the oldest daughter *Paula,* Mr. O. smiled and nodded to his wife, indicating (for one of the few times) that she should answer. Mrs. O. demurely replied that she liked the name as both her husband and father were named Paul. When the interviewer persisted and asked how Paula had reacted when the baby was given the masculine equivalent of her name, Mr. O. replied sternly, "She was honored!" Later, in an interview separate from her husband, Mrs. O. acknowledged that her husband had hoped that their first born would be a boy and had made it clear to her that he assumed she would name him Paul. She felt she had failed him by having a girl and hoped to appease him by naming her after him anyway. When he decided to name the baby Paul, she did not voice her disagreement, even though it occurred to her that Paula might feel hurt or confused. As far as Mrs. O. could observe, Paula appeared to ignore the contamination of names. Questioned further, Mrs. O. became flustered and denied hotly that the subject was ever discussed. When the topic was broached later with Mr. O. he attempted to debate the interviewer; assuming a mock injured air, he accused the interviewer of the *argumentum ad hominum,* adding slyly that the interviewer was unfairly using "Freudian tactics." When the psychiatrist asked Paula her feelings about the similarity of the names, she suddenly became completely impassive, turned away, and would answer nothing else for the rest of that hour. She remained immobile in her hospital room the rest of that afternoon, unresponsive to anyone or anything. That night she slashed both of her wrists.

Progress in Treatment. During the next three weeks, Paula sat in her room as much as possible and was unresponsive to everyone. She continued to read Dostoevsky and Plato or to listen to the radio. Occasionally, she would play the piano. She would not respond to any questions, and would sit in silence with the psychiatrist for the entire hour if permitted. Nor did she respond to any of the psychological tests. She was very tense when urine specimens were taken and ran and stood in the corner in obvious terror when the physical examination was begun. She would not disrobe for the physical examination which was abandoned because she seemed so upset. Later it was thought that Paula would be less embarrassed by a woman physician, but Paula seemed terrified even when a woman physician attempted to examine her. The nurses and occupational therapists made efforts to include Paula in the ward activities, but it was extremely difficult to get her to leave her room. She ate sparsely but there was no noticeable drop in her weight. Her parents visited almost daily; she would come out to see them but said very little to them, which upset her father.

At the end of three weeks, despite interviews with the parents, Mr. O. signed the patient out of the hospital against medical advice. This was his vacation and he had decided months in advance to take the family on a trip. Four days later, the parents returned with Paula and reported that she had refused to go camping and that after her father had raged at her, she had gone to her room crying. Later, after everyone was in bed, she had slipped out of the house and walked down a main boulevard, where she was picked up by the police in her nightwear. Sometime during the evening, she had again slashed both of her wrists with a piece of glass. Paula was readmitted to the hospital on the understanding that both parents would come regularly to interviews with the social worker and psychologist. Gradually Paula began to talk to her therapist, at first mainly about irrelevant topics, e.g. her interest in music, what she was reading, her poetry. At the end of another six weeks, it was felt that Paula could be seen on an outpatient basis and she continued coming into the clinic three times a week. Meanwhile, Mrs. O. was seen regularly by the social worker once a week. More of the history of the family was obtained. A beginning was made in helping Mrs. O. to explore her feelings, first about Paula, and gradually about her husband. Mr. O. was also seen in therapy.

Approximately four months after outpatient treatment Paula appeared still to be making little progress in her individual interviews with the psychiatrist. She had made several further suicidal threats, though less definite than before. Then one morning on the way to school, she came across a pre-school child, entirely a stranger to her, and suddenly she began throttling him. His mother rescued him and called the police, and Paula was brought in to the hospital.

During the ensuing year, both parents continued in treatment in the outpatient clinic. Paula's homicidal attack on this child sobered the father and made him realize, finally, the necessity of looking at what was going on in his family. He argued less and less with his therapist, talked increasingly more about himself, his wife, and his daughter. The changes in Mrs. O. were even more dramatic. One day after a brief holiday, her therapist looked for her in the waiting room, but did not at first see her, for she had cut her hair, was wearing make-up, and a very modish dress. Mr. O. was irritated that his wife was talking back to him, was spending a lot of money on clothes, and wanted to be taken places at night. On the other hand, he allowed his wife to take the lead in handling Paula on her visits home from the hospital and to take Paula shopping, which she had not done before. Mr. O. reported with some pride that he was able to be less critical of Paula. During this second stay in the hospital, Paula's behavior swung to the opposite extreme. She lost about 35 pounds, smeared make-up across her face in an amateurish fashion, dressed in shorts and a dirty blouse, and tried to avoid wearing her glasses. She behaved in such a seductive and almost vulgar fashion toward the male patients that it was at times necessary to restrict her behavior. Her father was scandalized when he saw her and was prevented from writing a letter of protest to the governor only by the quick work of the hospital social worker. However, on his wife's insistence, he began to accept a little of the change in Paula and at the end of the year, when she was returned home, he was able to accept her greater freedom in talking back to him, and her general independence. When the clinic's contact with the family ended, Mr. O. was reporting that he could accept Paula's first date, even though he felt very tempted to bring the young man in from the hallway and cross-examine him. However, Mrs. O. had foreseen that Mr. O. might do this and had warned him against doing anymore than saying good evening to Paula's date. A year later, Paula wrote a brief letter to her therapist in which she indicated that she was completing high school and had no further problems.

Questions for Paula O.

1. What are the significant symptoms which are to be understood in this case?

2. Identify the stresses which, over the preceding three years, may have acted to precipitate Paula's illness.

3. On the basis of the evidence available evaluate the role of the following in producing Paula's illness:

    a. the separation from her father during her first two years

    b. the relationship between Mrs. O. and her mother

    c. Paula's relationship with her father

    d. Paula's relationship with Karen and Paul

4. What psychological defenses do we see operating in Paula? Why did these defenses fail to stabilize her anxiety level?

5. What are some possible underlying reasons for *attempting* suicide and which of these seems most appropriate in Paula's case?

6. Paula showed a marked departure in her behavior after her second hospitalization. She changed from a prim, asexual girl to a seductively behaving, less controlled woman. Was this change predictable from Paula's past history? Defend your answer.

7. Why, do you think, did the interviewers press the O.'s so closely about Paula's name? What might have been the significance of her name in:

    a. her relationship with her father

    b. relation to her "lack of femininity"

    c. her feelings about Paul

8. What might be the significance of:

    a. Paula's drive toward intellectual achievement

    b. her dress and appearance

    c. her dread of physical examination
    d. her attack on the neighbor child
9. What two diagnostic classifications suggest themselves to you? Attempt to choose between these two classifications by weighing the evidence for each one.

References

DEUTSCH, H. *The psychology of women.* New York: Grune & Stratton, 1944. Read Chap. 3, Puberty and adolescence.

JACKSON, D. Theories of suicide. In SCHNEIDMAN, E., & FARBEROW, N., *Clues to suicide.* New York: McGraw-Hill, 1957.

LIDZ, T., et al. The intrafamilial environment of the schizophrenic: the father. *Psychiatry,* 1957, **20:** 329–342.

LYNN, D., & SAWREY, W. The Effects of father absence on Norwegian boys and girls. *Journal of Abnormal and Social Psychology,* 1959, **59:** 258–262.

THE CASE OF DAVID Z.

The Choice of God

While waiting in the reception room of the hospital, David stood rigidly motionless, staring straight ahead, unresponsive to the nurse's invitation to have a seat. He was a strikingly handsome ten-year-old, olive-skinned, with large dark eyes and jet black hair, which was combed in an old-fashioned part. He was dressed up in his "Sunday best": dark suit, white shirt and tie, and well-polished shoes. After the admission papers had been filled out by his parents, the nurse asked him to follow her but he did not budge. His father took him by the hand and half-dragged him along; David moved his legs only enough so that he did not fall completely forward. Once on the ward, David did not return his father's goodby nor look around after him. Although he retained his impassive stance, he permitted the nurse to dress him in hospital clothes and to lead him to a chair where he was seated.

David's father reported that for the preceding five days and nights David had remained in the same chair in their living room, silent and immobile. He had not even eaten nor gone to the bathroom. The parents had scolded, threatened, cajoled, and offered bribes but to no avail. Mr. Z. regarded David's behavior as willful disobedience but had been prevented by his wife from physically punishing the child. Mr. Z. believed that the immediate incident which set off this reaction in David was a scolding which he had given David for similar behavior at school. Shortly after David had entered a new class in a new school, approximately six weeks earlier, he told his parents that he did not like the teacher and found no friends at school. Then the teacher had called Mr. Z. to report that David had not spoken to her or any of the children for several weeks and was not doing his schoolwork. The teacher was outraged and intimated that Mr. Z. was neglectful as a parent since she had sent several notes home to him by David, which Mr. Z. had not received. Mr. Z. was quite embarrassed, and, after apologizing to the teacher, he returned to scold David very harshly, threatening to send him away to an institution if David continued in his behavior.

According to Mr. Z., David had always been a rather quiet, serious child who tended to his own needs in an independent fashion. Mr. Z. immediately apologized for his lack of information about David, saying that much to his regret he knew little of the child's behavior or of his training, since he worked long hours in his business, usually leaving home before the children were up for breakfast and returning after they were in bed. During the previous eight months he had seen nothing of David because Mrs. Z. and the children had been in Turkish Armenia visiting her parents. Mr. Z. said that David spoke both English and Armenian, the latter being the preferred language in the home. Mrs. Z. spoke very little English, despite the fact that she had been in this country over twelve years; only recently had she begun taking night-school lessons for the foreign-born.

Although Mr. Z. had left most of the discipline and care of the children to his wife, he was not entirely in accord with her methods of rearing them. He immediately attributed a great deal of David's behavior to what he called his wife's "inconsistencies." He complained that Mrs. Z. was very impatient with David, never listened to what he had to say, and was very suspicious of any of his explanations or observations. At the same time, Mr. Z. felt that his wife often coddled David, buying him things even when David did not request them and yielding too often to David's demands. Although Mr. Z. was away from the house a great deal, he claimed that he tried to attempt to keep in touch with the family by returning home for the noon meal, and his wife occasionally helped him in his business and brought the children with her. However, he was usually too busy to intervene in any way in the care of the children. Also, Mr. Z. avoided crossing his wife since her behavior was similar to David's current pattern, that is, she would refuse to speak to Mr. Z. for over a week, would ignore anything that he said to her, and even refused to eat if he were present.

Mr. Z. was a short, stocky, dark-skinned man with graying hair; he was neatly dressed in a business suit. He tried to approach the problem in a co-operative and intelligent manner, but it was the interviewer's impression that he was a little too formal and guarded.

Nevertheless, he frequently spoke with considerable feeling; there was no doubt of his affection for his son or of his concern over David's condition. His voice and face also revealed his impatience and anger with his wife.

Mrs. Z. appeared to be at least ten years younger than her husband. It was evident that David resembled his mother much more closely than he did his father. She was dressed neatly but conservatively; her dark hair was tied up in a bun at the nape of her neck, and she wore no noticeable cosmetics or jewelry. During the initial interview she said nothing, and Mr. Z. answered all questions directed at them. Subsequently it was discovered that she understood English quite well and was able to respond to most questions. Both she and her husband were seen in subsequent and separate interviews several times during the ensuing weeks.

Past History. Both Mr. Z. and his wife were born in Armenia, in a section now part of the Republic of Turkey. Two older cousins of Mr. Z. brought him to the United States at age five, after his family had been wiped out by one of the several invading armies in that region during World War I. He had been raised by these cousins and other Armenian friends in a small city in central California. When he reached adulthood, he was taken into their fruit and vegetable distribution business; he later branched out on his own and became a successful and prosperous businessman in his own right. He did not marry because, he explained, there were almost no Armenian girls his age, and he considered the younger women to be far too Americanized and "greedy." However, he yearned for a family. Therefore, after prolonged correspondence with a marriage broker in the village of his birth, a marriage was arranged for him and he returned to his homeland to meet his bride. Mrs. Z., who was twelve years her husband's junior, was the youngest daughter of a large family and "the apple of her father's eye." Her family had once been a wealthy and politically powerful clan but in recent decades had lost much of their property and influence. The marriage of this last daughter to what was considered by the community to be a "rich American" was openly touted by Mrs. Z.'s father as a revival of the family's community standing. Mrs. Z. admitted that she had not liked the idea of an arranged marriage since this custom had largely died out, but she had been very protected by her parents and had had no chance to meet young men and make a choice of her own. Despite the family's limited finances, she was very well educated and had even been abroad to Switzerland for a year of schooling. She spoke several languages and was well read. She had often dreamed of coming to America and was very excited at the prospect of leaving home. She found her new husband to be a charming and handsome man, and in the long run was very happy about the marriage. Mr. Z. reported that he was immediately attracted by his young and beautiful bride and pleased to find that she was so intelligent and, for one reared in a remote village of the Caucasus, relatively cosmopolitan in outlook.

Upon the couple's return to the United States, Mrs. Z. was very disappointed to find that her husband's little apartment was much less luxurious than she had expected; indeed, though it had many modern appliances, it was much less spacious and beautiful than her own home. She had never had to do any housework before and was ill-prepared to care for a home or to do her own marketing. She was very lonely as her husband was away from home most of the time. She had nothing in common with the other women of the Armenian community, for the older women were not as well educated, and the younger women spoke little Armenian and were preoccupied with their own American-type activities. In addition, she became pregnant almost immediately, and during this first pregnancy she was often ill, quite depressed, wept a great deal, and was morose and irritable with her husband. Mr. Z. regarded her reaction as childish and scolded her. The dissension between the Z.'s increased when the first child turned out to be a girl, as Mr. Z. had hoped very much to have a male heir immediately. Burdened with the care of the new baby, Mrs. Z.'s depression increased, and deepened even further when she became pregnant a few months later with David. She began to make demands upon Mr. Z. for help around the house, and asked that he get her a servant. He made fun of her because she was not able to care for their three-room apartment and she reacted with morose silences.

She suffered with nausea, vomiting, and weakness during her pregnancy with David. Mr. Z. was overjoyed at David's birth, and invited all of his friends and relatives in for a huge celebration. David was given a list of names, honoring Mr. Z.'s ancestors. However, Mr. Z. referred to him by an ancient Armenian term which translated roughly as "the choice of God." Mr. Z. was somewhat disappointed that his wife did not appear to share his joy and excitement over the birth of the son. She did not show David any particular favor over her daughter or the subsequent children. She did not use her husband's term to address David but rather called him by a diminutive of one of his other names which was the same as her older brother's. This often irritated Mr. Z., but Mrs. Z. paid no attention to her husband's protestations. It is possible that Mrs. Z. gave no extra attention to David because she soon became pregnant with a third child; she subsequently bore another girl, another boy, and a third girl—a total of five children in twelve years.

As far as could be ascertained, David's birth and early development were relatively normal. Mr. Z. remembered almost nothing of David as an infant and Mrs. Z.'s English was too limited to describe David as a baby other than to say that he was in good health. He was breast-fed for the first several months and gradually weaned to soft foods. It was Mrs. Z.'s impression that David learned to walk and talk much earlier than her other children. She could not remember exactly when he was toilet-trained, and she used no particular methods that she could identify as toilet-training. She said, however, that he seemed to be naturally clean and was no longer soiling himself about the time that she was giving birth to her third child, which must have been when David was only slightly over a year old.

Mr. Z. remembered David as being an excessively curious child who got into everything and wanted to know about everything. He reported with pride how Mrs. Z. telephoned one day when David was about two to report that David was missing from the house, after he had announced that he was going over to Mr. Z.'s store several blocks away. Before Mr. Z. could wind up his immediate business and go look for the child, David appeared at the store saying that he wanted to see his father and help in his father's work. Although the parents were frightened by the prospect of a two-year-old who wandered the streets, Mr. Z. was very proud and excited by this incident and took it as an omen that David would follow in his footsteps. David seemed to enjoy being around adults and listening to their conversation. He liked to watch the news on TV as well as the cartoons; he looked at the pictures in the magazines and before he started kindergarten he was reading. As further proof of David's intelligence and perceptiveness, Mr. Z. cited an incident when David

was four: David had refused to attend Sunday school, arguing that
because the Russian rocket to the moon had not hit any angels David
no longer believed the things that were taught him at church. This
amused the Z.'s very much, and they did not insist that David return
to Sunday school. The Z.'s were socially and financially contributors
to the local Armenian church, but both regarded religion with intellectual skepticism.

In his first several years at school David made excellent grades. He
read voraciously and was intensely interested in science. Mr. Z.
bought him many expensive toys, which David picked out himself.
However, Mr. Z. had no time to play with David and did not know
what David did with the scientific toys he bought for him. Mr. Z.
seemed to regard David as brighter than their other children but
otherwise normal; however, from their description it seemed clear
that David was a social isolate almost from the start. He had little
to do with his brothers and sisters, except to complain frequently
that they interfered with his activities. His parents also felt that he
was much less obedient than the other children and were often irritated that he did not immediately follow their commands. They tried
depriving him of things, but this proved ineffective. Mrs. Z.'s method
of punishment was to isolate the children in a room away from the
rest of the family; David's reaction was to remain in the room after
permission was given him to return. As far as they knew David had
few friends at school, for he always returned home immediately after
school and never spoke of any playmates. However, the Z.'s had no
contact with the school prior to the current incident.

Although Mrs. Z.'s depression decreased gradually, she remained
very discontent with her lot in life. Even though her husband acceded to her demands for larger living quarters and a few more luxuries, she constantly complained about the burden of her children
and her lack of any social life. She continually expressed the desire
to return to her homeland at least for a visit. However, such a trip
seemed out of the question in the face of the unsettled conditions of
the world during and immediately after World War II. Moreover,
for over a decade she was either pregnant or caring for a newborn
child. Shortly after the birth of their fifth child two years previously,
Mrs. Z.'s sense of frustration seemed to reach a new peak. She again
became extremely irritable with her husband and nothing seemed to
satisfy her. Mr. Z. decided to teach her a lesson and told her that he

was leaving her. He packed his bag and left the home intending to stay away only briefly. Mrs. Z. retaliated by withdrawing the family savings with which she bought herself and the children a ticket back to her homeland. Mr. Z. wrote her many letters, begging her to return and promising her a new home and many other luxuries. When Mrs. Z. and her children returned to the United States, Mr. Z. had purchased them a new home in a tract some distance from the rest of the Armenian community. He also had made arrangements for household help so that Mrs. Z. would be relieved of some of the burdens of caring for the house and children. He convinced her that if she would attend night school and improve her English she would have wider social opportunities. David seemed quite discontent with the new home, for he used to enjoy being around the Armenian community, hanging around his father's place of business and running little errands for his father's employees or other people in the business neighborhood. Mr. Z. was even less able to spend any time at home, for the distance between his business and the new home prohibited his coming home for lunch or other daytime visits. David dreaded the idea of attending a new school and begged to be returned to his former school, but this was not possible under the school board rules.

Course in the Hospital. For several days after his hospitalization David continued to refuse to eat, did not go to the bathroom, and had to be led from the chair where he usually sat in the dayroom to his bed in the evening. He spoke to no one and responded to no one. The night nurses observed that he often seemed awake in his bed but did not arise. In the morning, he had to be lifted from his bed and placed on his feet. He made no voluntary movements of any kind and gradually would neither stand nor sit, but slid over on the floor in a heap. His doctor spoke to him, explaining to him that no harm would come to him in the hospital and that the doctors and nurses were there to care for him and to get him back to his home and school. David made no response, and it was difficult to know whether or not he understood. Mr. and Mrs. Z. visited almost daily, but David refused even to look at them. Finally, it was decided that it would be best not to have his parents visit. When this was explained to David, he responded for the first time with a slight smile and a movement of his eyes, suggesting that this idea met with his approval.

Because he refused to eat, he rapidly lost weight and became weak and emaciated. It was firmly explained to David that no matter how angry and depressed he might be, the doctor would not permit him to endanger his life by refusing food. David permitted a tube to be inserted into his throat and was force-fed. The following day, however, David responded to the nurse's invitation to join the other children at mealtime and consumed small amounts of food and liquid. He had to be encouraged to more frequent intake of liquids. Because it was feared his bowels might become impacted, an enema was necessary. The necessity for this procedure was also explained to David in terms of the doctor's resolution that David would not be allowed to come to any harm. During the ensuing weeks his doctor spent several hours a day talking to David, usually for fifteen- to twenty-minute periods. David made no verbal response, but his facial expression changed from complete impassivity to flashes of anger, excitement, and even gratitude as the doctor revealed to him that he understood David's situation. Once when the doctor told him how he understood David's extreme feelings of depression and anger, David broke into tears and continued to cry for almost an hour. Gradually, David permitted himself to be led into the games and activities of the other children of the ward. He read books and magazines that were handed to him, and then began to select books from the hospital library on his own.

His first speech came on slowly and shyly with the ward schoolteacher. After that he began to talk with his doctor and the nurses on the ward. He admitted to his doctor that he felt that his father had disowned him. The hospitalization confirmed for him a fantasy that he had long nursed to the effect that he was really an adopted child and that someday his true parents would appear and take him away from the Z.'s. He felt that his father's many gifts and praises of him were not at all sincere and that his father did not really love him. However, after saying this, he again broke down in tears and said that his father's approval and affection were what he wanted most in life. He was far more reticent to discuss any feelings about his mother. He admitted that his mother's irritability and flashes of anger made him at first angry in return and then frightened. However, he refused to say anything negative about her and appeared to be quite guilty when he mentioned that he ever felt angry toward her. There were also many indications that he felt keen rivalry with his younger brother, whom he regarded as his mother's favorite.

At David's request his parents were allowed to visit again after approximately two months of hospitalization. Shortly thereafter he made two weekend visits home. He was discharged from the hospital three and a half months after admission. He continued to attend weekly outpatient psychotherapeutic sessions with his doctor. His parents were seen in separate interviews with the social worker throughout the time of David's treatment. David returned to the school he had been attending prior to hospitalization and seemed to be making a fair adjustment there. Approximately a year after his release from the hospital he was discharged from the clinic as improved and with no immediate need for further treatment.

Questions for David Z.

1. First, if you have not already done so, read the part of the case of Merry L. which describes her psychological and physical development during her first two years of life. Compare the facts of Merry's early development with David's. In what ways are they dissimilar? (Cover, in particular, speech development, motor development, and emotional responsiveness.)

2. In many child guidance clinics, Merry L. would be diagnosed as an "autistic child," while David might be diagnosed as a childhood schizophrenic with catatonic features. What dissimilarities in the development of these two children support the use of different diagnoses?

3. How might events in David's environment immediately prior to his hospitalization have been associated with the onset of his severe withdrawal symptoms?

4. Can you offer some explanations why David developed this particular reaction pattern rather than some other symptoms (i.e. aggressive acting out, bed-wetting, and so forth)?

5. What chronic tensions appeared to exist in the home during the years preceding David's symptoms? How might these tensions be related to his sudden emotional disturbance?

6. Do we have any reason to suspect that these tensions might have

been more stressful for David than for the other children in the family? Take into account:

    a. David's intellectual level.

    b. the phases of emotional development which one would expect David to be going through.

    c. the father's threat to leave the mother.

    d. the mother's trip to Armenia.

7. During the course of his stay in the hospital, David finally verbalized an intense need for his father's approval. Can you give some reasons why this need was so intense in David, and what role it may have played in David's symptom pattern?

8. While in a state of withdrawal, David refused to eat or go to the toilet. What meanings might these bodily functions have had for David and how do they help us to understand what David was trying to express at the time of his withdrawn episode?

References

BENDER, LAURETTA. Evidences from studies of childhood schizophrenia. *Archives of Neurology and Psychiatry*, 1953, **70**: 525.

BRADLEY, C., & BOWEN, MARGARET. Behavior characteristics of schizophrenic children. *Psychiatric Quarterly*, 1941, **15**: 296–315.

DESPERT, LOUISE. Schizophrenia in children. *Psychiatric Quarterly*, 1938, **12**: 366–371.

WEIL, ANNEMARIE P. Clinical data and dynamic considerations in certain cases of childhood schizophrenia. *American Journal of Orthopsychiatry*, 1953, **23**: 518–529.

THE CASE OF MERRY L.

The Model Child

Even before Merry was four, her pediatrician had expressed concern over her emotional and social development and had advised her mother with increasing urgency, to seek a psychological evaluation. Mrs. L. did not believe there was really anything wrong with Merry, but was disturbed by the pediatrician's insistence. She agreed that Merry's development could be considered slow, but she was not worried. It was her opinion that Merry would develop at her own pace and would eventually be quite normal. She believed "in letting children develop at their own pace rather than pushing them," but could not convince the pediatrician that Merry would "grow out of it." The confident manner with which Mrs. L. voiced her opinions made it clear that she expected the psychologist to support her point of view.

Asked to describe Mary's slowness, Mrs. L. first mentioned that Merry did not seem to "talk clearly." As Mrs. L. explained further, the problem was not that Merry could not express herself in words, for she had been using brief sentences since approximately the age of two, but rather that Merry talked to herself when she played and did not seem to converse with anyone else. She repeated words over and over in sing-song fashion, and did not seem to pay attention to what other people said. In fact, Merry's parents had suspected that she might be hard of hearing, but an examination by the pediatrician had revealed no auditory defect. Furthermore, Merry had not responded to efforts to toilet-train her until age three and continued at age four to have "accidents" during the day and to wet the bed at night. This rather puzzled Mrs. L. since, in other ways, Merry seemed excessively concerned with neatness and would become almost panic-stricken if she got her hands dirty or if something were spilled or dropped. Otherwise, in Mrs. L.'s eyes, Merry seemed to be an ideal child. She was quite independent; she seemed to be able to get many of the things she wanted and seldom was any bother to her mother or others. Although occasionally she would inexplicably burst into tears, she was comforted easily with some favorite doll or her blanket. She had several such objects, the favorite of which was a small blanket, but she was also very attached to a hair brush which she had brought home from her grandmother's, and a couple of small stuffed animals which were always in her bed or crib. To illustrate how "well behaved" Merry could be, Mrs. L. cited an incident of the previous New Year's Day: she and her husband had been out most of the night before and when she awakened the next afternoon, Mrs. L. suddenly realized that Merry had not been fed or taken care of in any way. To her surprise she discovered Merry at the other end of the house by herself in her play pen; in the kitchen was evidence that Merry had helped herself to cereal and milk. Merry seemed undisturbed by the fact that her parents had slept through most of the day.

Merry knew how to feed herself fairly well and even was quite independent in bathing herself. However, a great deal of Merry's care was given over to a Negro housekeeper, who usually fed and bathed Merry, and, if the parents were not home in the evening, saw that Merry got to bed. Mrs. L. thought that perhaps some of Merry's slow development was due to the fact that there were no other children her age in the immediate neighborhood with whom she could play. She had hoped to put Merry into a nursery school class, feeling that the example of the other children would be helpful, but the nursery school would not accept Merry until she was completely toilet-trained.

Petite, blonde, blue-eyed, and dressed in an immaculate crinoline skirt which stuck out stiffly, revealing several petticoats underneath, and wearing patent leather shoes, Merry looked like a very beautiful little doll. During the interview with her mother, Merry at first clung to her mother's coat, but Mrs. L. pushed her toward another chair. Merry promptly climbed up and knelt on the chair, facing away from her mother and the examiner. There she stayed for the entire hour of the interview, rocking up and down, rhythmic fashion, and making small cooing noises to herself. Mrs. L. paid no attention to Merry throughout the interview. At the end of the hour, when the examiner asked to see Merry in the playroom, Mrs. L. spoke to Merry, but

Merry did not move. Merry looked up when Mrs. L. touched her, but did not respond to Mrs. L.'s introduction to the doctor. The examiner reached out his hand and Merry took it and followed him down the hall for a short distance. She did not look at the examiner but seemed to be staring at the ceiling. She walked on her tiptoes in an odd dancing fashion. Finally, she broke loose from the examiner's hand and began to whirl around in large circles, up and down the hall, still on her tiptoes. When the examiner neared her and reached out his hand, she again grasped it and then clung to him for a moment, all the time silent. She permitted herself to be led into the playroom, where she once more whirled about the room for a few moments. She did not respond to the examiner's directions or voice, and seemed to be almost unaware that he was in the room. Finally she stopped in the corner and began to repeat the cooing noises that she had made previously. Occasionally there would be words interjected in these noises, which would be repeated over and over again. Only two of these words were distinguishable; the first was "darling," and the second was her name. She did not respond to any offers to play with the toys nor otherwise pay any attention to the examiner. However, if the examiner came close to her, she would move to another part of the room. She began to move her hand up and down in front of her face, sometimes touching various parts of her body. Finally she crouched in the opposite corner from the examiner and began rocking back and forth. She permitted the examiner to come closer to her and sit down beside her. When she was touched, she reached out her hand and rose to her feet as if expecting to be led from the room. Taken back to her mother, she continued to gesture in front of her face and make her cooing noises as she left the clinic.

Prior History. Mrs. L. reported that her pregnancy with Merry had been entirely uneventful. She mentioned that she had been very pleased since she had gained very little weight during this pregnancy and had been able to continue her work as a model in a dress shop until the last three months. Even during these final three months, she had continued to work as a saleslady in the office. Merry's birth was without complication; Mrs. L.'s labor was quite brief and parturition was achieved with only an ordinary anesthesia. Although, as far as could be determined, the pregnancy had lasted nine months,

Merry, who weighed less than four pounds at birth, was considered "premature" and was put in an incubator for five days.

Mrs. L. left the hospital before Merry but fell ill shortly thereafter and returned to the hospital again, remaining in the hospital for three months. At first, she passed over the details of this illness, saying that she had a mild, but persistent fever of unknown origin. Later, however, she admitted that she had had "a nervous breakdown," and had been treated with electric shock. She claimed that the electric shock had erased from her memory her feelings and experiences during this "nervous breakdown," but agreed that perhaps she had been quite depressed. During this interval, Merry remained in the hospital for another month and was then sent home in the care of a practical nurse. When Mrs. L. returned home from her hospitalization, she was still too weak to care for Merry. It was difficult to find a permanent nursemaid and there was a succession of people taking care of the child. Mrs. L. reported with pride that Merry seldom cried; she would lie for hours in her crib often without moving. However, she readily adapted to a routine feeding. Mrs. L. never did breast-feed Merry, partly because a special formula was recommended to help Merry gain weight, and secondly because, after she returned home, she had no lactation. All in all, she could recall very little about Merry's development during the first two years of her life. She could not remember when Merry sat up or began to stand. Merry did seem quite different from her eight-year-old brother, Mark, in that Merry lay so inert in her playpen. She remembered Mark as climbing out of the playpen and getting "into everything." She described Mark as making many more demands upon her for attention. She went on to describe how Mark was a very cuddly baby whom she loved to hold. On the other hand, she remarked, "Sometimes I would just forget for the whole day that Merry was there."

THE MOTHER. Mrs. L., age twenty-eight, was a beautiful, shapely, blonde, chic in dress and appearance. As she sat, she seemed to pose in the chair in a slightly seductive fashion. She wore a slight, set smile as if it were part of her stylish costume and lacquered coiffure. About the only change in her facial expression occurred when she began to talk about some of her own personal problems—then her smile changed to a pout.

Prefacing her remarks with a denial that she had any difficulties in adjustment, Mrs. L. seemed to enjoy talking about her background. She was an only child. Her father had deserted her mother soon after Mrs. L.'s birth, and her mother was forced to work to support them. In her early years, Mrs. L. was cared for by her maternal grandmother, whom she remembered with considerable fondness. There was more than occasional dissension between her mother and grandmother, as her grandmother repetitiously insisted that she had warned Mrs. L.'s mother about her father's unreliability before they were ever married. Mrs. L.'s mother did not deny her mother's accusations against Mrs. L.'s father, but resented being reminded of her marital mistake. Mrs. L.'s mother also tried to quiet the grandmother, saying that this topic should not be "brought up in front of the child." Mrs. L. was quite curious about her father, but her grandmother would tell her nothing about him, saying only that she hoped that Mrs. L. never made such a mistake. In Mrs. L.'s words, her mother "devoted her life to me," providing "everything that I ever wanted." Although they were not well-to-do, Mrs. L. always had all the playthings and all the clothes that she ever needed. As a dressmaker, Mrs. L.'s mother was able to provide the finest clothes for Mrs. L. She also began music lessons and dancing lessons for her at an early age. Mrs. L.'s mother was disappointed when Mrs. L. did not turn out to be talented; about the only frustration Mrs. L. could remember in her childhood was the many long hours of practicing her piano or ballet lessons. Otherwise, she said her childhod was quite happy. She made average to above-average grades in school and had many playmates. In junior high and high school, she was quite popular, went to many parties, and always had dates.

Both her mother and grandmother continually warned her in rather vague terms about "watching herself" with boys. She laughed, as she remembered feeling guilty when she was first kissed by a boy at age fourteen. However, despite her mother's warning, she began to pet heavily on her dates and had her first sexual experience at age sixteen. She completed high school at age seventeen, took a brief course in modeling clothes, and obtained a job as a model. She met her husband shortly thereafter and became pregnant by him at age nineteen. Her mother and grandmother were very upset but became mollified by the fact that her husband came from a wealthy family and that his parents agreed to their marriage. Her husband was one of the most handsome boys in the high school class, a basketball star, and one of the top students. His father was a leading physician in the community, and it was he who paid for the extravagant and elaborate wedding. Although Mrs. L. felt a little uncomfortable about the fact that she was pregnant at the time of the wedding, she had gained no noticeable weight and she believed that no one, other than her immediate family, was aware of the pregnancy. It was understood that her husband's plan to go on to university and medical school was not to be interrupted and her father-in-law agreed to pay for his education. She saw little of her in-laws as they never invited her over or spoke to her. Her father-in-law occasionally dropped by their apartment, but only to make financial arrangements with her husband. During her ensuing pregnancy with Mark, she suffered considerable illness, with continual nausea and vomiting. She also had prolonged labor and continued to be weak and depressed after Mark's birth. Nevertheless Mark seemed to be a healthy baby and she enjoyed caring for him and devoted a great deal of attention to him. During the next eight years, Mr. L. was forced to devote all of his energies to his studies and there was little opportunity for them to have a good time, to do much together, or to go anywhere. However, having a baby to care for at least partially compensated Mrs. L. for the isolation from her husband. She also spent considerable time visiting her mother and grandmother.

The year before Merry's birth, her grandmother died. Mrs. L. was again depressed and her depression seemed to increase when, six months later, her mother remarried. She denied that she was disappointed that her mother was not near her when she became pregnant and gave birth to Merry, saying that since she had been through this once before with Mark and since Merry's birth was so easy, she really did not miss her mother. When Mrs. L. was asked about the aspects of her environment which could have produced her nervous breakdown following Merry's birth, she smiled wanly, remarked again that she did not know the nature of this "nervous breakdown," and said she regarded the whole incident as unimportant and probably merely resulting from fatigue.

Soon after recovering from this "nervous breakdown," Mrs. L. decided to go back to work and had been steadily employed nearly ever since. She hired a nursemaid to care for Merry, and Mark was enrolled in a private school, where he stayed most of the day. There were frequent changes in nursemaids, probably because Mrs. L. expected them to do all of the housework in addition to caring for Merry. She expressed considerable dissatisfaction with these maids, complaining that they were sloppy and disobedient. Critical as she was about their inability to keep the house exactly as she required, she made no mention about their care for Merry. Exactly why she decided to go to work at this time was not clear, except that she had enjoyed her work as a model and had, for a long time, been determined to return to it. This decision seemed even more inexplicable because by this time Dr. L. had completed his medical training and was beginning his practice. Thus, their income no longer depended upon the father-in-law and was much larger than it had been throughout the previous nine years of their marriage.

Regarding their marriage, Mrs. L. maintained that she and her husband had an ideal relationship. Although he had seldom been free from his studies, whenever they did have a little money he would make sure that they went someplace together. He was always buying her little presents, and encouraged her to buy the clothes that she wanted, and praised her for her beauty and taste. She did intimate that she had hoped that when he finished his medical education they would have a great deal more time together, but while building up his practice he had many night calls, was off early in the morning for operating schedules, and seldom seemed to be available for personal contact, let alone social activity. She might not see him from morning to night. They used to play golf together but since he began his practice they did not have the same day off. She expressed considerable annoyance with his friends, since all they talked about was medicine and she could not endure the wives of the other physicians. She considered them all snobs who talked about nothing but their husbands and children. Asked about her sexual relations with her husband, she responded with her oft-repeated "wonderful" and declined to discuss the topic further.

THE FATHER. Doctor L. was a tall, blondish man with an athletic build. He expressed considerable willingness to come in and discuss his daughter's condition, but it proved difficult to arrange an appointment because of his busy schedule. When he finally came, he seemed quite relaxed and jovial, in an expansive mood. Offering the therapist a cigar, he proceeded to describe his daughter and wife as if they were cases of his own he was discussing with a colleague. He began by stating, with a laugh, that he was afraid he was a very poor informant since, because of his extremely busy practice he was not home enough to really say much about Merry's development, and "I don't even know what my wife is up to these days." He said that he also had been unaware that Merry presented any particular difficulties until he was advised of it by their pediatrician. Even then he was inclined to disregard the pediatrician's advice because "All of us knew that this guy is off on a psychiatric jag in his ideas." However, he did observe that Merry seemed somewhat slow in development and that many of her mannerisms were annoying to him. He had one of his colleagues in neurology examine her, but there were no findings indicative of any neurological defects and her electro-encephalographic record was normal for this age. His colleague also advised that Merry's difficulty was probably some sort of emotional disturbance, which Dr. L. said that he accepted although he could not immediately see what the nature of the disturbance was or the possible causes of it.

With only slightly more questioning, Dr. L. began to express considerable dissatisfaction with his wife. He started by saying that he now realized that, in many ways, she did not seem to be "well-adapted to being a mother." He felt that she was very unhappy with her first pregnancy with Mark, that she continually complained that Dr. L. had ruined her life, and, to this date, really never let him forget that their marriage had been forced by the fact of her pregnancy. In neither her pregnancy with Mark nor with Merry had Mrs. L. worn maternity clothes and, indeed, Dr. L. had been concerned because Mrs. L. had made many efforts to hide the fact of her pregnancy by wearing tight undergarments and by going on a much more severe diet than was recommended by the obstetrician. During her pregnancy with Merry, Mrs. L. ate almost nothing, to the point that she was often weak and he feared she would become anemic. She appeared extremely tense during her pregnancy with Merry. Since she was always on edge, he constantly had to avoid upsetting her. "We never really quarrel, but that's only because I shut up and get out of the way." When asked about Mrs. L.'s "nervous breakdown" following Merry's birth, Dr. L. said that she had been extremely depressed, unable to talk to anyone, and wept constantly. She was hospitalized in a private sanitarium and given a brief series of electric shock treatments. Following these treatments she improved rapidly but seemed to have no memory of her experience. He could not account for her depression, adding with a laugh, "There's a great deal I cannot account for in my wife's behavior." Questioned further about their marital relationship, Dr. L. became a little sad and said that originally he had been very much in love with his wife and considered himself extremely lucky to have had such a very beautiful "doll," but things had really not turned out as well as he had hoped. He said that he himself felt somewhat guilty in that he had devoted so much of his time to his studies and had so little time for his wife. On the other hand, he felt she always seemed extremely wrapped up in herself and her own needs, and had really never understood his educational or vocational goals. He agreed she seemed "attracted to" Mark when he was a baby and had attempted to take care of Mark, but that this seemed to be largely a matter of "pride in her production"; when Mark grew into "a naughty little boy" she quickly made plans to put him into a day school. He did not believe that she wanted to have any more children after Mark's birth since she so resented being pregnant. Their sexual relations had never been very frequent and never really satisfying to either of them. He was very surprised when she became pregnant with Merry since he thought that she was preventing pregnancy by use of contraceptives. Since Merry's birth, sexual relations between them had been almost nonexistent. He agreed that he felt extremely frustrated and often wondered if their marriage was going to continue. He hinted that he found his sexual satisfaction outside of marriage, but when questioned on this, laughed, held his hands up in front of his fact, and protested that he saw no connection between Merry's disturbance and his own sexual problem.

Course in Treatment. Merry was placed in a psychiatrically oriented nursery school which she attended daily for a two-hour period along with other children of her age who had similar disturbances. In this setting, the teacher, a person specially trained in work with emotionally disturbed preschool children, directed her efforts chiefly toward helping Merry to find a relaxed atmosphere in which it was hoped that she could establish emotional relationships with others. At the same time, Mrs. L. was seen in individual, periodic interviews with the psychologist and attended a group discussion with other mothers whose children were in the nursery school. In the individual interviews Mrs. L. spent most of her time reporting on Merry's current behavior at home and resisted any attempts to encourage her to talk about herself or her own feelings. In the group, she sat silent, posed, and staring straight ahead. She protested that she got nothing out of the group discussions. Often she missed these sessions or came quite late. Several times, the other women in the group remarked on her silence and one woman in particular, kept remarking that she did not understand how anyone who seemed as poised, calm, and beautiful as Mrs. L. could possibly have a child that was disturbed. This remark did not seem to faze Mrs. L.

Merry very gradually became more and more attached to the teacher. At first there was little change in her behavior in the nursery school playroom; she stuck to her own corner, continuing her gestures and noises. From time to time, however, she began to accept things from the teacher or bring over toys to show the teacher, but would permit very little interaction with the teacher or with the other children. She became attracted by the teacher's coat and loved to sit and rub the teacher's coat or the teacher's arm. At first she seemed unwilling to handle any of the materials which would at all soil her hands or her clothes, but one day she became fascinated by the sandbox and, thereafter, seemed almost to enjoy getting messed up, much to the annoyance of her mother. The teacher encouraged Mrs. L. to dress Merry in playclothes, to which Mrs. L. finally acceded. Then Merry seemed a little more relaxed and willing to paint or play with the toys in the yard. After approximately three months, Merry seemed to be running and playing fairly well, although she remained verbally uncommunicative. Her rocking and whirling behavior was much less frequent.

About this time, Dr. L. called to report that his wife had disappeared and had notified him that she was in Las Vegas to obtain a divorce. He would not discuss the conditions of the break-up of their marriage but seemed relatively cheerful. He requested that Merry be continued in the playschool, but said that he did not have time to come in and discuss Merry's behavior, suggesting that perhaps the maid would be a better informant. Although the clinic felt that, under these conditions, it was improbable that Merry would continue to progress, they saw no other possibilities and agreed to continue Merry in the nursery school.

During the following several months Merry reverted to much of the behavior she had shown when she began treatment. Dr. L. was called in for an interview and advised that it was quite probable that Merry would need hospitalization. Again, he begged that the clinic continue to work with Merry, saying that the only progress he had ever seen in her development had occurred during Merry's stay there. He agreed that Merry's relapse probably was related to the fact that her mother had left, but said that he hoped to rectify the situation soon as he planned to marry again. A week later he called and asked for a further interview and requested that his fiancée be seen also. The second Mrs. L., who looked very much like Merry's own mother, had previously been the nurse in Dr. L.'s office. She expressed considerable interest in Merry, saying that she had discussed the situation with Dr. L. and that she planned to take an active part in Merry's treatment and rehabilitation. Dr. L. remarried within the month after the divorce and Merry's stepmother began to attend the mothers' group. She had left her job and stayed at home caring for Merry and Mark. She often came and observed Merry in the playroom along with the teacher. She seemed to be a fairly warm-hearted woman who was quite disturbed at first over Merry's behavior and puzzled by it. During the group sessions, she expressed her feelings of uneasiness about taking over the care of the children of her husband's previous wife, but apparently was quite attracted by Merry and determined to help out with Merry's recovery, motivated by her devotion to her new husband. Very gradually Merry seemed to accept her stepmother and a second period of improvement in Merry's behavior ensued. At the end of a year and a half, Merry was playing quite actively, talking a little bit, and showed very few of her old mannerisms. It was agreed to try Merry in a public kindergarten, continuing the nursery school treatment in the afternoon. Merry's problem was discussed briefly with the kindergarten teacher and she was accepted. Her interaction with the other children, at nursery school and the kindergarten increased markedly during her year at kindergarten. She remained a silent and somewhat withdrawn child but was able to start school at age six in the first grade. At this point her attendance at nursery school was dropped.

Questions for Merry L.

1. What aspects of Merry's early development appear unusual according to any set of developmental norms? Group these deviant trends according to the following categories:

    a. motor development

    b. development of personal habits

    c. responses to people in her environment

    d. verbal development.

2. What aspects of Merry's early life, particularly during the first year, could provide a fertile ground for learning each of these categories of behavior?

3. Which categories of behavior listed in response to question 1 do not seem to follow from the pattern of Merry's early environment? How might we account for the appearance of these other classes of behavior?

4. What needs and conflicts present in Merry's parents made it difficult for them to perform their parental roles comfortably? In particular, what aspects of Mrs. L.'s early life situation set up conditions which made it difficult for her to assume the role of the mother?

5. How can one account for the fact that one child in this family was ostensibly normal and the other seriously emotionally disturbed?

6. Escalona (ref. 4) has suggested, on the basis of her research with children like Merry, that at times, we may be confusing cause and effect in understanding this type of child. Her research indicates that children like Merry are deviant from birth and that much of the parent-child friction grows out of the parents' frustration in not receiving the normal response that they need from a child. What support for this point of view is present in the case of Merry? How would you reconcile Escalona's point of view with the changes shown by Merry in the preschool?

7. In studying this case, what questions arise in your mind that you would like to see attacked by research? List these questions and summarize how we might go about finding the answers to them. (Don't let your lack of experience hinder you!)

References

EISENBERG, L. The autistic child in adolescence. *American Journal of Psychiatry*, 1956. (Also reprinted in REED, C. F., ALEXANDER, E. E., & TOMPKINS, S. S., *Psychopathology*, Cambridge: Harvard Univer. Press, 1958. Pp. 15–24.

EISENBERG, L., & KANNER, L. Early infantile autism—1943–1955. *American Journal of Orthopsychiatry*, 1956. (Also reprinted in REED, C. F., ALEXANDER, I. E., & TOMPKINS, S. S., *Psychopathology*, Cambridge: Harvard Univer. Press, 1958. Pp. 3–14.)

ESCALONA, SIBYLLE. Some considerations regarding psychotherapy, with psychotic children. *Bulletin of the Menninger Clinic*, 1948, **12**: 127–134.

GOLDFARB, W. Effects of psychological deprivation in infancy and subsequent stimulation. *American Journal of Psychiatry*, 1945, **102**: 18–33.

SPITZ, R. A., & WOLF, K. M. Anaclitic depression: an inquiry into the genesis of psychiatric conditions in early childhood. *The psychoanalytic study of the child*, Vol. II. 1946. Pp. 313–342.

THOMPSON, W. R., & HERON, W. Effects of restriction early in life on problem solving in dogs. *Canadian Journal of Psychology*, 1954, **8**: 17–31.

THE CASE OF OLIVER N.

Child of the Follies

Except for his incipient baldness, Oliver N. gave the impression in appearance of an overdressed, old-fashioned little boy, rather than a man of thirty. He was of slight build, scarcely over five feet in height; his thinning, sandy hair was slicked back from his receding forehead; and he was dressed in a neatly pressed but well-worn blue serge suit, a stiffly starched white shirt, and an outsized striped tie. He sat tensely upright on the front of the chair, his lips pursed, and his palms perspiring. His voice was high-pitched and he spoke in a hesitant fashion, although he seemed impelled to talk. He was obsequious in manner, always addressing the examiner as "sir," and apologizing for taking up so much of the examiner's time.

Oliver N. began by stating that he had been very tense and nervous for many years, and, at various times, he had sought psychiatric consultation. However, he had never been in a position to maintain extended treatment. He asked hopefully if psychotherapy would be available to him at the clinic. When asked the reason for his coming to the clinic at this time, he explained that it was on the instigation of his attorney, since he found himself in a "slight jam." He hurriedly explained that for the past ten years he had been able to alleviate his feelings of overwhelming tension through use of a commercial drug which he could purchase over the counter at the "chemist's shop" in Canada where he had been living. Since his return to the United States several months ago, he had not been able to purchase this particular drug as it proved to be a barbiturate available only on a physician's prescription. The several physicians whom he had consulted had refused to prescribe such a barbiturate for nervous tension. Oliver N. complained that the milder tranquilizers which were prescribed for him gave him little relief. A few weeks ago he had made the acquaintance of a woman who told him she had formerly been a nurse; she had given him some "little white pills" which he found more effective. Two days prior to his first visit to the clinic, Oliver N. was arrested for the possession of narcotics. Oliver N. was very upset by this arrest, claiming that he had always been very law-abiding; in fact he had never been arrested before in his life. He considered the whole affair as "one of those mistakes"; once the court heard his explanation, he felt sure that the case would be dismissed.

Further questioning of the patient revealed the following circumstances regarding his arrest: Oliver N. had been unable to find employment since his return to the United States, and this added to his tension. Although he denied that he had ever used alcohol at all before, Oliver N. discovered that sweet wine made him relax. With increasing frequency he started drinking wine earlier in the day, so that for the balance of the day he would be in a benign haze. On the day of his arrest he had been job-hunting most of the morning, without success. He then returned home, and, carefully avoiding his parents, he stayed in his room where he consumed a fifth of muscatel. Around six in the evening he awoke to find that he had a violent headache. Also, he had feelings of nausea which he tried to counteract by consuming more wine. He was too embarrassed to go to dinner with his family, so he left the house and wandered the streets for a while. He then remembered that he had agreed to attend a prayer meeting of the Pentacostal sect with which he had recently become affiliated—also in the hopes of finding some release for his tension. He recognized the fact that his semi-inebriated state would not be appropriate at this prayer meeting, but, nevertheless, he decided to attend, hoping to find some solution for his difficulties. He believed that his drunken condition was not noticeable to his friends at the church. However, instead of experiencing relief, Oliver N. found himself growing more and more uneasy. He became fearful that he might say something which would shock the congregation, although he could not remember what he might have had in mind. He then left the meeting and sat in a park where he consumed some more wine. Shortly afterwards he found himself talking to "a very nice man" who turned out to be a plain-clothes policeman. He spent the night in the city jail; the following morning his father came to bail him out.

As the interview proceeded, Oliver N. became increasingly vague about the current incident in which he was involved. Also, in giving his life history, he seemed mildly confused, skipping from topic to topic, indefinite as to the sequence of events or even his age when certain things happened. He seemed anxious to answer the questions completely and honestly, yet he often hesitated; he sounded puzzled and began to talk about other unrelated topics. He volunteered that his attorney would probably be of more help in ascertaining the facts regarding his legal status. He himself was not clear regarding the charges which he faced in court. It was suggested to him, therefore, that he have his attorney call the clinic. Since he could not remember much about his early childhood or even his adolescence, it was also suggested that his parents come to the clinic. Later that day, at the patient's instigation, his attorney called. He stated that the initial charge for the arrest was that the patient had made "lewd and lascivious" suggestions to the plain-clothesman, which was a felony under the laws of the state. In a "shakedown" search of the patient at the time of the arrest, it was discovered that he was in possession of a tranquilizing drug which was obtainable only upon a physician's prescription. The patient had admitted that he had obtained it from his girl friend. Both the court and the law enforcement authorities took into consideration the emotional condition of the patient and, in view of the fact that he had no previous court record, accepted the attorney's argument that the charges should be reduced to the misdemeanor of being drunk in a public place. Oliver N.'s attorney was of the opinion that, at the time of trial, the court would probably grant probation on the condition that the patient seek psychiatric help. The attorney further advised that, as far as he could ascertain, neither the patient nor his parents had funds for private psychiatric care and that it would be necessary for the patient to receive help through a public clinic. The attorney himself was a court-appointed defender from the Legal Aid Society.

Within twenty-four hours, the patient called, even more anxious than before. After thanking the intake-worker effusively for talking with his attorney, he requested with some urgency an appointment for his parents, who were interviewed several days later. The elder Mr. N. looked very much like the patient—indeed, could be taken for his older brother. Although considerably balder than the patient, he showed few effects of aging and appeared much younger than his stated age of sixty-eight. He volunteered little during the interview, seemingly content to let his wife do most of the talking. The patient's mother, although the same age as her husband, was still a strikingly beautiful woman. In contrast to the shabby dress of her son and husband, she was attired in what must have been a rather expensive suit in the latest style, with purse, gloves, shoes, and costume jewelry to match. Her face was relatively unlined and her make-up, although theatrical, indicated considerable care for her appearance. The only sign of age was her snow-white hair, immaculately arranged as if she came directly from the hairdresser. Both parents seemed unaware of the nature of the incident in which the patient had been involved. They regarded the charges as an error in the law and believed that the patient's only mistake was in trying to obtain the medication. The patient's father vaguely agreed that perhaps the patient did need some kind of psychiatric care, saying, "Oliver has always been a nervous boy." Mrs. N. was much more definite about Oliver's condition and his background. However, she made it very clear that she resented the intrusion of her family privacy and that she had come to the clinic only because the attorney had advised her to do so. She did agree that many times in the past she had thought that Oliver was in need of some medical help, perhaps psychiatric, but that she herself did not want to be involved in it, nor did she feel that the personal history requested was really necessary. Her general attitude was that Oliver had gotten himself into this trouble and that he was responsible for getting himself out of it. She demanded to know how long the interview would take, explaining that she had another appointment that morning. As the interview progressed and she became more irritable, she pointed out that Oliver had been in trouble before and that she was about fed up with it.

Past History. Mrs. N. began by stating rather proudly that this year she and her husband were celebrating the fiftieth anniversary of their careers in show business. Mrs. N. had once been a Ziegfeld Follies Girl and her husband one of the comedians in the Follies. Both came from theatrical families and had been in show business all their lives. They were married when they were eighteen, and a daughter was born the year after. Mrs. N. said proudly that she managed to return to the stage almost immediately after her daughter's birth. Her career was phenomenal, and soon she became a "Music Hall Star" and leading lady in several comedies during the 1920's.

Her husband became her business manager. In later years the couple worked in vaudeville and then U.S.O. stage shows during World War II, and even recently obtained occasional bit parts in the movies and on television. "We were on the top of the heap when we got Oliver," said Mrs. N. Asked what she meant by ". . . we got Oliver," she smiled sardonically and looked at her husband. Mr. N. said quickly, "when Oliver was born." When asked about the conditions of Oliver's birth and infancy, Mrs. N. was a little vague and avoided the question. Finally, when she was pressed, she looked at her husband and said, "I don't care what you think, I'm going to tell the truth." She explained that her husband had long wanted a son but that she did not want any more children, since she felt they interfered with her career. The year prior to Oliver's birth the N.'s had separated, partly because of business disagreements but basically because of Mr. N.'s discontent with their lack of real family life. Their daughter had been in private schools or with other people who cared for her throughout most of her childhood. During their separation Mr. N. had an affair with a younger woman who was Mrs. N.'s protégé. Oliver was the son of this other woman, who died in childbirth. The N.'s reconciled soon after this incident, and Mrs. N. agreed to her husband's request to keep Oliver and to rear him as their son. Mr. N. added quickly that they had never told Oliver of this situation and fervently begged that he not be told at this time. His wife disagreed, saying that he should have been told many years before. She said that she believed that this family secret might be one of the causes of Oliver's disturbance, although she had no definite proof.

Despite Mr. N.'s hopes, the informal adoption of Oliver did not create a settled home life for the N.'s. They continued to live in hotel rooms or one-room apartments, moving frequently, as Mrs. N. was usually in a road show. This nomadic life continued for the next twenty years until the family ended up in western Canada about ten years ago. Mrs. N. never assumed any maternal role. Indeed, Oliver always referred to his mother as "Lily," although he spoke of his father as "Dad." All of the care of Oliver as an infant was left to his father. The conditions of Oliver's birth were unknown to the N.'s. As far as they knew, he was in good health at the time they began taking care of him, which was three months after his birth. Until then he had remained in the County Hospital on the infant ward. Mr. N. described him as a very good child "who absolutely never

cried." In Mrs. N.'s words, "He was a doll." Mr. N. fed, bathed, and
diapered the baby. He could not remember much of the details of
Oliver's development during the first year or two. When asked about
feeding Oliver, he described with pride how he had invented a wire
tripod which held the bottle to the baby's face so that Oliver could
nurse from the bottle at any time he wished, whether or not the parents were present. Neither of the N.'s could remember when Oliver
began to walk, talk, or when he was toilet-trained. However, much
of this must have been accomplished by the time Oliver was two
since the N.'s remembered losing all of their possessions, including
Oliver's baby clothes, crib, and so forth, in a hotel fire about that
time. After that they did not bother to buy another baby bed but
took the two-year-old into their own bed, where he continued to
sleep throughout his childhood. He did not soil himself either during the day or at night from that time on. Mrs. N. described Oliver as
a real "trouper," denying that their traveling about caused any in-
convenience to the child, nor he to them. They usually ate their
meals out or in a boarding house. Mrs. N. laughingly remembered
Oliver's first words as "coffee shop." Although Oliver was never
really under a doctor's care, he was described by his parents as always being a sickly child. He had a constant cough most of his childhood, which Mr. N. doctored with various patent medicines. His appetite was poor and he was always underweight. Mrs. N. labeled
her husband "a fussy old mother," who was always worrying over
Oliver's appetite or trying out a different cough syrup on the child.
She complained that Oliver wheezed when he breathed, which disturbed her sleep.

As far as could be ascertained, Oliver's childhood must have been
an extremely lonely one. The N.'s had no close friends with children,
nor did they have any relatives. Oliver's world must have consisted
largely of the four walls of the hotel room, with an occasional visit to
the lobby and coffee shop. Oliver's own earliest memory was of the
enjoyment of being taken to the zoo by his father. His other memory
is of being awake for an entire three days and nights traveling in the
train coaches from one end of the country to the other. Train rides
made him ill and he spent much of his time in the restroom, nauseous and vomiting. Every time his mother's show moved from one
town to another, Oliver would become apprehensive about the prospect of another train trip. Oliver remembered seeing a large poster

describing his mother as an exotic dancer, which he later realized meant that she was the star in a burlesque show. He also remembered hurried exits down the back stairs of a hotel, in order to avoid paying the bill. As might be expected, Oliver's education was "catch as catch can." Seldom did he have the opportunity to finish a whole semester at one school. Mr. N. said defensively that he had been Oliver's teacher and that Oliver was a very bright boy and an apt pupil. He claimed that Oliver was able to pass his examinations in any school which he attended. Oliver, however, admitted that he was a very poor student, that he hated school, and often failed to attend when his parents thought he was in school. Oliver loved to hang around the theater when his mother was performing. He helped out with the costuming and the stage setting. His mother boasted how he became very expert in helping her dress and putting on her make-up and giving her her cues. "All the girls loved Oliver," she said.

Asked about Oliver's sexual development, the N.'s became very defensive. Mr. N. again repeated his frequent phrase, "Oliver was always a good boy." Asked what preparation on sex they gave their son, Mrs. N. went into a long explanation of life in the theater. She pointed out that, contrary to the general public's opinion of the theater, show people were actually very proper in their sexual behavior. "On the other hand," she said, "no one is ashamed of his body." She said that she felt that there was very little that one had to teach Oliver; he was in and around women's dressing rooms and that it was all very natural. Mr. N. agreed and said that the only thing he remembered explaining to Oliver was that Oliver should avoid being mixed up with any of the "fags," i.e. homosexuals, who hung around the edge of the theatrical business as costumers, stage hands, or other service people.

Asked about Oliver's nervousness, the N.'s explained that he had always been "a sensitive child" who was upset by any little thing. He would easily become tearful, uneasy, or excited, and it was often difficult to get him to sleep. As early as Oliver's infancy his father started to give him a sleeping pill, not only to get him to sleep but also to try to alleviate his night-time wheezing. Oliver remembered that during his childhood his father would frequently give him some medication to quiet his nerves. Oliver first visited a psychiatrist at the age of seventeen because he had become involved in an incident similar to the one which brought him to this clinic currently. Neither he nor his parents could remember the exact details; he had been arrested allegedly for wandering into a strange home where he surprised a woman who was taking a shower. He was accused by the woman of an attempt to molest her sexually, but Oliver denied this. He claimed that he had been ill, and that he had been wandering about on a cold night and accidentally walked into the wrong house. This incident upset the N.'s and made them realize that possibly something was wrong with Oliver. They did not continue with the psychiatric care ordered by the court at that time; instead, they shipped him off to live with his sister, seventeen years his senior, who was married and living in Florida. Oliver had seen his sister only once or twice in his entire life. This arrangement lasted only a couple of months; his sister complained that Oliver had "nasty habits," and that she did not want him around her children. Asked about his own sexual behavior, Oliver denied that he had had any sexual experiences, but, under direct questioning, admitted that he had masturbated frequently since childhood. He had had one or two experiences with prostitutes, but said they had been entirely unsatisfactory to him. During his adolescence he had had no girl friends, because the family never stayed in any location long enough for him to know any girls. His mother denied that he had ever shown any interest in girls.

When Oliver was approximately twenty, the N.'s settled fairly permanently in a small city in western Canada. Mrs. N. gave dancing lessons and she also had a radio program which together provided them with a meager living. Oliver and his father kept house and worked at odd jobs from time to time whenever they could find them. Here, as everywhere else, the family made very few friends and stayed much to themselves. They frequently moved within the city. Oliver claimed that he never had enough money to take a girl out on a date. His health continued to be poor, and much of his time and energy was spent in doctoring himself. "No one can be happy with bad nerves," he said.

Although Oliver claimed that the family left Canada to seek employment in the United States, Mrs. N. admitted that their exodus was precipitated by "another one of Oliver's screwball acts." He had been arrested for appearing nude in the public along with a large group of Dukhobors, a religious sect who rebelled against the social order by stripping off their clothes. Oliver was not actually a member of this religious group, and the N.'s were unaware that he had any association with them until the time of the arrest. This arrest was complicated by the fact that Oliver was already on probation for having allegedly exposed himself sexually to children. Again the N.'s protested that Oliver's behavior was misconstrued, claiming that he had merely had to go to the bathroom and had used a children's toilet at a public school. Asked if there had been other such incidents, Mr. N. denied it, but Mrs. N. reminded him that a few years prior to leaving Canada, Oliver had been accused of sexually molesting a neighbor girl whereupon he had to leave town for the following year to avoid prosecution. At this point of the interview, Mrs. N. began to upbraid her husband, claiming that it was his fault that Oliver had such a "twisted mind." She accused him of "bringing those magazines into our house," magazines which she claimed had many nude pictures in them and which she felt were "bad for a young man's mind." Mr. N. argued that these were not lewd magazines, but were part of a course in body-building to which Oliver had subscribed on his own initiative. During his early twenties Oliver had spent many hours exercising with barbells and other gymnastic equipment which he had purchased through the ads in these magazines. He had taken a course to be a masseur and also another to be a chiropractor, but he had failed the licensing examinations which were necessary prerequisites to practice either vocation. As discussion of Oliver's sexual behavior ensued, Mrs. N. became very upset, again blaming her husband, saying that if he had stayed out of trouble and never gotten mixed up with other women they would have never had Oliver in the first place.

In a subsequent interview, Oliver denied that he had ever been in any other trouble than the incident when he was seventeen. Regarding the Dukhobors, he claimed he was merely an observer and denied that he had been arrested. He became increasingly anxious during this interview, and so confused that further inquiry into the incidents related by his parents was curtailed.

Disposition. The probation officer at the court requested a report from the clinic. The court was advised that, due to a long waiting list at this clinic, no psychiatric treatment was immediately available for Oliver. The clinic was also of the opinion that he was motivated to seek help chiefly because he was under pressure from the court and under such circumstances it was unlikely that he would become involved in psychotherapy. The clinic attempted to get Oliver N. to accept hospitalization voluntarily in the state hospital, but both he and his parents rejected this advice. The clinic finally decided to accept Oliver for treatment and his name was put on a waiting list. Three months later when treatment became available, it was discovered that the N.'s had left town.

Questions for Oliver N.

1. Under what circumstances has Oliver usually sought psychiatric assistance?

2. What does your answer to question 1 tell us concerning Oliver's way of handling anxiety?

3. How does the use of drugs fit in with Oliver's mode of handling anxiety as outlined in your answer to question 2?

4. If Oliver were unable to obtain drugs for a prolonged period of time, what other types of symptoms would you anticipate?

5. What aspects of Oliver's behavior led you to predict the behaviors cited in your answer to question 4?

6. How would you characterize Oliver's sexual behavior and level of maturity?

7. Relate the following specifically to Oliver's sexual difficulties:
   a. the nomadic life which the family lived
   b. the fact that Oliver was cared for exclusively by his father
   c. Oliver's experiences around the theater when his mother was a performer

8. When you put together Oliver's social isolation, his sexual behavior, and his behavior in the interview, what three psychiatric diagnoses occur to you?

9. What evidence argues for each of the three and what contradictory evidence do we have for each diagnosis?

10. It is obvious that Oliver had a great many unpleasant experiences in his early life, but do you see any evidence for any positive factors which might have helped him to resist a complete breakdown up to the present?

11. Although Oliver's life and behavior were bizarre and seemingly out of the ordinary, at least two situations related to his adjustment are relatively common in our society today, especially among the lower socio-economic groups: (1) frequent changes in residence in search for employment, and (2) increasing participation of fathers in infant care when mothers are forced to become breadwinners. Discuss briefly what difficulties in personal adjustment these social situations might create for children. How might parents help children to adjust to such circumstances? What was the N.'s chief failure?

12. The type of social problem which Oliver represents is all too common, although the exact statistical frequency is difficult to estimate because such cases appear under different psychiatric diagnoses or legal categories of offenses. Although they appear in our prisons, probation lists, and even mental hospitals, they often seem outside the pale of either the law or psychiatry. Imagine yourself appointed by the governor of the state to a citizens' commission to study the social problems created by such persons. What social agencies, either already in existence or to be created, might you recommend as further assisting in the prevention of such problems, the rehabilitation of such persons, and in the protection of the community from the disturbances they create?

References

ARIETI, S. *The interpretation of schizophrenia.* New York: R. Brunner, 1955. Pp. 61–74, The schizoid personality.

BRANCALE, R., ELLIS, A., & DOORBAR, RUTH. Psychiatric and psychological investigations of convicted sexual offenders. *American Journal of Psychiatry,* 1952, 109: 17–21.

BOWEN, M. A family concept of schizophrenia. In JACKSON, D. D. (Ed.) *The etiology of schizophrenia.* New York: Basic Books, 1960.

KANT, O. Clinical investigations of simple schizophrenia. *Psychiatric Quarterly,* 1948, 22: 141–151.

KARPMEN, B., *The sexual offender and his offenses.* New York: Basic Books, 1954.

THE CASE OF DR. McD.

The Lonely Sex

Dr. McD., a 54-year-old, white, unmarried physician was originally admitted to the Veterans' Administration hospital in 1954. A major in the army reserve, Dr. McD. had re-entered active service in the Korean conflict as a lieutenant colonel. Soon after he had been placed in command of an overseas hospital, the War Department in Washington began to receive letters directly from him complaining of graft in both the American and Korean forces. Since these letters did not come through the usual "channels," an investigator from the Inspector General's office was assigned to his hospital. When evidence of this alleged graft was requested of Dr. McD., he presented the investigator with boxes containing slips of paper, most of which appeared to be laundry receipts or old prescriptions from his home town pharmacy. In addition, Dr McD. made rash accusations against many of his fellow officers and the United Nations command, intimating that many of the high command in Korea were actually on the side of the Communists. On the advice of the base psychiatrist, Dr. McD. was hospitalized in a psychiatric ward and given a medical discharge with the recommendation that he be immediately hospitalized in a veterans' hospital.

Although Dr. McD. protested what he regarded as the extreme injustice of this move, he did accept the hospitalization. At the time of this first admission to the V.A. hospital, Dr. McD. explained to the admitting physician that he regarded the entire war as a conflict between Christianity and Judaism and had accepted the hospitalization only because he felt he could better report to the proper authorities what he regarded as the machinations of Jewish psychiatry against the government.

At this time, Dr. McD. remained in the hospital approximately five months. However, he never assumed the role of a patient but continued to behave as a physician on the staff of a hospital. Thus, he refused to discuss any of his private life with any of the staff. Although at first he openly expressed his opinions regarding graft in Korea and the nature of the war, he gradually ceased to mention these ideas and subsequently denied them. Since he had been a fairly prominent physician in a nearby city, and a clinical instructor at the university, he succeeded in awing some of the younger staff, who found themselves being queried about their knowledge of medicine, defending themselves rather than investigating the patient's case. His overt and snide anti-Semitism also angered many of the staff members, both Jewish and Gentile. Many of the staff had had brief professional contact with him, but no one knew much about his personal life. As far back as anyone could remember, Dr. McD. had been regarded as an eccentric lone wolf. He never confided in anyone and seldom consulted with any of his colleagues on any case unless invited to do so by them. He never hesitated to air his views about psychiatry; he was quite critical of its tenets and enjoyed mocking psychiatry and psychiatrists to their faces. He said several times at public meetings that he regarded psychiatry as an extension of the Jewish faith. Only because of his brilliant record as a research worker and as a diagnostician had he been granted professional status within the medical community.

Dr. McD.'s ability to buffalo the hospital staff was furthered by his appearance and demeanor. Although a slightly built, gray-haired man, he had an erect military posture, and as he sat stiffly upright, his hands gripping the arms of the chair, he seemed to command the situation. His rimless spectacles and his tiny gray moustache seemed to add to the severity of his countenance. He was always impeccably dressed in his military uniform, with his brass buttons gleaming, and his shoes highly polished. (Hospital regulations prohibiting the wearing of military uniforms had been relaxed in this case, since Dr. McD. had brought no other clothes with him and he adamantly refused to wear hospital clothes.) Despite his grim appearance, he was always polite and overtly pleasant, albeit his smile seemed forced and artificial. He spoke slowly and precisely, in a modulated voice, even when expressing his most violent opinions or strongest protests against being hospitalized. Although he made what seemed to be rash accusations against other people, he remained overtly calm and reasonable.

Throughout this initial hospitalization, his attitude and behavior continued to annoy and upset the staff. He ordered the nurses and medical attendants about in an authoritative manner, to which they often responded in complaint fashion before they realized who was giving the commands. On several occasions he seated himself in the doctors' offices when no one was present and made notes in other patients' charts, prescribing medicine or other medical procedures. Because the hospital was large and many of the staff new, his orders were sometimes carried out. On most occasions his orders and prescriptions were innocuous or even appropriate. However, he also made bizarre entries into the chart which had nothing to do with the patient, such as the following:

> 3:00 a.m. Heard shots being fired at the back fence. This is obviously another case of failure on the part of the hospital administration. 5:00 a.m. I could not locate the body. 9:00 a.m. Freshly burned refuse in back of building 504. Contains what must be human bones. The administration has gotten rid of the evidence.

For the most part Dr. McD. was allowed full range of the hospital grounds. However, it was twice necessary to place him on a locked ward. Typically, he merely raged or threw objects such as shoes at patients whom he claimed were insulting him, but once he wrestled a much larger patient to the floor and was attempting to strangle him when attendants came into the room. Later he laughed off this incident as the kind of thing one might expect when one tried to protect oneself from psychotic patients. His second outburst occurred when the attending psychiatrist attempted to inquire into his sexual adjustment. Dr. McD. calmly responded that he believed his sexual adjustment was beyond question. He suggested that the psychiatrist might be sexually maladjusted since he knew that psychiatrists were particularly "sexually minded," and he had expected them to bring this question up. The same evening following this interview the patient disappeared from the ward and did not return until after midnight. When he returned he raged up and down the ward, disturbing everyone and finally had to be forcibly restrained and put in a private room for the night. The next morning he denied that his behavior had been in any way unusual, claiming that the night staff always made such accusations against him.

During the admission staff conference, a month after Dr. McD.

was admitted to the hospital, the staff discussed the patient's behavior, the difficulties which they had encountered in interviewing
him and finding out anything of his background, and their own reactions of frustration and anger in response to his resistance, his ar-
rogance, and his prejudiced social attitude. Under the circumstances,
it was agreed that direct exploration of the patient's anxieties and
personal life was futile, but that continued detailed notes on his behavior by the psychiatric nursing staff would be helpful in planning
hospital management. It was decided to accord him the deference
and respect which his status as a senior member of the medical pro-
fession would be granted, but to avoid, in as kindly a manner as possible, carrying out his orders and to prevent his gaining access to
medical charts. Because of his difficulties with other patients, he was
given a private but unlocked room. This approach to Dr. McD. was
reinforced by the clinical director who invited Dr. McD. to his office
"for a chat," asking whether there was anything else he needed and
offering his personal attention should Dr. McD. have any requests.
At the same time, the director explained to him that under the circumstances, it would not be possible for him to practice medicine
without a formal appointment to the staff, much as they appreciated
his efforts. Dr. McD. accepted this explanation in what appeared to
be a most co-operative and understanding attitude. However, when
the clinical director requested permission to meet with the patient's
sister (his only living relative), Dr. McD. demurred, explaining that
she was elderly and had been ill.

During the ensuing months, Dr. McD.'s stay in the hospital was
without incident. He accepted even the usual frustrations of daily
hospital routine with an imperturbable nonchalance. He avoided all
contact with other patients, remaining by himself in his room, or pac-
ing the perimeter of the hospital grounds alone. He made no effort
to order the nurses around, although his sharp commanding voice
continued to snap them to attention from time to time. He greeted
the medical staff in a friendly manner, stopping them to exchange the
time of day or to discuss articles he had been reading in his professional journals or in the medical library, to which the director had
granted him access. After four months he requested permission from
the director to visit his sister, which was granted. After the second
such visit, he informed the director that he believed he had "served
his time" and was ready to leave the hospital. The director agreed to

consider his request, but expressed the hope that, as his patient, Dr. McD. would accept his medical opinion. The next day, Dr. McD. was more demanding, and when the director recommended to him that he remain in the hospital, Dr. McD. argued that he was not legally committed and therefore could leave of his own volition. Agreeing that Dr. McD. had voluntarily committed himself, the director pointed out that if Dr. McD. left, it would be "against medical advice," and encouraged him to consider the matter further. Nevertheless, Dr. McD. immediately signed the formal papers requesting release from the hospital and, after the legally required wait of three days, he returned to his home.

Thirteen months later, Dr. McD. was involuntarily recommitted by the Superior Court on the petition of his sister. At the time of this readmission, Dr. McD. denied vigorously that there was anything wrong with him, and averred that his hospitalization was a plot by his sister and the government. Dr. McD.'s sister alleged that during this year his behavior had become increasingly bizarre, culminating in an attack on his Japanese houseboy, whom Dr. McD. accused of plotting to attack him in the near future.

After returning home from his initial hospitalization, Dr. McD. attempted to resume his practice as an internist. However, he found that many of his patients had transferred to other physicians and did not return to him. Dr. McD. felt very bitter about this and blamed his colleagues for stealing his old patients and for refusing to refer new patients to him. Many of his colleagues were shocked by these accusations and reacted to them by not referring any new patients to him. When Dr. Mc.D. was fortunate enough to get a new patient on his own, his gruff manner and his insistence in inquiring in detail into the patient's social and sexual adjustment, even when appropriate, frequently drove these new patients away. He spent many hours sitting alone in his apartment and claimed to be working on a new book which "would revolutionize medicine." However, his houseboy reported that Dr. McD. did not appear to be doing any writing, but seemed instead to spend a great deal of time playing with his model railroad, his telescope, or just sitting by the hour staring into space. Although not previously a religious man, Dr. McD. began to attend church services regularly, often stopping at the door to argue about the sermon with the minister. He often attended other church meetings including those of the board of the church. At these meetings he criticized the behavior of the board members, intimating that they were not good Christians. He also became involved in one petty complaint after another against his landlord, and, when the landlord attempted to break his lease, Dr. McD. took him into court on three different counts regarding the care of the building. During the month prior to his readmission to the hospital, Dr. McD. had called the police fifteen times regarding what he felt to be suspicious looking characters who were entering the lobby of his apartment house or strolling through the neighborhood streets. He could not make any definite complaints against any of these people nor could he identify any of them, but he became quite irritated when the police pointed out that they could not investigate further without some direct evidence or charges.

Although he had not physically attacked anyone prior to his attempted assault on his houseboy, Dr. McD. had recently purchased two new revolvers. He had been in contact with his sister only twice during the year, but on both occasions had mentioned in passing that she should not be surprised if he were found dead within a year.

Upon admission to the hospital, Dr. McD. vigorously denied that he had attacked his houseboy but rather accused the houseboy of being a thief and a sexual pervert. He further claimed that instead of wanting to harm his houseboy he had tried to protect and befriend "this fellow" for the twenty years that he had worked for him. Dr. McD. claimed that the houseboy had threatened him because he had advised the houseboy's fiancée of what he regarded as the houseboy's alleged character defects. At other times, Dr. McD. defended his behavior as an effort to prevent the houseboy from making an unsatisfactory marriage. The patient was also very critical of the houseboy's fiancée, claiming that she was merely after the houseboy's money.

At the time of this readmission, Dr. McD.'s sister visited the hospital, and, in interviews with the psychiatric social worker, further information concerning his early development and background were obtained. His houseboy was also interviewed. In addition, a member of the medical staff recalled that he had attended the same private high school as Dr. McD. for two years, and was able to shed some light on Dr. McD.'s adjustment as an adolescent.

Prior History. Dr. McD. was born and reared in the city in which he was currently practicing medicine. His father, a prominent physician, had married late in life to a widow, then also in her forties, who had an eighteen-year-old daughter from her previous marriage. His, father died when Dr. McD. was four years old, leaving him with a very comfortable inheritance and a trust fund which financed all of his schooling. Dr. McD.'s mother died two years later leaving him in the care of his sister then aged twenty-six. As far as his sister could remember, his early training and development had otherwise been uneventful. Their mother had been sickly and her brother had been under the care of various housekeepers in the home. Dr. McD.'s sister had been in a boarding school during the patient's early childhood. After she was given guardianship of Dr. McD., she placed him in a boarding school and seldom saw him except on holidays. As far as she knew, Dr. McD. adjusted well in this school, always made top grades, and was a well behaved and polite little boy. During the summer periods he was usually sent to camp. He seldom spent as much as a week in her home during the holidays.

Dr. McD. graduated with full honors from a private high school at age sixteen. The staff physician who had attended high school with him recalled that Dr. McD. had demanded and been granted many special privileges at the school which were not ordinarily accorded the other boys. The other boys were jealous of him, teased him, and refused to include him in their cliques. They identified him with the headmaster, a gruff disciplinarian who seemed to protect him, and felt that he tattled on them to the headmaster. At one time, Dr. McD. had the nickname in the school of "the little head." One of the privileges granted the patient by the headmaster was a private room, allegedly because the patient refused to dress or bathe in front of the other boys. The patient did not participate in any of the school's sports activities or other extra-curricular activities and the boys thus considered him a "sissy." There was considerable sexual curiosity and homosexual play among the other boys in the school from which the patient was specifically excluded because it was thought that he would report them to school authorities. One incident the staff physician recalled specifically: the boys had discovered that Dr. McD. was on the toilet and would not come out while they were present. They accused him of masturbating and stood guard over him for several hours until the situation was broken up by one of the teachers. In reminiscing further, the staff physician was of the opinion that possibly the headmaster may not have been as cold and distant as the boys regarded him, and that perhaps he had taken pity on the patient because of the treatment accorded him by the other boys. Possibly this pity was motivated by the fact that Dr. McD. was an orphan. It was reported that one Christmas Dr. McD. could not go to his sister's home because the family was ill, and the headmaster suggested to several of the other boys' parents that they invite him to their homes for the holiday. Since no one accepted this suggestion, the patient spent Christmas with the headmaster and his wife which only furthered the boys' impression that the patient was a "pet." Because the patient was a brilliant student, the teachers praised and rewarded him, adding to the jealousy of the other boys.

Following graduation Dr. McD. went on to the university to take his premedical training. He finished this undergraduate training in two and a half years rather than the usual three. Since he was six months too young to be admitted to medical school, he was sent abroad for a period of travel by himself. During this year abroad, he attempted to look up relatives in the country in which his mother had been born and was quite disgusted and upset to find these relatives living in a ghetto. Although he mentioned this to his sister upon his return from Europe, he acted and spoke as if he were unaware that his mother was Jewish.

On returning to this country, he entered medical school where he was again a top student in his class. Dr. McD. spent his summers at the medical school on research scholarships. During these medical school years Dr. McD. lived at a boarding house near the university in a room by himself. He had almost no social life as a student and lived as an isolate, spending most of his time either in the laboratory or in his own room. His sister and several older women members of the family frequently invited Dr. McD. to come to their houses or saw that he got frequent invitations to parties, which he usually attended and at which he seemed to enjoy himself. His sister and the other women attempted to pair him off with many of the young ladies in their social group, and although he went along on theater parties and other affairs, he never followed through with their hopes that he would continue to date one of these girls on a steady basis. Indeed, Dr. McD. seemed amused by his sister's efforts to get him "hooked up" with some girl, and he once informed her that he was determined to outwit her and her friends in their plans for him. In a cynical fashion, which gradually began to alienate other people, Dr. McD. informed his brother-in-law, and other married men of his acquaintance, that he would never marry any girl who was not a virgin, and that, furthermore, his medical training and experience had led him to believe that there were few, if any, women over the age of twelve who were virgins. Dr. McD. also took every opportunity possible to make fun of married life and to argue for the joys of celibacy.

Outside of medicine, Dr. McD.'s only enduring interest was in railroading. He had read many books on the topic and built a large and elaborate model railroad in his apartment. He had a similar fascination with astronomy; on his balcony were mounted several powerful telescopes. His fellow medical students kidded him when they discovered that these telescopes could be trained at the windows of the nurses' home at the medical school down the block. Dr. McD. took this kidding good-naturedly, but pointed out that it was his fellow students who had thought of this use of the telescope.

After being graduated *cum laude* from medical school, Dr. McD. was immediately admitted to an internship at the same university, and thereafter, a residency in internal medicine. He continued to pursue his research interests during his residency and completed a study on the functioning of the kidney which was regarded as revolutionary and was widely quoted in medical textbooks. The year after he finished his residency, he authored a text on the office practice of internal medicine which was so well received that it became a standard work in that field.

Following the completion of his residency Dr. McD. engaged in the private practice of internal medicine. He was moderately successful and his life went along in a comparatively uneventful fashion until the outbreak of World War II. No one was aware why Dr. McD. was not immediately called up for duty at the outbreak of World War II. The colleagues who disliked him voiced the opinion that he had been rejected on psychiatric grounds. However, while staying at home, Dr. McD. became extremely busy since he was one of the few physicians left in his community. He was appointed Acting Assistant Medical Director at one of the large hospitals. Shortly before the end of the war Dr. McD. was given an appointment as captain in the U.S. Army and served briefly at a military hospital nearby. During the physical examination, when first admitted to the veterans' hospital, Dr. McD. was asked about a surgical scar on his scrotum. He mentioned that he had had an operation for an undescended testicle in 1944. He at first denied that there was any special purpose for this operation at that particular time, but later mentioned that this physical abnormality was the reason he had been denied a commission in the service earlier. Apparently the surgery corrected this abnormality and he was accepted in the service in 1944. As far as could be determined, Dr. McD.'s year of service in World War II was uneventful, and he showed none of the unusual behavior which he manifested during his Korean period of duty. After World War II, Dr. McD. continued in the military reserve, attending all reserve meetings faithfully and going on brief periods of active duty every summer. He rose to the rank of major and entered active duty at the onset of the Korean war with the rank of lieutenant colonel. Dr. McD. seemed very proud of his military activities and rank and wore his uniform at every possible opportunity.

Course in the Hospital During Second Admission. On readmission to the veterans' hospital, Dr. McD. was found to be in good physical health. He denied any history of illness or injury and did not recall having even any of the usual childhood diseases. He claimed to keep himself in good health by walking. The examination by the admitting psychiatrist revealed that the patient was "well-oriented as to time, place, and person" and that except for his ideas concerning the nature of the war and the reasons for his hospitalization, appeared to be able to reason logically. Various tests of intelligence and abstract reasoning indicated that Dr. McD. was of superior intelligence and, in general, showed no obvious deterioration of his thought processes. The psychologist noted, however, that while the patient seemed to reason well enough, his logic was defective in that he often argued on the basis of false premises. Emotionally, Dr. McD. showed no overt anxiety or depression. On the ward and around the hospital, except for the occasional outbursts mentioned above, Dr. McD. was well-behaved and co-operative. Although a patient, Dr. McD. continued to play the role of a physician and behaved toward other patients as he might if he were a member of the hospital staff.

Since Dr. McD. was so reluctant to discuss his personal life and seemed so defensive about it, he was not considered a favorable candidate for individual psychotherapy. One attempt was made to include him in a psychotherapeutic group but once again he took the role of the physician rather than the patient, and interviewed the other patients in the group rather than talk about himself. When the other patients challenged his attitude, Dr. McD. failed to appear at any future group meetings. Although generally aloof, Dr. McD. did seem to form some sort of continuing relationship with a student psychologist assigned to study his case. The student had been advised by his supervisor of Dr. McD.'s defensiveness and was cautioned not to attempt any direct inquiry into the patient's personal life. It was emphasized that the student should attempt to form some kind of relationship with Dr. McD. and to merely listen to him. Dr. McD. permitted the student to accompany him on his walks around the hospital and regaled him with his attitudes about the war, medicine, psychiatry, and the details and history of railroads in the United States. However, the student's curiosity and impatience grew from week to week and finally one day, in a pause during their daily walk, the student haltingly inquired about one small aspect of Dr. McD.'s personal life. Dr. McD. turned to the student and said in a stern but friendly fashion, "Young man, I am an old and lonely man, and there is nothing you can do about it."

Dr. McD. continued to reside in the hospital and it was the opinion of the psychiatric staff that he will probably remain there for the rest of his life.

Questions for Dr. McD.

1. The hospital notes on Dr. McD. indicated that he was not visibly anxious and could discuss his accusations against others in a calm and detached manner. How can we reconcile the fact that Dr. McD. was so disturbed psychologically with his apparent lack of overt discomfort?

2. What anxieties are present in Dr. McD., although not directly observable? Suggest a theoretical formulation which permits the existence of anxiety and no overt manifestations of anxiety operating concurrently.

3. Taking a long term view of Dr. McD.'s life, what are the personality traits which seem to herald the form of his later disorder?

4. What kinds of approach-avoidance conflicts appear to underlie the learning of the traits suggested in your answer to question 3?

5. What were the conditions in Dr. McD.'s early life that appeared particularly conducive to the learning of the conflicts listed in question 4 above?

6. What psychological defenses did Dr. McD. learn to use in reducing anxiety?

7. Obviously these defenses eventually resulted in a psychotic reaction rather than a neurotic one. Can you explain why the more serious reaction (psychosis) pattern occurred rather than the less serious one (neurosis)?

8. One popular theory of Dr. McD.'s disorder (that offered by Freud) emphasizes the central role of latent homosexuality. Do you see any evidence in Dr. McD. of homosexual trends, latent or otherwise?

9. How can you account for the following:
   a. Dr. McD.'s celibacy
   b. Dr. McD.'s enjoyment of the army role
   c. Dr. McD.'s need to maintain the role of the physician even when hospitalized

10. Do the results of the psychological examination fit with the usual criteria for diagnosing a person as paranoid schizophrenic? If not, what diagnosis also might be said to cover Dr. McD.'s' pattern of symptoms?

11. Dr. McD. expressed openly his religious prejudice and in general his behavior might be called "authoritarian." Compare this case with those reported by Maria Levinson in *The Authoritarian Personality* (see reference below). In what way does Dr. McD. fit the characteristics of the authoritarian personality, and in what ways is he different?

References

CAMERON, N. The paranoid pseudo-community. *American Journal of Sociology*, 1943, **49**: 32–38.

FROMM-REICHMAN, F. Loneliness. *Psychiatry*, 1959, **22**: 1–15.

LEVINSON, MARIA. Psychological ill health in relation to potential fascism: a study of psychiatric clinic patients. In ADORNO, T. W., FRENKEL-BRUNSWIK, E., LEVINSON, D., & SANFORD, R. N. *The authoritarian personality*. New York: Harper and Bros., 1950. Pp. 891–970.

Ovesy, L. Pseudo homosexuality, the paranoid mechanism and paranoia. *Psychiatry*, 1955, 18: 163–173. (Also reprinted in Reed, C. R., Alexander, I. E., & Tompkins, S. S., *Psychopathology*, Cambridge: Harvard Univer. Press, 1958. Chap. 25.)

Phillips, L. Case history data and prognosis in schizophrenia. *Journal of Nervous and Mental Diseases*, 1953, 117: 515–525.

Seitz, P. Infantile experience and adult behavior in animal subjects. II, Age of separation from the mother and adult behavior in the cat. *Psychosomatic Medicine*, 1959, 21: 353–378.

THE CASE OF MARLA T.

The Dance on the Precipice

Marla T.'s entrance into the hospital's reception room was most flamboyant. A petite but plump woman, in her early thirties, she was garishly clad in a sleeveless sheath dress of a silver-colored metallic cloth and wore elbow length gloves of the same material. A pair of elaborate and gaudy earrings dangled below her platinum-blonde hair, which was cut in a Dutch bob. Her make-up was so heavy that she looked ready to appear on stage. However, this layer of cosmetics failed to hide the "crow's feet" around her eyes; very near-sighted, she peered through the thick lenses of her plain, dark-rimmed glasses—which contrasted starkly with her otherwise ostentatious costume. Since Marla and her husband arrived about noon, her dress and appearance seemed even more bizarre. Somewhere between her car and the hospital door, she had kicked off her shoes, which her husband was carrying. As she entered the hospital door, she was talking rapidly in a loud, raucous voice, and continued to chatter incessantly for the next hour to anyone and everyone. Her husband was an immense, dark-complexioned, handsome Negro, who was dressed much more modestly in dark sport clothes. He said very little, except to attempt periodically to quiet her and to suggest that she listen to the doctor.

In the initial interview, Marla insisted that everything was "copacetic" (a slang term from World War II, meaning "in smooth running order"). She saw no reason that she should enter the hospital but then agreed that "perhaps" she could use some rest. Her husband was "perfectly wonderful to be so concerned about my health," and if he thought she should be hospitalized, she certainly was willing to "do anything to please him." She was "very delighted" with the condition of the hospital grounds and with the "handsome" doctors. She was sure that she would get the rest that her husband thought she needed. However, she was equally sure that she probably would be home either that evening or the next morning. Marla kept demanding that her husband check through her overnight bag to make sure that she had all the things she needed. Repeatedly she sought reassurance that he would visit her that evening, and pleaded with the doctor to admit her husband with her. However, she avoided the questions of the admitting physician, saying only that she felt perfectly all right. She immediately changed the topic when any specific questions were asked. Marla talked very rapidly, skipping from one topic to another with apparent ease. She read out loud the diplomas on the doctor's wall, mentioned persons she knew who had attended the university where the doctor got his degree, and went on to tell the personal history of these people, the towns from which they had come, other people she had known there, how this was related to her feelings about world politics, particularly the problem of racial segregation in the United States. She went on to tell how she had been engaged for the past week, almost night and day, in programs dealing with the abolition of segregation. Any attempts to question her about her other behavior or her life in general were answered briefly and politely, but she quickly came back to her ideas on how to solve the problems of race prejudice. Her husband sat by silently, with a pained expression on his face. As Marla became increasingly incoherent she was given a heavy sedative, which she accepted without question, and was led into another room with the suggestion that she should take a brief nap. She continued to talk to an accompanying nurse for almost another hour before the sedation took effect.

Mr. T. reported that the behavior which his wife demonstrated had come on rather gradually, over the past six weeks. He described her as usually a garrulous and sociable person whom everybody liked. She was always "on the go," and was considered the "life of the party." Over the past six weeks, however, she had become increasingly involved in several allied organizations that were conducting active programs to combat race prejudice. She went to one meeting after another, participated in parades and demonstrations, and seemed to be able to talk or think about little else. Marla's husband had become increasingly embarrassed by the loudness of her voice, as had others who spent any time in her company. She had gotten herself onto a TV program, and argued in an angry and abusive fashion with the moderator. Marla had spent one night in jail after fighting with the police, in a scuffle which occurred in a demonstration picket line. For the past four days she had eaten very little, slept only sporadically, and had not taken off her dress, the one she was wearing when she came to the hospital. Her general appearance had also changed; she usually dressed much more modestly and wore little or no make-up.

As far as her husband knew she had never had such passionate devotion to any cause. Usually she was much more calm and level-headed. She transacted a great deal of the financial side of his work, often traveling about the country selling the modern artistic jewelery which he made. Indeed, she had built his art hobby into a thriving business. Only twice in their two years of marriage had he been concerned about her emotional adjustment. Once on her return from a selling trip, seeming very tired and unusually quiet, she had gone to bed immediately and slept for well over forty-eight hours. He had discovered later that she had taken a heavy dose of sleeping pills. Another time she had frightened him when, after a late party, she had climbed atop a twelve-foot wall overlooking the ocean and proceeded to dance the length of the wall, threatening to jump into the water. When he expressed his concern she said it was all a joke.

Mr. T. could offer little information about his wife's background, as she had told him only of intermittent parts of her life. They had met a little over two years before in one of the organizations fighting race prejudice. Soon afterward they began living together in a common-law marriage, which Mr. T. felt has been essentially very happy and satisfying to both. Her ability to create a business out of his artistic work had enabled him to quit his job as a truck driver and devote himself entirely to his art, and to return to his college education. Several times he had urged his wife to legalize their marriage, but she had put this off, joking that if they became legally married they would not be acceptable in the artists' colony in which they lived. Asked what he had hoped might be added to the marriage by legalizing it, he sheepishly admitted that he would like to have children, although he quickly assured the interviewer that he realized that neither their economic nor their social situation was very amenable to raising of children.

The past summer his thirteen-year-old niece had been left in their care, which delighted his wife. Marla and his niece had become very close. Marla had devoted considerable energy to seeing that the girl was entertained, and spent a great deal of their budget in buying her clothes. She was disappointed when the niece returned to her own family at the end of the summer. This had raised Mr. T.'s hopes that she might want children, but he had not reintroduced the topic with her.

Asked specifically about their sexual relationships, he said that they were usually quite gratifying to him, and he supposed to her. Regarding her current sexual adjustment, Mrs. T. said only that "everything is wonderful; my husband is a wonderful lover," and refused to discuss the matter further. Mr. T. knew that Mrs. T. used a diaphragm, but had never discussed the matter of contraceptives with her, and he denied that he felt any need to discuss it. He did remark that during her menstrual period she seemed excessively irritable, and would either completely reject any sexual advances on his part, or demand repeated intercourse.

On further inquiry he agreed that, although she was generally an affectionate and warm-hearted person, she also could be very irritable and difficult to please at times. While she was always trying to do something for other people, it always had to be *her* way of doing it, and often she seemed to be doing things for others whether or not they wanted anything done for them. During the preceding weeks several of the organizations to which she belonged had at first suggested to her that she take it easy, and finally the leader of one organization had told her to stay away from their meetings entirely. She was very hurt and wept for days after the quarrel with this organization president, but finally resolved her tears by deciding that this man was emotionally disturbed and that she could help the organization best by not irritating him further. Even before her present disturbance, however, she frequently cooked fancy dishes for the neighbors, which she insisted her husband take to them, even though the neighbors protested that they did not need her gifts of food. Marla was always bringing someone home to dinner or for a drink. Marla's husband denied that either of them used alcohol at all, although they kept some alcoholic beverages in their home to serve guests. The couple lived in a one-room studio in a community largely inhabited by artists and writers.

Past History. Marla's past history was pieced together from further statements by the patient and her husband, and by a subsequent interview with the patient's grandmother, Mrs. H. An only child, Marla was reared chiefly by her maternal grandmother, as her parents had separated shortly before her birth. Marla's father never reappeared, and her mother, who was secretary for a prominent politician in Washington, left Marla entirely in the care of her grandmother before Marla was a year old. Marla remembered her mother chiefly as a stranger who visited the home at less than six-month intervals. Her earliest memory of her mother was of a large heavily perfumed fur coat in which Marla buried her head and cried. At other times her mother would greet her at the door and grasp her in her arms, and Marla would wiggle out and run into the other room crying. The grandmother remembered Marla as a very happy and pretty child. She ate well, according to the grandmother, and gained weight very rapidly, and was always a heavy-set child. The grandmother could not remember exactly when Marla learned to walk or talk, but believed that there was nothing unusual about her development during infancy. She did remember that Marla continued to be fed from the bottle until she was almost three years of age, but the grandmother did not regard this as anything unusual. She said, defensively, that she had fed Marla baby foods and solid foods at the same time that Marla was also carrying the bottle around. Asked about Marla's toilet-training, the grandmother claimed that Marla had always been a very clean child, and that she had been successful in toilet-training Marla before she was a year old. Mrs. H.'s only child had been Marla's mother, and Mr. H. had died five years before Marla's birth. The child and grandmother lived in a large, old house near the center of town.

About the only outward evidence of emotional disturbance in Marla's early childhood was her social isolation. Her grandmother enrolled Marla in a parochial school, believing it would provide "better discipline for the child," although she could not say why she thought Marla needed any special discipline. Marla denied any definite memory of her early school years, saying only that she made fair grades and "got along well" with the sisters and the students. Her grandmother reported that at times Marla seemed very unhappy, and was called "fatso" by the other children because of her mild obesity. She had little in common with the other children; she was not a member of their social clique at the school, nor did she associate with the children outside of school. She had almost no friends in her neighborhood, which was largely inhabited by older people, with no young children. Marla spent many hours playing by herself, especially with her puppets. From early childhood, she showed evidence of artistic taste—if not artistic talent—and was skillful and interested in various handicrafts. Her grandmother taught her to sew and, using sewing scraps, she constructed a large collection of elaborate hand-puppets, including costumes from many nations, fairy-book characters, and a royal family. Her favorite, however, was a rag-doll "orphan," the central character in Marla's chief puppet play. In this play the orphan, after having been abused by bad step-parents, was rescued by the prince, and it was then discovered that the orphan was really royalty.

Mrs. H. praised Marla for her being a well-behaved and helpful child who voluntarily helped with the housework and who was always obedient. Mrs. H. was convinced that Marla's disturbance began about age thirteen, when Marla's mother returned. Marla's mother had been married and divorced twice in the interim, had lost her job in Washington, and returned home broke and unmarried. Quarreling broke out between Marla and her mother almost immediately. Marla was critical of her mother's dress and her mother's habits. Her mother always wore fine clothes and went out a great deal, dating various men. At home Marla's mother slept till noon, then spent most of the afternoon grooming herself at home or at the beauty shop. Marla felt that her mother's attention to her dress and grooming was "sinful." At the same time Marla's mother made fun of Marla for quoting religious dicta on behavior, and called her "a little prissy." She blamed the grandmother for Marla's overweight, and insisted that Marla be put on a diet. She removed Marla from the parochial school, and put her in public school. Instead of the simple uniforms which Marla had been wearing, her mother bought her fancy clothes and Marla felt out of place in the public school with her silk dresses and patent leather shoes.

Once, when quite inebriated, Marla's mother described in detail her sexual exploits with her boy friend the night before. Mrs. H. then insisted that her daughter leave the house and have nothing more to do with them. The mother responded that if she left she was taking Marla with her. This quarrel, which lasted for twenty-four hours, was climaxed by Marla, who ran away from home. She was picked up by the police two hundred miles away from home, in a motel with two sailors. Mrs. H. reported that she had given Marla no sexual instruction at all, other than on the use of feminine hygiene during her menstrual period. Marla had started developing secondary sexual characteristics at about age eleven, and her first menstrual period was a month before her twelfth birthday. The grandmother denied that Marla had shown any interest in boys up to this time whatsoever and had never so much as been on a date. Marla admitted that she had spent the night in the motel with the sailors, but refused to divulge to the grandmother whether or not she had had any sexual relations with them. Marla, in giving her own history, did not mention this episode, but stated rather that she had engaged in sexual play with both girls and boys from about age eight on, and had had her first heterosexual experience with a neighbor boy when she was about ten.

Shortly after this episode Marla's mother remarried and took Marla to live with her. Marla would have preferred to stay with her grandmother, but she was also excited by the idea of having a stepfather. "I adored him the first time I met him." He treated her as a little adult, brought her presents when he came on dates with her mother, and teased her about her developing figure and attractiveness. Marla was very excited over the prospect of her mother's marriage to this man and was thus extremely disappointed when they went out of town to get married. After her mother's marriage, however, Marla saw little of her stepfather; he worked the "swing shift" in a wartime industry, departing for work before she returned from school and not awakening in the morning before she left the house. Even his day off occurred in the middle of the week, rather than on the weekend.

Marla remembered her mother at this time as being excessively strict and concerned with Marla's social behavior. Marla began to meet boys at the public high school and to go to parties and dates; she had sexual affairs with several boys. Her mother was very suspicious of her, and kept accusing her of being sexually loose. After about a year of frequent quarrels with her mother she left her mother's home when her mother accused her of attempting to seduce her stepfather, which Marla hotly denied. Mrs. H., who seemed unaware of Marla's sexual behavior, described Marla at age sixteen as being a very beautiful and attractive girl, having lost much of the excess weight of her childhood. Mrs. H. was very proud of the fact that many boys were attracted to Marla and had great hopes that Marla would make a successful marriage to a rich and ambitious young man. She thus encouraged Marla's dating and spent a great deal of money in helping Marla buy clothes and go to the beauty shop. Despite the fact that Marla was out on a date almost every night and for long weekend parties during high school, she succeeded in graduating from high school with high honors. She had developed an interest in writing, and won a state poetry writing contest. Graduating from high school before she was eighteen, she received a scholarship to the local university.

When Marla entered the university, she became enamored of a slightly older woman graduate student and moved into her apartment, where she quickly became involved in a very intense, overt homosexual relationship. This relationship lasted about three months, at which time Marla began to demonstrate many of the symptoms she showed at the time of the present hospitalization. Her grandmother remembered that Marla upon returning home talked incessantly and was unable to sleep. She recited poetry by the hour, speaking in blank verse. The grandmother believed that her behavior was associated with the heavy use of alcohol, although Marla denied this. This incident was climaxed when Marla ran out of the house in excitement and was hit by a truck in the street. She was badly injured, and it was believed for a while that she would be crippled for life. She was returned in a wheelchair to her grandmother's home, and the grandmother proceeded to nurse her and care for her like a baby. Marla remembers her grandmother rubbing her legs and helping her with the exercises prescribed by the orthopedist. Within the year Marla was able to get around on crutches, and the following year seemed almost entirely recovered. Current medical examination revealed scars of the orthopedic surgery, but there was no muscle or nerve loss.

Once Marla was able to be up and around she did not attempt to return to the university, but obtained various short-term jobs as a secretary. Marla herself reports that she was most interested in getting married, but never seemed to decide on any one man. She volunteered that she took great joy in seeing how quickly she could seduce every new man that she met. She also had one or two brief homosexual affairs. Mrs. H. reported that Marla often seemed to be at loose ends, and that she was fearful that Marla would never "amount to anything." By this, Mrs. H. meant that she hoped that Marla would return to her college education, and find either a good job or a rich husband, or both. At times Marla did engage in alcoholic bouts, which sometimes resulted in complete incapacitation for several days at a time. Mrs. H. was quite worried about Marla and tried to discourage her use of alcohol, but always nursed her back to health whenever she went on one of these binges. For the first time Marla began to quarrel with her grandmother, and to deride her old-fashioned ways. Mrs. H. was very hurt and blamed Marla's dissension on the alcohol.

Marla's interest in poetry, the fine arts, and music continued, and many of her friends were artists and writers. She became involved in various social movements, particularly in the organizations concerned with the amelioration of race prejudice. Much to her grandmother's dismay she had dated several Negroes prior to meeting her husband. Marla was very proud of her open-minded approach to sociological questions, and often engaged in prolonged arguments with people regarding the accepted institutions and prejudices of the community. It was after an extended and bitter quarrel with her grandmother, the subject of which neither could remember, that Marla went to live with her husband, Mr. T. Although Marla and her grandmother did not speak for almost three months following Marla's common-law marriage to Mr. T., thereafter Marla and her husband moved in with the grandmother and took over the house, with almost no objection on the part of the grandmother. At times the grandmother protested, saying that she was very ashamed to have a Negro in her home, which was in an all white community. Marla would become angry at her grandmother and curse at her in loud tones, telling her that she was narrow-minded and Godless, which hurt the grandmother very much. Finally, at the insistence of Mr. T., the couple moved away to their present studio, approximately six months ago. Marla continued to visit her grandmother occasionally, but always parted in a fit of anger. Their last contact was approximately six weeks before, at which time Marla swore she would never have anything more to do with her grandmother at all.

Course in Hospital. During the first week of hospitalization Marla required considerable sedation. However, she soon began to quiet down, and to follow the hospital routine. She would occasionally burst into tears and demand that the hospital get in touch with her husband, whom she said she missed dreadfully. During the second and third weeks she refused to eat and she sat at the window for hours on end, silent. This depression lifted spontaneously, however, and although still considerably quiescent she once more returned to joining in ward activities. At the end of five weeks she was allowed to go home on a visit, and upon her return seemed to be quite happy and at ease, but without the excitement she had shown on admission. The following week, after another home visit, her husband requested that she be discharged. She was put on a three months' trial home visit, at the end of which she was formally discharged from the hospital. In closing her case, the psychiatrist noted "prognosis is guarded."

During her hospitalization several interviews were conducted by the psychiatrist with Marla. She seemed eager to talk about her life, but kept denying that any such discussion had any bearing on her adjustment, or that she needed any type of psychotherapy. She brought her poetry with her, and made several attempts to write more poetry while in the hospital, but complained that she was unable to be creative at this time. Her poetry consisted of several volumes of handwritten pages of blank verse, which was largely incomprehensible. She smiled when the doctors asked her about the meaning of it, and explained that one had to know something about modern poetry to be able to understand it. The wording of the poetry was extremely morbid, and often overtly sexual. Many of the words referred to death and violent destruction or to the unhappiness of the world in general. At the doctor's request Mr. T. brought in some of Marla's published poems, which were only slightly more formal and comprehensible, and in which the themes of death and meaninglessness were prominent.

Questions for Marla T.

1. Cite the critical experiences and relationships in Marla's early life that provided a fertile ground for learning various conflicts.
2. What need (or needs) appear to have been particularly frustrated as a result of these experiences?

3. How did Marla learn to react to the frustration of these needs?

4. What additional conflicts appear to have been stimulated when Marla's mother returned home when Marla was thirteen?

5. How can we account for the fact that in spite of their poor relationship, Marla appears to have patterned a substantial part of her behavior after that of her mother?

6. Marla's sexual history is bizarre in many ways, yet it may be seen to be quite explicable when studied in some detail. First, try and explain Marla's motivation in running away with the two sailors at age thirteen.

7. How much of Marla's later sexual behavior might be seen as being based on the same motivation? Consider the following in your answer:

    a. Marla's promiscuity and enjoyment in seducing all men

    b. Marla's homosexual affair with the graduate student

    c. Marla's interest in dating men of other racial groups

8. How can we reconcile Marla's sexual looseness with the other side of her personality, namely the desire to help others, to give things to them, and to fight for the cause of minority groups?

9. Marla's first acutely excited episode occurred during her homosexual affair with the graduate student. Do we see any common features between that situation and the events preceding Marla's present breakdown?

10. Can you trace any relation between Marla's conflicts and the types of symptoms she developed during her acute episode, i.e. garish dress, excited talking, expansive feeling of well-being, and so forth?

References

CAMERON, D. E. Some relationships between excitement, depression and anxiety. *American Journal of Psychiatry*, 1945, **102**: 385–394.

CAMERON, N. The place of mania among the depressions from a biological standpoint. *Journal of Psychology*, 1942, **14**: 181–195.

GIBSON, R. W. The family background and early life experience of the manic-depressive patient. *Psychiatry*, 1958, **21**: 71–90. (Also reprinted in SARBIN, T. (Ed.) *Studies in behavior pathology.* New York: Holt, Rinehart, Winston, 1961. Pp. 210–228.

RENNIE, T. Prognosis in manic depressive psychoses. *American Journal of Psychiatry*, 1942, **98**: 801–814.

THE CASE OF "BUDDY" A.

The Attainment of Nirvana

Buddy's admission to the psychiatric ward of the county hospital was precipitated by the following events, which took place several hours earlier. He informed his mother that it would be necessary to sacrifice her in order for him to "attain Nirvana"; he threw her to the floor and, with his knee on her chest, began choking her. After a violent struggle she was finally able to free herself and fled, screaming for the police. Buddy left the house and wandered about the streets. When the police located him he surrendered without protest.

His entrance into the hospital emergency room was most dramatic: a huge, muscular man, he strode across the lobby, dragging behind him the two policemen to whom he was handcuffed. He was clad only in a filthy towel wrapped around his waist. His unkempt hair reached his shoulders and a massive beard covered most of his face. His body, hair, and beard were caked with dirt, and blood flowed from the scratches inflicted by his mother. Barely visible was the elaborate tattoo of a battleship across his chest; his arms were also decorated by a tattoo of a reverse swastika and of a heart-and-dagger. He voluntarily seated himself on a bench at the admission desk, forcing the officers also to sit. Aside from the glassy stare of his eyes, his face was expressionless. He paid no attention to questions addressed to him and said nothing to anyone. Staring at the ceiling he occasionally mumbled indistinctly to himself.

Released from the handcuffs, he allowed himself to be led to the general admitting ward where, for the next four hours, he squatted on his haunches at the foot of his bed, his head bowed as he muttered to himself. Several times the nursing attendants tried to get him to shower and dress in preparation for a physical examination. Finally, two of them attempted to lift him to his feet, hoping to lead him to the shower, at which time he savagely attacked them and began destroying the furniture and bedding. Forcibly restrained and put in a separate room, he continued briefly to pound on the walls before he finally settled back into his buddha-like squat on the floor and resumed his trance-like appearance.

Later in the evening he appeared in the door of his cell and asked for a cigarette, whereupon the attending psychiatrist came to see him and brought him cigarettes. He was eager to talk but seemed somewhat confused. He was not sure where he was or how he got there. He did remember the assault on his mother, an act which he said he regretted but had felt compelled to commit because of what the "voice" had told him. He said that for several years he had regularly heard voices telling him what to do, although in the past year, since he had been studying religions of the Far East, the voices had been less frequent. In a rambling confused fashion he attempted to explain his need to find "unity with nature" and "a higher level of enlightenment," referring vaguely to Yoga, Zen, and the Bhagavad-Gita. He apologized for being "incommunicado" earlier in the day, explaining that he was being "bombarded with knowledge." Increasingly preoccupied with expounding his philosophy, he became unable to discuss anything else. Near the end of the hour when asked again if he knew where he was, he was able to respond correctly. He was also oriented as to the date, and was even aware of the time of day. When asked about such facts as his age and occupation, he again launched into a philosophic discussion of the unimportance of such information, saying that he felt ageless and that his life was devoted to the problem of "self-realization and enlightenment." Shortly thereafter, he gave his age as twenty-three, said he usually worked as a dishwasher but had been unemployed for approximately a year and a half, except for occasional employment at a coffee house.

This question reminded him that he had not eaten for the past twenty-four hours. Told that it would be necessary for him to bathe and dress before he would be given food, he complied. During his bath he again got into an altercation with the nurse's aides, cursed them loudly and threatened them with bodily harm, but calmed down after a few minutes and apologized to them for his outburst. He put on a hospital gown but refused shoes and stockings. Since it was near midnight, a dinner had to be ordered from the employees' kitchen and there was a slight delay. He accepted the meal silently but after eating, again became violently angry, throwing the dishes and shouting vulgar threats. Although Buddy could not say what it was that upset him, the nurses guessed that he had overheard them discussing their difficulty in obtaining food for him. Heavy doses of a combination of psychotropic drugs were prescribed, which quieted him, and he did not repeat any of his violent and destructive behavior during the next eight days in the county hospital receiving ward.

At the request of the social worker, Buddy's mother and sister came to the hospital for interviews several times during the ensuing week. Still very fearful, they did not visit Buddy. However, he did not appear perturbed, and requested only that they bring some of his books and other possessions from home. He spent his time peacefully reading his books on occult religion, and practicing his Yoga exercises. He graciously permitted his contemplations to be interrupted twice daily for psychiatric interviews and even seemed to enjoy talking about himself and his ideas. Although the tranquilizers made him drowsy and inert, his conversation was much more lucid than when he first arrived at the hospital and his thought processes did not seem slowed down or quite as confused.

Mrs. A.'s heavily lined face and dry blotched complexion made Buddy's mother appear at least ten years older than her stated age of forty-seven. An obvious wig of a reddish-brown hue grotesquely capped her tiny figure, contrasting oddly with her drab and shabby clothes. Her tremulous voice and downcast expression suggested considerable depression. She kept repeating such phrases as "I don't know what I've done to deserve all this," or "God knows I've tried, I've tried." At times she gave bits of information pertinent to Buddy's current illness and childhood, but on the whole she was not really able to give a comprehensive history in anything approaching a chronological order. Buddy's sister, Trudy, was built more along the lines of her brother, almost six feet tall, raw-boned, yet not exactly lacking in attractiveness. She was better dressed than her mother and seemed to pay at least average attention to her appearance. During the first two interviews she accompanied her mother and occasionally attempted to clarify her mother's rambling account of Buddy's history. On the third interview the sister seemed markedly under the influence of alcohol and contributed little to the discussion. Mrs. A. was seen for two further interviews, but her daughter did not appear again at the hospital.

In Buddy's memory his emotional disturbance began during adolescence when, in his words, he was "a very mixed-up kid." However,
he regarded himself as having matured considerably over the past
two years since he began the study of religion. He attributed much
of his aberrant behavior as an adolescent to the fact that he had
once or twice smoked marijuana. It was during a period of drug in-
toxication that he first heard voices telling him that he was Christ.
Later, without the drug, he again conferred with these voices to be
reassured that he should take up the study of religion and that this
would be the answer he was seeking. As his conversations with these
voices progressed, he began to see visions of holy figures from different religions floating before his eyes. In thinking over his attempt
to murder his mother, Buddy realized he might have misinterpreted
a command from the voices. Or he thought possibly this attack was
caused by an experiment with peyote, even though his use of this
drug had occurred several months previously.

Buddy's mother was also unable to give a coherent picture of the
immediate events surrounding Buddy's murderous outburst. Seemingly unable to stick to the immediate event, she kept interjecting
disconnected vague references to her troubles, past and present.
From what she did say, and from what her daughter added, it appeared that Buddy had been a worry to her during his adolescence,
but she was not really concerned about his "mind" until approximately two years ago, after he returned home from military service.
At that time he seemed moody and restless and easily irritated.
Often, he would absent himself from the house or would refuse to
speak to anyone for several days at a time, seemingly wrapped up in
his own thoughts. His irregular sleeping and eating particularly worried Mrs. A. Employed briefly on several different jobs, he found
nothing to interest him. Mrs. A. knew little of Buddy's activities
away from home, but her daughter added disparagingly that "he
hung around a bunch of bums and 'beatniks'." At first Mrs. A. and
her daughter thought little of Buddy's interest in religion as he had
always been an avid reader and was always "off on some kick or
other."

Over the past year Buddy had become even more morose. He was
easily angered into violent outbursts, sometimes smashing furniture
to the point of injuring himself, and often threatening his mother
with violence on the slightest provocation. "He had always been a

hard boy to control," Mrs. A. said sadly, "but now you don't dare say anything to him." For the past year he had not even bothered to seek unemployment insurance benefits and was entirely dependent on his mother. (His sister lived by herself in another part of town.) When he was not reading, Buddy devoted himself to his Yoga exercises. As he usually paraded around the house and yard wearing only his sandals and a towel, the neighbors had protested several times and the police had been called twice to investigate. Each time Mrs. A. had taken pains to keep Buddy away from the door as she was afraid he would become embroiled in an altercation with the police.

Past History. Mrs. A. lost both her parents during the influenza epidemic of World War I, when she was still an infant, and was reared in a series of foster homes. Her last set of foster parents forced her to quit school after the eighth grade in order to work in their delicatessen. Throughout her childhood she had felt like a cast-off, unwanted and lonely, and as an adolescent she was also withdrawn and friendless, deprived of any kind of social or family life. To add to her misery, she suffered an endocrinological defect which left her completely bald. When she was seventeen her foster parents arranged a marriage for her with Otto A. Sr., Buddy's father. Although he was twenty years her senior and a stranger, she accepted the marriage without question, since in the past her life had always been arranged for her. At the time she had at least a faint hope that someone wanted her and would care for her. She learned indirectly that Mr. A.'s parents, then deceased, had emigrated from Germany and raised a large family, but she met none of them. Other than this, she knew nothing about her husband's background or his personal life. She was not even sure how he earned his living or spent his time when away from home. A minor political "ward-heeler" in a Midwestern metropolis, Mr. A. always seemed to have plenty of money but no definite means of earning a livelihood. Mrs. A. thought it probable that he had made most of his money illegally during Prohibition. Although he provided his family with at least the bare essentials, he showed no affection or regard for either his wife or children. Whenever the slightest demand was made on him, he became angrily abusive, frightening them into submission. Mrs. A. wondered why he ever married, since he was seldom home and seemed to have little need for a wife, either as companion or sexual partner. Buddy himself spoke of his father more fondly, but his recollections were vague. He recalled two occasions when his father had thought to bring him a birthday present, but had no other definite memories of his father. Buddy seemed proud of the fact that he resembled his father physically.

Buddy was born six years after his parents' marriage, four years after Trudy's birth. Mrs. A. skipped over the details of Buddy's birth and early development, remarking only, "Buddy was a very sweet baby and never gave me any trouble." Later in the interviews, she described him as "being quite a handful after he learned to walk . . . he grew very fast and was always too big for me to manage." . . . "He had quite a temper and there wasn't anything you could do when he threw a tantrum." Mrs. A. believed that one of the sources of Buddy's problems throughout his life was the fact that he had no father to discipline him or teach him self-control. On the other hand, she insisted that during his early childhood, Buddy was usually "a pretty good boy" or, at least, got into no serious trouble either at home or at school.

His health was, in general, excellent—except for the fact that he was bald, since he suffered from the same endocrinological defect as his mother. Mrs. A. used to be concerned about the effect Buddy's baldness might have upon him, but, so far as she could remember he had never been bothered by it. His sister agreed, but said that this was only because Buddy would "beat the tar out of any kid who so much as looked at him cross-eyed." Apparently, even as a child Buddy towered over other children. An above-average student, he enjoyed going to school. His athletic prowess commanded respect among his companions, not to mention his ability to cow them into submission if they were critical of him. According to his sister he was the "kingpin of the school" throughout his grade-school years.

For reasons she could not explain, Mrs. A. decided, when Buddy was about eleven, to leave her husband and move to southern California. She did not admit to the children that she was separating from her husband, but told them instead that he had a job elsewhere and would join them soon. For several years he continued to send her money, which she invested in several apartment houses. However, for the past decade she had not heard from her husband. Buddy and his sister would occasionally ask after their father, but since they had seen so little of him in their childhood, it did not seem to Mrs. A. that his absence made any difference to them. Buddy, who could not recall this period of his life, said only that he knew his father "always had been a bum and probably still was." In any case, Mrs. A. was more concerned with Trudy, then thirteen, who had run away from home several times, traveled with a "fast" crowd, and was in frequent conflict with the law for truancy and being loose on the streets late at night. Whenever Mrs. A. attempted to confront her daughter with her behavior, Trudy became truculently defiant and Mrs. A. wept helplessly. Buddy also recalled these scenes, mentioning that he remembered being left at home at night, lonely and scared, while his mother went out to look for his sister. At fifteen, Trudy was finally placed by the court in a foster home where she remained until she finished high school. Since then her adjustment has been, at best, marginal, marked by several marriages and increasing alcoholism.

Buddy's adolescent problems followed shortly upon Trudy's. Not long after the family moved to Los Angeles, Mrs. A. became determined to do something about Buddy's baldness and took him to a physician, who began hormone treatments which proved quite effective. About the time Buddy turned thirteen a light fuzz of red hair appeared across the top of his head and shortly afterwards on other parts of his body in normal fashion. However, Buddy seemed to resent intensely the hormone treatments and the resulting hair growth. At school he was no longer able to beat back every taunter and, indeed, seemed to feel he had nothing to fight about. Having moved from a school where he had been a physical and social leader, he now had to take a back seat. He was often in trouble with the school authorities for fighting. Now the other youngsters shunned him. In recalling this period of life Buddy associated the growth of his hair with a sense of failure and inadequacy, for which he blamed his mother. Once he shaved his head bald again, but his hair returned thicker and longer than ever before. He gradually became more and more of an isolate, "hating myself and everyone else too."

During his later teens he seemed to make a brief effort to break away from this social isolation. He joined with one and then another of the delinquent groups at high school, engaging in behavior which seemed specifically aimed at defying the school authorities. According to Trudy, Buddy had dressed in black leather coat and tight

jeans, and sported a "duck-tail" haircut; he swaggered about, inso-
lent to adults, much to the dismay of his mother. Buddy himself recalled that he had tried to act like a "big shot," but later discovered
that this was not the "true way to self-realization." He admitted that
he had become so attached to and so admired one of the gang leaders that he actually had "a crush on him" and tried to imitate his
idol, submitting to everything that he was asked to do. However, the
gang leader seemed to take particular pleasure in embarrassing
Buddy by ordering him to carry out either difficult or silly tasks. For
example, the only time Buddy really was in trouble with the law,
other than for truancy, was when he was commanded by the gang
leader to "strip" (steal exterior accessories) a car—which turned out
to be a police car. Buddy was promptly apprehended and the gang
thought this a great joke. On his own Buddy would think up
"crazy stunts" which sometimes amused his peers but more often
confirmed their opinion that he was an "oddball." Not sure they
could trust him, the gang excluded Buddy from their group sexual
activities and much of their other asocial behavior, which made him
feel very much of an outsider. Even before this he had begun to
worry about his sexual adequacy; from age thirteen on he had been
masturbating several times a day, with elaborate daydreams of sexual prowess. Discovered once by the gang, he was forced to masturbate in front of them while they roared in laughter, especially because he was unable to maintain an erection.

Buddy's educational achievement was at best erratic. He made
barely passing marks in most of his subjects, but occasionally he
would become fascinated with some particular topic and would be
among the top in his class for a semester. His teachers were surprised
by the display of miscellaneous knowledge derived from his extensive reading, or when they received a satisfactory paper after he
had done absolutely no work in class. Even his performance on intelligence tests varied so extremely that one school counselor sought
to refer him to the school guidance clinic; however, due to a long
waiting list, he never received attention. His surly and defiant attitude toward teachers and school authorities became so extreme that
he was suspended from school several times during his junior and
senior years. As he grew increasingly disgusted with school, his at-
tendence became more and more irregular; approximately three
months before the time he might have been graduated, he dropped

out of high school altogether. His mother had always supplied him with petty cash on his demand, so Buddy had never had to work. However, his expenses were small since he never dated. After he quit high school he sat around the house doing little except watching TV and eating constantly. He gained so much weight that his mother became worried. As she recalled her concern, during the interview, she sighed and remarked, "Whenever Buddy starts something there is no stopping him; he seems to have no control over himself."

Shortly after his eighteenth birthday, Buddy was drafted into the military service. Even before he had completed his basic training he had been reprimanded twice by "company courts-martial" for minor infractions of army regulations. Although Buddy pleaded ignorance, these rules were common knowledge to every soldier. After approximately six months' service he was convicted of the use of narcotics and sentenced to a dishonorable discharge plus a year's hard labor in the military prison. Buddy admitted that he had previously tried smoking marijuana as a "joke" with the gang, but maintained that this incident in the army was a single occasion when in his loneliness he sought the company of young men similar to those he had known in high school. The other men fled when the military police appeared, leaving Buddy in possession of the marijuana cigarettes. In the military prison Buddy was screened by a psychiatrist, who, Buddy believed, had recommended to the military courts that his sentence be commuted. After four months in prison he was dishonorably discharged from the service. Upon return to civilian life Buddy was unable to obtain a job because of his lack of education and experience. The nature of his military discharge deprived him of his veteran's rights to further education. Furthermore, when prospective employers ask about his military service he became evasive and left without making further application for employment. He rapidly came to believe that everyone knew about his military conviction and imprisonment. He therefore returned to his former behavior of sitting around the house with nothing to do or wandering aimlessly about the streets. His mother and sister, concerned about his behavior, hired an attorney who agreed that the sentence had been unusually harsh for a crime which in civilian life would be a misdemeanor. However, the attorney was unable to effect any reversal of the court-martial sentence.

Depressed and bitter, Buddy withdrew in silence from all social contacts, even with his family. Though Mrs. A. and Trudy were concerned, they did not know how to comfort him and were hurt when he ignored their overtures.

When he began his bizarre religious practices his family became even more uneasy, but since he seemed to find surcease from his troubles they avoided disturbing him. Even when Buddy began to talk with his "voices" and to lie around the house almost naked, masturbating openly in the living room, Mrs. A. tried to maintain an air of composure, hoping he suddenly would "come back to his old sweet self." When she finally admitted to Trudy how frightened she was by Buddy's outbursts of violence, Trudy tried to convince her to take him to a psychiatrist. Overhearing them, Buddy threatened to kill them and himself if they interfered with his freedom in any way. Cowed by his belligerence, they had despaired of taking any action, until the incident occurred which led to Buddy's hospitalization.

Disposition and Treatment. At the end of eight days of observation in the county hospital, the staff recommended to the courts that Buddy be committed to the state hospital. The psychiatrist was able to convince Buddy that he should go to the hospital as a "voluntary" patient, which avoided legal procedure. Buddy's mother and the police dropped all criminal charges against him. About a week later, Buddy reappeared at the outpatient section of the county hospital asking to see the psychiatrist to whom he had talked previously. He waited around many hours until that particular doctor was free. He explained that he could not peacefully practice his religion behind hospital walls and so had signed himself out against medical advice. However, he wanted to let this doctor know since he respected the doctor's opinion. It appeared also that Buddy was very afraid that he might be given electric shock treatment. After talking to him for several hours the psychiatrist permitted Buddy to return home with the promise that he would return on appointment. Buddy did not keep the appointment, but did reappear without an appointment several days later. He continued to appear, sometimes on appointment although more often without. Most of his discussion with the psychiatrist concerned his current adjustment at home. He was able to move away from home to a boarding house, which was arranged for him by the clinic social worker. He found a job as a dishwasher, which he held for two or three weeks, but thereafter shifted from one menial job to another over approximately a year's period. The psychiatrist insisted that if Buddy could not keep appointments with him that at least Buddy should come to see him or telephone him when any crisis arose. Several times Buddy called him at night for long telephone conversations without apparent reason, but at such times he usually seemed panicky or depressed. After approximately a year Buddy became considerably depressed and finally admitted that he again had an urge to kill someone. He voluntarily returned to the state hospital, where he remained for approximately two years, at which time he was discharged as being "in remission." Over the next several years Buddy contacted his psychiatrist at the county hospital only twice. Both times he came on the pretext of seeking advice about some change in his living situation, but really seemed to need the assurance that assistance was available whenever he might need it. On neither occasion did he appear unusually depressed. He remained emotionally and socially isolated but appeared to have dropped his religious fanaticism and other bizarre behavior and, in general, was less overtly disturbed. When last heard from, he was continuing his marginal existence outside the hospital, maintaining himself away from home through intermittent employment at unskilled jobs.

Questions for "Buddy" A.

1. List Buddy's symptoms and behavior at the time that he was first brought to the hospital. What clinical diagnosis best fits Buddy's behavior? Defend your answer.

2. Trace Buddy's social development since childhood. Recount what you see in terms of the following:

   a. the quality of relationships with his mother and father

   b. the quality of his relationships with friends of the same sex

   c. the quality of his relationships with members of the opposite sex

3. In later years, Buddy evinced an interest in certain Far Eastern religions:

   a. What are some of the fundamental concepts of Yoga and the Buddhist religions?

    b. In the light of your answers to the above, why might some of
these concepts have been perceived by Buddy as a possible
source of relief for his anxieties about his (1) relations with
members of his own sex; (2) relations with members of the opposite sex; (3) masturbation?

4. Read the Phillips and Rodnick and the Garmezy articles listed in
the references.

    a. According to the criteria advanced by Phillips, would you
classify Buddy as a "*good* pre-morbid" or a "*poor* pre-morbid"?
    b. To what extent do Rodnick and Garmezy's descriptions of
family organization for each pre-morbid group fit Buddy's
family constellation?

5. How would you characterize Buddy's relationship with his
father? What effect did this relationship appear to have in Buddy's
concept of himself as a man?

6. Can you see any relation between your answer to question 5
above and some of Buddy's psychotic symptoms (i.e. his feeling
that he was Jesus Christ; his attempt to kill his mother to achieve
Nirvana)?

7. Surprisingly, Buddy reacted very unfavorably to the successful
treatment of his endocrine disorder. How can you account for this
reaction? (*Hint:* Consider the gratifications which his affliction provided Buddy earlier in his life, and the age at which the successful
treatment occurred.)

8. During his most disturbed period, Buddy showed some profound
disturbances in his thinking. This thinking has been termed pseudo-
logical by some writers. For example, one bit of psychotic thinking
has been reconstructed in syllogistic form as follows:

    George Washington was a man

    I am a man

    Therefore, I am George Washington

Attempt, following the above example, a reconstruction of the syl-
logism underlying Buddy's conclusion that in order to achieve Nirvana he had to kill his mother.

9. From what you know of psychology, how can you account for the
fact that thinking, as it exists in the psychotic, can go so awry? Attempt an explanation either from a learning theory or psychoanalytic
theory of the thinking disturbance shown by Buddy.

10. Make an estimation of the likelihood that Buddy will return to a

mental hospital at some time in his life. Base your estimate on statistical figures or factors that point to a return of psychotic symptoms after a first episode and not upon a personal judgment. (*Hint:* See Phillip's article, ref. 3.)

References

ARIETI, S. *Interpretation of schizophrenia.* New York: Robert Brunner, 1955. P. 192.

CAMERON, N. Deterioration and regression in schizophrenic thinking. *Journal of Abnormal and Social Psychology,* 1939, **34**: 265–270.

PHILLIPS, L. Case history data and prognosis in schizophrenia. *Journal of Nervous and Mental Disorders,* 1953, **117**: 515–525.

RODNICK, E. T., & GARMEZY, N. An experimental approach to the study of motivation in schizophrenia. In JONES, M. R. (Ed.) *Nebraska Symposium on Motivation.* Lincoln: Univer. of Nebraska Press, 1957. Pp. 109–183.

SULLIVAN, H. S. *The interpersonal theory of psychiatry.* New York: W. W. Norton & Co., 1953. Pp. 325–327.

THE CASE OF LUCY Q.

A Woman's Work

Although Mrs. Q. had just passed her sixty-second birthday, her behavior and appearance gave the impression of marked physical and mental deterioration. She stumbled feebly up the steps of the state hospital, grasping at her daughter's arm for support, and had to be helped to a seat in the reception hall. Her wispy snow-white hair was sparse; her face was pinched and heavily wrinkled; and her blood vessels were visible through her pale, dry skin. Although dressed neatly in a little black bonnet and a relatively new pink wool suit, her clothes hung loosely on her tiny, thin frame. Apparently uncomfortable, she pulled nervously at her collar and blouse until scolded in a stage whisper by her daughter. In the office, she sat tensely on the edge of a chair, tremulous but tight-lipped, clutching at her purse.

Her daughter, Vicki, described Mrs. Q.'s condition and background to the doctor in front of her mother as if Mrs. Q. could not hear her, although later it proved that she had no hearing defect whatever. However, Mrs. Q. seemed either unaffected by or inattentive to anything her daughter said to the admitting physician. When the physician turned to Mrs. Q. and introduced himself, she smiled politely and shook his hand and asked anxiously if he had met her husband—despite the fact that her daughter had told the physician in Mrs. Q.'s presence only five minutes before that Mr. Q. had been dead for two years. Without waiting for an answer, Mrs. Q. went on to describe what a wonderful man her husband was and how sorry she was that he was not with her that day to meet the doctor. Asked how she felt about going into the hospital, Mrs. Q. grabbed her daughter's shoulder and began to weep. When her daughter pushed her away, Mrs. Q. sat back in her chair, looked very dejected, dabbed at her face with her handkerchief, and said bitterly,

"They hate me! They all hate me!" Her daughter also began to cry and tried to reassure her mother, "We don't hate you, Mother, it's all for your own good." She turned to the doctor and remarked, "I was afraid she would make a scene." Mrs. Q. seemed to recover her aplomb for a moment and retorted, "I'm not making a scene; you'll have to excuse me, doctor; I haven't been feeling well and we must leave now." Asked about her health, Mrs. Q. relaxed and told in detail of her many pains, her weakness, and especially her sensation that something was eating away at her stomach and bowels. Throughout her recitation of her physical miseries, she kept hinting that none of her children understood or sympathized with her disabilities. She seemed reassured for the moment by the doctor's statement that in the hospital she would receive the medical care, rest, and attention she needed, but when the nurse came Mrs. Q. cried out plaintively, "Where are you taking me? Where are you taking me?"

When examined several days later on the ward, Mrs. Q. appeared even more deteriorated. Her daughter had brought no additional clothes for her other than a nightgown. Mrs. Q.'s suit had been stored in a locker and she was dressed in "hospital clothes," a faded and ill-fitting house dress which drooped around her emaciated body. In the interim, she had broken both her glasses and her dental plate while washing up in the ward bathroom. Her toothless condition increased her appearance of severe aging. The nurse reported that she had eaten little and seemed very depressed. She sat in a chair in one corner of the room, not responding to anyone. She had not voluntarily washed herself, and at the end of two days she was given a shower bath by one of the nurses, to which she submitted without question. She dozed at times during the day in her chair, slept fitfully at night, and arose once or twice and wandered about the hall muttering to herself until led back to bed.

She shuffled into the examining room in her hospital slippers and stood rigidly in the doorway, pouting in anger. Introduced to another doctor, she protested, "You're not my doctor; I want to see *my* doctor." Before the situation could again be explained to her, she reassured herself with a declaration that her son was coming and that everything would be all right. Again by inquiring about her health the doctor was able to calm her, and she launched once more into a recitation of her physical ills. Asked what medication and treatment she had received, she replied that doctors and pills had done her no good and explained that she found the greatest relief through "the power of prayer." Although born and reared a Catholic, she no longer had any use for the Catholic Church and had taken up "faith science." A brief mental examination was conducted, during which it was ascertained that she had no idea of the date or year. Although she could give her birth date correctly, she was not sure of her age. At one moment in the examination she recognized that she was in a hospital, but did not know the name of the hospital or why she was there; later she appeared to be confused as to exactly where she was. Her speech often trailed off and she would sit silent for a moment, seemingly collecting thoughts. Many of her remarks were irrelevant and she was difficult to follow as one idea seemed to float into the next in tangential fashion. At the end of the examination she repeated her hope that her son and daughter would come and take her home. Physical examination revealed an undernourished individual with mild signs of arteriosclerosis. There was a well-healed scar at the base of her throat, confirming the daughter's report that Mrs. Q. had had a goiter removed several years ago. There were also suggestions that she might be suffering from a mild kidney infection. Her gums were so deteriorated that the dentist wondered how she was able to utilize the dental plate, which had been ill fitting.

Past History. Since Mrs. Q. was unable to give a coherent account of her background, most of this information was obtained either from her daughter, Vicki, at the time of admission, or from her son, Steve, who made several visits within the next two weeks. Neither of these informants knew anything of Mrs. Q.'s birth and childhood development. She emigrated from Ireland to this country in her late teens. They believed that her parents died when she was quite young and that she had been reared by various older brothers and sisters. So far as they knew, she had no relatives in this country and never spoke of her kinfolk in Ireland. Steve remembered that his mother had spoken of "working out" before she emigrated, which he took to mean that she had been a servant girl in her early teens. Mrs. Q. had pointed out to them at one time the wealthy home where she had worked briefly before her marriage. She was barely twenty when she married their father, then a rookie patrolman in a small manufacturing city on the Atlantic coast. Vicki, their eldest, was born approximately a year after her parents married. Steve was approximately five years her junior, and there survived one other living child, Emily, who was six years younger than Steve. Vicki believed her mother was pregnant at least twice after she was born and before Steve was born but that there was only one live birth and this child died in its first year of life. Mrs. Q. was also pregnant twice between the middle and youngest child but both times suffered miscarriages. One other child was born after Emily, but it also died in infancy.

Both Vicki and Steve described their mother as an extremely hard-working, vigorous woman who devoted all her energies to her home and children. She scrubbed her house until it was "hospital clean." She hovered over her children's every move, constantly correcting them and threatening them with punishment from their father or from God if they did not obey her immediately. "We weren't afraid of our father," said Steve with a laugh, "because he was never home." Apparently they weren't afraid of God either, for they did not carry out their mother's wishes that they attend church. Steve had completed more religious training than his sisters but had rebelled against it in his adolescence; his mother was very disappointed that he did not become a priest.

Although Mrs. Q. never made any complaint against her husband even privately, her children realized when they became adults that she felt sorely mistreated by him. He expected her to wait on him hand and foot, never showed her any open affection, and gave her only the barest allowance on which to run the house. It was common gossip in the community that he was a "ladies' man," unfaithful to his wife. As the children grew older, Mrs. Q.'s patience with them grew shorter. She seemed to have little understanding of their social or emotional needs and they rebelled against her scolding and ignored her fears. Her husband labeled her a nag and laughed at the children's misdemeanors. Steve admitted that in his adolescence he was involved in several serious delinquencies and would have been sent to jail if his policeman father had not intervened for him. Vicki, in an act of rebellion, ran away and got married in her early teens, a marriage which was annulled shortly afterwards. However, her mother was furious, called her a slut, would not take her back in the house, and did not speak to her for several years. Emily also married soon after she left high school and moved to another part of the country. Neither Steve nor Vicki had seen much of her since and they did not believe that she had written her mother in years. They admitted with some guilt that they had never felt close to either their mother or father. As soon as they became adults they went their own ways, became involved in their own lives, and had only infrequent contact with their parents. Letters from their mother were replete with accounts of her physical suffering, but they were unsure of the nature of her illnesses. "She was the kind of person who enjoyed poor health." Vicki could not remember exactly when her mother had been operated on for the goiter.

About ten years prior to Mrs. Q.'s present hospitalization she had been very depressed and disturbed. Their father, who never wrote to them, had telephoned to ask their advice as to whether she needed "to be put away." Months before, in a sudden pique, she had stopped speaking to him. She remained in her room, often weeping to herself and neglecting her housework. More religious than ever before, she built a small shrine in her bedroom and frequently repeated her prayers. Steve visited her at this time and found her much as his father had described. In a long, involved, and not too coherent tale she confided to Steve that the neighbors were plotting against her and asked him to prevail on his father to get her a gun. When Mr. Q. demanded that Steve sign papers to commit his mother to the state hospital, Steve refused on the grounds that this was his father's responsibility. Mr. Q.'s excuse that any such action on his part might jeopardize his position on the police force seemed unreasonable to Steve. After a bitter argument with his father, Steve returned home, angry and guilty, having left his mother in the same situation in which he had found her.

In more recent contacts with their mother, Steve and Vicki found her emotional condition ameliorated, although she remained depressed and suspicious of everyone in general. Steve's wife, in an effort to make friends with her mother-in-law, made a long and tiring visit with their children only to find Mrs. Q. uninterested and weary. Vicki, about a year prior to her father's death, invited her parents to her home for Christmas. Mrs. Q.'s caustic criticism of Vicki's handling of her children and of her housekeeping had irritated Vicki intensely. She scarcely knew her father and found that she and her husband had little in common with him.

Mr. Q. had died suddenly of a heart attack within the first year of his retirement from the police force. Steve and Vicki discovered that he had taken his entire pension out in cash, and there was no account of what had happened to his money. It also appeared that he had heavily mortgaged their home. Mrs. Q. was of the opinion that her husband had gambled heavily and lost a great deal. She was financially destitute, depressed, and bitter. Both Vicki and Steve lived in small houses which had no separate quarters for their mother, and neither were at all eager to take her into their homes. She was not at that time eligible for any type of old-age insurance or public pension. Although Steve could ill afford any further expenses from his own modest salary, he attempted for almost a year to make payments on the mortgage and to cover his mother's ultilities. Vicki agreed to furnish her mother's food and clothing. Mrs. Q. shrugged her shoulders and looked away when informed of her children's plans. Steve was able to keep up his end of the bargain for approximately nine months at which time he lost his job. Vicki had informed him that her mother continued to be depressed and was not eating well. Most of all, Vicki was upset because Mrs. Q., neglecting her personal care, had become dirty and unkempt, in contrast to her previous obsession with cleanliness. Abandoning her Catholicism, Mrs. Q. had become involved in a small religious sect known as "Truth Science," to which, Vicki discovered, Mrs. Q. contributed much of her food and clothing allowance.

Steve and Vicki despaired of what to do with their mother. For the next year she lived with each of them alternately. At Vicki's home, she slept on a couch in the dining room, keeping her meager belongings in the guest closet in the front hall. She was annoyed and impatient with Vicki's teen-age children and was constantly correcting them. She complained of the noise of the television, only to demand her own programs. Because she only washed and changed her clothes when Vicki pressed her, she was often unpresentable, which embarrassed Vicki in front of her friends. At Steve's home, Steve's wife gave her mother-in-law their bedroom while she and Steve slept in the living room. Mrs. Q. was a little happier here, but her complaints and corrections of Steve's behavior and of Steve's young children sorely strained their tolerance. As Mrs. Q.'s mental confusion and depression increased, both of her children realized they could no longer care for her.

Treatment and Disposition. Mrs. Q. was put on an immediate "total push" program of rehabilitation, aimed at her physical, social, and emotional needs. Medications were prescribed to slow down the process of her arteriosclerosis and to clear up her kidney infection. New dental plates and new glasses were fitted for her, with extra pairs in case one was broken. As the state did not supply the glasses cost free, Steve was very happy to carry this expense, and Mrs. Q. was informed that her son was making this contribution. Vicki volunteered to take her mother shopping when she was advised of her mother's need for clothes. Place on a ward where there were other ladies her age, Mrs. Q. was engaged in a busy program of occupational therapy. She learned to knit, at which she proved very adept. A beauty shop operator volunteered to teach the women patients to set one another's hair and manicure their nails. Mrs. Q. took a renewed pride in her personal grooming. She had no recreational interests whatever and could not be involved in the card games or other activities of the patients on the ward. She did enjoy, however, taking long walks with one of the psychiatric aides. First assigned a job helping to serve food on the ward, she later, on her own initiative, asked to be transferred to helping to feed the patients on the children's ward. Here she was allowed to do some cooking, making special treats for "her" children. The hospital was too distant from town for Vicki and Steve to visit their mother regularly, but, with the encouragement of the hospital social worker, occasionally they did take their mother to their homes. Her weight returned to near normal and she ceased mentioning her illnesses and seemed much more cheerful and a little less confused. One of the other women patients on her ward, also born and reared in Ireland, attached herself to Mrs. Q. and enjoyed exchanging childhood memories. When Mrs. Q.'s friend was placed in a foster home, Mrs. Q. requested to be transferred there also. The foster home provided Mrs. Q. and her friend with a small kitchen where they could do some of their own cooking. They soon became popular as baby sitters throughout the neighborhood. Mrs. Q. seemed much less depressed and much better oriented to everyday affairs the last time she was visited by the field social worker.

Questions for Lucy Q.

1. List the symptoms which Lucy Q. expressed at the time of admission to the hospital classifying them into

    a. emotional features

    b. intellectual features

2. Which of these symptoms are known to be the psychological consequences of arteriosclerosis? Which are not?

3. If you have listed some symptoms to the second part of question 2, indicate what diagnostic category could subsume these additional features.

4. There are certain ideas about herself which Lucy manifests which are more or less characteristic of mental disorders in advanced years. What are these ideas? How can you account, on a psychological basis, for the prominence of these symptoms in people of advanced age?

5. Ordinarily, mental illness, even when it has an organic component, reflects the long-standing personality adjustment of the individual to stress. What evidence do we see in Lucy for pathological modes of adjustment over her adult life-span?

6. Which of the pathological modes of adjustment remained intact during Lucy's illness and which yielded to other, more regressive, behavior patterns?

7. From your answers to questions 5 and 7, speculate as to which drives or emotions Lucy was striving to keep out of awareness during her pre-illness period of life.

8. What factors existed in Lucy's environment which placed unusual stress upon her ability to master her environment?

    a. 10 years previously

    b. at the time of the present illness

9. What role did Lucy's relationship with her husband appear to play in her two illnesses?

10. How can you account for the fact that Lucy's relationship with her children deteriorated over the years? What effect did this alienation from her children have upon her self-concept?

11. *a.* What specific things were done to Lucy during her stay in the hospital?

    b. What psychological needs did they satisfy for Lucy which evidently permitted her to reintegrate her personality during this period?

12. What are some specific psychological problems unique to the fifth and sixth decade of life?

13. Using your answer to question 12 as a base, attempt to account for the fact that the modal pattern of abnormal behavior in the late adult years is depression?

References

BUSSE, E. Psychopathology. In BIRREN, J. (Ed.) *Handbook of aging and the individual.* Chicago: Univer. of Chicago Press, 1959.

DAVIS, D., WEISS, J. M. A., GILDEA, E. F., & MENSH, I. Psychiatric problems of later life. II. Clinical syndromes. *American Practitioner, Diagnosis and Treatment,* 1959, 10: 61–65.

FERRARO, A. Psychoses with cerebral arteriosclerosis. In ARIETI, S. (Ed.) *American handbook of psychiatry.* New York: Basic Books, 1959. Pp. 1080–1086.

RECHTSCHAFFEN, A., et al. An intensive treatment program for state hospital geriatric patients. *Geriatrics,* 1954, 28–36.

REISMAN, D. Some clinical and cultural aspects of aging. *Selected essays from individualism reconsidered.* New York: Doubleday Anchor Books, 1955. Pp. 164–173.